"Thought-provoking and genuine, *Good People* is a must read for anyone interested in creating prosperous, wholesome, and resilient teams and businesses."

—Beth Comstock, vice chair of General Electric

"This book reminds us of what really matters in life: the goodness we find in ourselves and the goodness we pass on to others."

—Shep Gordon, Hollywood talent manager and "Supermensch"

"*Good People* reminds us that good business and human fulfillment really can go together, that goodness and productivity aren't enemies, that being whole and being successful are one and the same. This book is a manifesto for twenty-first-century business and also a wake-up call to all of us to be fully alive at work with our colleagues, in silence within ourselves, and in friendship with those we love."

—Tim Shriver, chairman of Special Olympics

GOOD PEOPLE

GOOD PEOPLE

THE ONLY LEADERSHIP DECISION
THAT REALLY MATTERS

· · · · · · ·

ANTHONY TJAN

PORTFOLIO/PENGUIN

An imprint of Penguin Random House LLC
375 Hudson Street
New York, New York 10014

Most Portfolio books are available at a discount when purchased in quantity for sales promotions or corporate use. Special editions, which include personalized covers, excerpts, and corporate imprints, can be created when purchased in large quantities. For more information, please call (212) 572-2232 or e-mail specialmarkets@penguinrandomhouse.com. Your local bookstore can also assist with discounted bulk purchases using the Penguin Random House corporate Business-to-Business program. For assistance in locating a participating retailer, e-mail B2B@penguinrandomhouse.com.

Image credits
Tables on pages 61–62 from Benjamin Franklin, *The Autobiography on Benjamin Franklin*. New York: Macmillan Publishing Co., Inc., 1962.
Images on pages 33, 46, 73, 94, 240, and 248 by Hilario Bango/Martian Arts.

Hardcover ISBN: 978-0-3995-6215-0
E-book ISBN: 978-0-3995-6217-4
International edition ISBN: 978-0-7352-1679-2

Printed in the United States of America

1   3   5   7   9   10   8   6   4   2

Book design by Fine Design

Dedicated to the Memory of Kaming Ng
For your creative wit, relentless stubbornness, and beautiful intelligence
For being a true cofounder, a true friend, and a true human being
And yes, for being one of the very good people
I'll always remember, and dearly miss

CONTENTS

. . . .

PART ONE

INTRODUCING GOODNESS AND GOOD PEOPLE   1

1 · A FIRST ENCOUNTER WITH GOODNESS   5

2 · A NEW FRAMEWORK AND LANGUAGE FOR
    GOODNESS   27

3 · THE FOUNDATION: TRUTH   41

4 · THE HUMAN FACTOR: COMPASSION   67

5 · THE ULTIMATE QUEST: WHOLENESS   91

PART TWO

BALANCING TENSIONS TO ACHIEVE GOODNESS   119

6 · PRAGMATISM VERSUS IDEALISM   127

7 · SHORT-TERMISM VERSUS LONG-TERMISM   143

8 · VULNERABILITY VERSUS CONVICTION   161

9 · IDIOSYNCRASY VERSUS CONNECTEDNESS   177

10 · GRIT VERSUS ACCEPTANCE   195

PART THREE

THE IMPERATIVE TO PUT GOODNESS INTO PRACTICE

THE IMPERATIVE TO PUT GOODNESS
INTO PRACTICE   205

11 · BEYOND ORDINARY MENTORSHIP   209
12 · BECOMING A BETTER JUDGE OF PEOPLE   237
13 · WRAPPING IT UP: IT'S ALL UP TO YOU   251

AFTERWORD   259
ACKNOWLEDGMENTS   265
NOTES   271
INDEX   287

PART ONE

• • • • • • •

INTRODUCING GOODNESS AND GOOD PEOPLE

I n 1953, industrial chemist Norman Larsen and his staff of two at the fledgling Rocket Chemical Company set out on a mission: to create a formula for the booming aeronautics industry that could coat space missiles and protect them from water. It took extensive trial and error to perfect the formula, but on the fortieth attempt they nailed it. Thus was born Water Displacement 40, better known today as WD-40.

WD-40 has a unique place in history and pop culture. It was first used on the Atlas space rocket, but then consumers began clamoring for it. Salesmen literally sold the now-iconic blue-and-yellow cans out of their car trunks. Today, WD-40 is a household name. Annual sales exceed $350 million, and the company is valued at more than $1.5 billion. WD-40's meteoric success makes it easy to overlook the most unique aspect of the company: the people who work there.

WD-40 has managed to retain its staff at three times the national average. Ninety-seven percent of employees report that they love—not just like—to tell people they work at WD-40.[1] The company's CEO, Garry Ridge, is unequivocal about the source of WD-40's remarkable success: "It's about people, it's about learning, it's about our culture, it's about our tribalism," he explained to me.[2] Obviously, WD-40's results aren't just the effect of organizational competencies. They reflect something deeper and more meaningful about the people at WD-40.

Under the leadership of Garry Ridge, who has been at the company for thirty years and has served as its CEO for twenty, there has been no question that the firm's first priority and most valuable asset is—well above anything else—its people. The WD-40 tribe espouses and leads with the people-first philosophy that Ridge and management guru Ken Blanchard describe in *Helping People Win at Work*: "Don't mark my paper, help me get an A." The primary core value of the WD-40 organization is "doing the right thing"—helping the people at WD-40 truly succeed.

In fact, at WD-40 mentorship is not just one expectation among many competing tasks; it is an imperative. The approval ratings for supervisors at WD-40 are through the roof, consistently around 96 percent. "The number one responsibility of a 'tribal leader' or coach at WD-40 is the success of his tribe members. Full stop," says Ridge. It's a simple concept for goodness, but one to which it is difficult to fully commit. But this is what makes WD-40 a paragon of a good company and its employees paragons of good people.

· · · ·

"Good people"—it's a phrase we hear all the time, both in the office and out of it. What do we *really* mean when we say those words? When we say that someone is good? We recognize that quality when we're around it, and we can feel goodness when we experience it, but to really describe it, specifically and fully, is challenging to say the least. Certainly we don't understand goodness to the degree it deserves.

"Good" and "goodness" are words so embedded in our everyday colloquies they've almost lost their meaning. They've become what my late neighbor, the illustrious intellect and MIT professor Marvin Minsky, termed "suitcase words": overused, overstretched phrases or expressions that have next to no practical meaning. Even formal definitions fall short. *Merriam-Webster's Online Dictionary*'s definition of "good," for example, is "something virtuous, right, commendable."[3] This is not incorrect, but we must build upon it and make it more concrete and understandable so that we may practice it in our daily lives.

If we take on the burden of creating a practical, actionable definition of goodness and putting that goodness into practice, we need to acknowledge that the topic has been a core question and source of inquiry for the world's greatest philosophers, psychologists, and spiritual leaders for millennia. As we can see from Aristotle's relentless quest to better understand the human condition and human spirit, from twentieth-century psychosocial explorations of different stages of desire and development by the likes of Abraham Maslow or Erik Erikson, and from many faiths' common principles of kindness, it is a near universal assumption that we should all live our lives striving to be good people.

But how can we think of goodness and good people as concepts that can be practically applied in the business world and understand their far-reaching benefits? First, we need to confront the ambiguities in the way businesses use the term "good." There are two sides of the word. When hiring employees and managing teams, we often use "good" as a synonym for "competent." But "goodness" is far more than a person's competencies; goodness is about people's humanity, their values, the qualities inherent in their character, and other intangible traits. We therefore need to distinguish goodness as competency from goodness as values, and we need to understand that the latter ought to take greater priority.

What makes WD-40 a special place to work is something that transcends the talent of its employees—which I am sure is great, but not far superior to the talent of competitors' employees. WD-40's greatest competitive advantage is its culture of good people. Its leadership has created a company that its employees believe in authentically. They genuinely find meaning both in their work and in their coworkers. And thus, WD-40's incredible results, year after year.

Despite the massive success of companies like WD-40, many people still believe that there's no place in the business world for "soft" concepts like *good, goodness,* and *good people.* Business is business after all, right? These people assume that leading a good business means focusing solely on getting results. But the truth is, now that prolonged competition, greater availability of information, and technological advancements have created a more level playing field, people matter more than anything else. They add value at every point in the organization. The best companies aren't just machines to maximize profits; they create widespread, positive change in their employees, their communities, and their industries. When good people imprint good values and qualities onto others, and they in turn do the same, they create enduring value and forward progress in businesses.

And even if you only care about maximizing profits and returns, goodness and good people benefit the bottom line as well.

This book is an attempt to explore the hard truth about soft matters. By putting the meaning back into the "suitcase term" of "good people," we can elevate ourselves and the people around us—and change the face of business, perhaps even whole societies and the entire world. After working in and advising organizations both good and not so good, starting a few companies of my own, and investing in about fifty others, I've come to believe that pursuing goodness in yourself while surrounding yourself with good people is the only leadership decision that really, truly matters. When we ask ourselves why we admire leaders (or for that matter, people in general), the answer is predictable: they put people first and understand and practice the values that underpin goodness. These leaders are committed to improving everyone around them just as much as they are committed to improving themselves. They feel a duty to serve others by inspiring and shaping them to become the best, fullest version of themselves. The leaders and people who do this, as management guru Tom Peters says, "don't create followers." Instead, "they create more leaders."[4] I have come to believe this, and I see people and their values as *the most critical* competitive advantage that exists—period.

1

A FIRST ENCOUNTER WITH GOODNESS

On one of the hottest afternoons in July in the Toronto suburb of North York, I schlepped up the three porch steps that belonged to the last house on the block, my bulky backpack biting into my shoulders. At age fifteen, I was eager to make whatever extra summer money I could, so I was going door-to-door selling picture frames. Even as a teenager, I wanted to feel like a big-shot entrepreneur, but instead people slammed doors in my face all day. Eight straight hours in the sweltering summer heat had left me ragged, sweat soaked, and feeling low. I was close to giving up, but I decided to attempt one last sale. I impulsively rang the doorbell.

I heard a soft shuffling of feet, and then a terse "Who's there?" As the door opened, I had to conceal my surprise. The owner of the house was elderly and tiny, much gentler looking in person than her voice had let on, with unkempt gray-white hair. Two minutes later, I was seated in her small, worn living room, but when I launched into my practiced pitch, she interrupted, turning her focus from the picture frames to *me*. She unleashed a barrage of questions: Who was I? Where was I from? Newfoundland? Then what was I doing in Toronto so far from home? Where were my parents? The frames weren't stolen, were they? And another question, one she asked repeatedly: *Was this something I really liked doing?*

An hour later, holding my second glass of iced tea, I'd hardly moved; the two of us were still deep in conversation. By now, I knew she was eighty-two, a retired social worker and a widow, and a graceful, even riveting, storyteller. She kept coming back to one point: the most important thing in life, she told me, was to figure out what I really wanted to do and who to do it with. She blurted it out: "Listen," and then stressed it in her slightly craggy voice—"You must *love* both that thing you are doing and *love even more* the people you do it with." Then, after a pause and with a wide, assuring smile, she added that she just knew I would have wonderful success in my life. And at that moment, for some reason, I believed her, even though she didn't buy even one picture frame.

· · · ·

Over the past two decades of my peripatetic career, I've tried hard to stand by that wisdom from the retired woman in North York: to love what I do, but to love even more the people with whom I'm doing it. I picked my first official job because of the good feeling I got from the people who interviewed me. Little did I know then that some of those same interviewers would serve as lifelong mentors, fund my first venture and subsequent ones, or become colleagues and collaborators in initiatives throughout my career.

One of those longtime mentors is a former partner of the management consulting firm McKinsey & Company, Tsun-yan Hsieh. I first met Tsun-yan when I was a young associate at McKinsey and he was a senior partner and then chair of McKinsey's Professional Development Committee globally. At the time of our conversation for this book, Dominic Barton, the worldwide managing director of McKinsey, had just recognized Tsun-yan for his mentorship, learning, and development philosophies. Both Dominic and I were in the same Toronto McKinsey office in the early 1990s, and Tsun-yan at that time was already a mentor to Dom. It all came full circle when Dom recently paid tribute to Tsun-yan as one of the handful of people who have had the most critical impact on leadership and people development at the firm.

It had been more than two decades since I had worked at McKinsey, but Dom's recognition of Tsun-yan's impact compelled me to ask him the question that I had always wondered. Why had Tsun-yan decided some two decades ago to take me under his wing and single me out for attention among the sheer number of people who sought his counsel? Tsun-yan paused, and after a moment said that he wasn't sure if he had chosen me or if I had chosen *him*. There was no arrogance in his voice or manner, but his response struck a chord. He was right. In pursuit of the same feeling I'd experienced as a teenager in North York, I *had* chosen him, and this choice occurred *before* he, in turn, chose to include me in a select group of mentees. He concluded, "Mentorship is mutual: the mentor must feel that they will get a deeply satisfying human experience out of building up somebody, just as the mentee must make a conscious choice with the hope that their mentor will impart life philosophy and professional wisdom, along with knowledge and skills."

This was classic Tsun-yan—thinking of each moment as a potential learning opportunity, implicitly making the point and recognizing that we all could work with the people that we wish to, if only we put a little more of ourselves into those we really want to be a part of our life story. Tsun-yan reminded me that twenty-two years ago I had come to him to propose a particular piece of intellectual capital on overseas Chinese family conglomerates that both he and I found fascinating. It was that common ground that laid the foundation for a relationship before a more formal mentorship occurred. Unconsciously or not, I'd put him in the category of "good people" alongside a cadre of others who would later go on to shape my life and career in profound ways.

I had always recognized that Tsun-yan saw putting people first and developing younger associates as an explicit part of his mission. But it was only in conversations of late that I learned that, for decades, Tsun-yan kept a diary to learn what he could do to further shape his own goodness and character, as well as the goodness and character of other people. A chance encounter with a former McKinsey associate whom he had once mentored had sparked the idea to keep the journal. Not surprisingly, the former associate had been excited to cross paths with his old mentor again, and he invited Tsun-yan to his home. Over dinner, he told Tsun-yan about his post-McKinsey career successes and the joy he felt in his new work in the music industry. He effusively thanked Tsun-yan for the critical role he'd played in this positive career change. When Tsun-yan asked him to elaborate, the man's reply surprised him. When he was consulting his colleagues on how best to explore his passion for music, the former associate said, "You were the only one who encouraged me to quit my job at McKinsey, and just follow my passion."

Tsun-yan dimly remembered the moment, but he hadn't realized its significance. The knowledge that he'd done good "in spite of what may have been an inconvenience at the time to lose a great associate" stayed with him. During his next airport layover, he went into a boutique and bought the biggest, thickest Montblanc journal he could find—nearly three hundred pages long. Once aboard the plane, Tsun-yan wrote a journal entry describing the context of the encounter he'd just had, why the man had thanked him, and what the conversation had made him feel: moved, and grateful to have had the opportunity to make a real difference to someone's life trajectory.

From that point on, Tsun-yan resolved to make a journal entry if and when another person expressed gratitude for his mentoring. Tsun-yan's motivation for recording these conversations had nothing to do with collecting accolades. Instead, he felt a calling to mentor as many people as possible and believed that the journal would encourage him to mentor as many people as possible. He decided that his career path—including his time as a senior partner at McKinsey—would have at its core a commitment to extensive mentorship. For Tsun-yan, people-first became both a personal mission and a lifelong practice. Ironically, while many of Tsun-yan's partners at McKinsey saw him as a thought leader and rainmaker, few initially regarded him as a potential people leader because he was an introvert. When Tsun-yan tried to enshrine this mission into his "professional program" (his "personal business plan") with McKinsey, he was told to "put it in the appendix" and emphasize other elements that were closer to his calling—like client conquests and knowledge development gifts to the firm.

For his journal, Tsun-yan set up a few ground rules. First, he couldn't and wouldn't go out and solicit an entry; someone had to thank him because he or she *wanted* to thank him. Second, the diary entry had to be specific. What exactly had Tsun-yan done to make a difference, large or small, in another person's life? How did it make him feel when he received that feedback? "I make each entry," he wrote on the inside cover of his journal, "so as to motivate myself to do even more good and do it better." Tsun-yan became convinced that people's character and goodness could be shaped and nurtured, and that his own character and goodness would flourish because of these relationships and experiences. Tsun-yan's diary created a virtuous circle—he would help others, and others would help him learn how to become a better mentor. Ultimately, the diary also served as a seminal exercise for one of Tsun-yan's evergreen themes for leadership: counseling others on leading and living with a sense of purpose toward wholeness. He encouraged people to pursue a larger and more holistic definition of success, in which success is defined in part by our capacity to make other people become more successful in life and leave the world a better place, too. "Most corporate executives are like racehorses whose entire existence has been devoted to 'running and winning races in an arena,'" Tsun-yan once wrote. "An alternative possibility is to proactively shape a life around activities that allow full expression of self in work and other arenas."[1] Hard results and soft outcomes like leaving behind better people are complementary, not mutually exclusive.

Tsun-yan made one last vow to himself: once he had filled all three hundred pages of the notebook, he would have accomplished his life's work and would then retire from McKinsey. More than a quarter century later, he completed the final journal entry and—true to his word—retired "in his own terms" from McKinsey. Since then, he has devoted his professional pursuits entirely to being a counselor, advisor, and mentor to leaders under LinHart, his own banner. Thanks to Tsun-yan, by now more than three hundred people are engaging more passionately and purposefully in their work, starting meaningful businesses, and serving their own mentees. Along with the woman in North York, Tsun-yan has shown me how change really begins: with a single person's determination to help others.

When I attended Tsun-yan's sixtieth birthday celebration a few years back, I noticed a remarkable common theme in the good-natured roasts delivered by generations of Tsun-yan's mentors. Every step of the way, the mentees all said, Tsun-yan saw more potential in them than they saw in themselves. And it was not until much later in life that they realized the goodness and potential in themselves that Tsun-yan believed was there all along.

THE POWER OF GOOD—REDEFINING SUCCESS

In the business world, success traditionally means maximizing profit. This view clearly fails to take into account the wide-reaching and long-term value generated by people like Garry Ridge and Tsun-yan Hsieh, who improve every aspect of their organizations simply by committing to their coworkers for the long term. Their work extends beyond them. It lives on through the strength of values, lasting relationships, and enduring cultures—goodness is indeed bigger than any one of us.

I imagine a new, expanded concept and definition for success that accounts for the power of good—a kind of success that's more purposeful, intentional, and profound than success based solely on profit or shareholder returns. There's nothing wrong with profit and shareholder returns, and I'm not arguing that goodness is a flat-out substitute for them. Of course performance in those areas matters, but we can do better.

In the end, performance and returns are the by-products of a set of principles, practices, and people. What is certain for me is that the sustainability and longevity of financial results is absolutely more of a function of people, values, and cultures than anything else. The good news is that the pursuit of goodness is not a trade-off. Even the conventional measures of value eventually catch up, as legendary investor Benjamin Graham has said: in the short run, the market is a voting machine, but in the long run, it is weighing machine. While many stock prices are driven in the short term by a popularity vote, over the long run, value reflects the true underlying quality and performance of a business.[2] It is not an accident that businesses like WD-40 that have managed consistent growth over such extended periods are rewarded accordingly by the market.

In and of itself, making money is not enough to serve as a guiding purpose to achieve long-term success. The pursuit of goodness makes us think deeper: What is the purpose of my work, and does it contribute to a larger organization? Do I cultivate my values and positively impact relationships that matter to create a lasting culture of kindness, compassion, and mentorship? Success must include much more than winning the popularity vote, so we must expand the meaning of success to incorporate goodness.

The late John Wooden, a Midwesterner who grew up on a small farm, understood the need to create a bigger, broader definition for success. Wooden is widely viewed as the most successful coach in college basketball history. With UCLA, Wooden won ten NCAA championships in twelve years, coached four teams that went 30–0 for the season, and led the Bruins to the most astonishing winning streak in NCAA history with eighty-eight straight game victories between 1971 and 1974. Over his twenty-nine-year career as a head coach, he held a winning percentage that was over 80 percent.[3] But surprisingly, Wooden eschewed the term "winning" and spent considerable time contemplating what success really meant. He did not like the term "winning" because, as he said, "you can lose when you outscore someone in a game, and you can win when you are outscored." To Wooden, success was something else.

Before coaching, Wooden taught English in South Bend, Indiana. In 1934, he coined his own definition of success to use with parents who complained about their child not getting the highest marks without regard to how other students in the class were doing. Wooden's father taught him to never try to be better than someone else, to learn from others, and yet to still make every effort to be his best.[4] This may seem contradictory—to *not* be better than anyone else and yet do everything to be your best—but that is the exact point and lesson. Success must stem from doing your best not only for yourself, but also for others. Wooden's definition of success guided his entire coaching career; for him, success meant "attaining the peace of mind and self-satisfaction of knowing that you made your effort to do the best of what you know you are capable."[5] It does not include a single word about winning.

This is what I have sought in pursuing goodness. I've not only looked to leaders and people who have won by the extrinsic and conventional markers of success—be it shareholder returns, materialistic possessions, or winning percentages—I have also asked *how* they achieved their success. And so it has been throughout my career and in the relationships and mentors that I have sought. I've always asked myself, would I want to be more like them or less like them in terms of their values and character? In terms of their substance? Wooden is right that there are many people who we might consider "winners" according to conventional definitions of success—those that have to do with the attainment of wealth and fame—but the truth is that reputational success and the long-term impact of one's life's work are far more important. This is the power of good people and goodness: to take what success means for oneself and for an organization to a higher level of meaning, substance, and impact.

In my view, a successful business should not only achieve the goal of realizing and optimizing long-term shareholder returns, but should also emphasize *how* it achieves that success, how sustainable it is, and how the business impacts everyone it touches. We need to move the business conversation in this direction, toward a discussion of how we can practice goodness and imprint goodness in others. Business can be a vessel and agent of tremendous positive change; to move beyond the cynicism and lack of trust, we need a movement of goodness. John Mackey, a cofounder of Whole Foods, outlined this principle in *Conscious Capitalism*:

> *The myth that profit maximization is the sole purpose of business has done enormous damage to the reputation of capitalism and to the legitimacy of business in society. We need to recapture the narrative and restore it to its true essence: that the purpose of business is to improve our lives and to create value for stakeholders.*[6]

I love John Mackey's quotation because it helps illustrate the power of goodness. It lays out an expanded vision of success in which businesses inspire profound change for their stakeholders as well as their shareholders. For shareholders, success can mean making or losing money—sometimes a lot of money. But a good business must positively impact the broader set of people connected to the business every day. Whole Foods has a small number of shareholders relative to its huge ecosystem of stakeholders—from the farmers and growers, to the people who pick, pack, and transport food to the stores, to the folks who serve on shop floors as brand ambassadors, to the customers. Businesses can choose to value their stakeholders, encourage them to succeed, and help perpetuate goodness in business. Mackey and Whole Foods have shown that goodness is a competitive advantage and is ultimately good for business. We can do good and still do very well for shareholders and stakeholders alike.

Doing good also begets more goodness and has the power to create long-term happiness, meaning, and significance in our lives and work. There is compelling scientific evidence that shows that investing in relationships over things like money and fame is key to living a healthy, happy, and successful life. In a 2015 TED Talk, Dr. Robert Waldinger, director of the Harvard Study of Adult Development, revealed the results of an extensive longitudinal study continuing to this day that has tracked the lives of 724 men over the last seventy-five years.[7] By systematically surveying these participants and conducting a battery of medical tests throughout this same period, Dr. Waldinger has concluded that the single most important driver of people's long-term happiness is the depth and the quality of their relationships. The most striking finding of the study thus far for Dr. Waldinger has been to see the direct correlation between investment in relationships and actual physical health. Citing research on the incidence of "chronic inflammation, circulating stress hormones, and the turning on and off of certain types of genes in certain environments," Dr. Waldinger reflected, "One of the surprises was the strong connection of relationships with physical health. There's a real powerful connection between our emotional lives and our bodies."[8] Putting time and work into other people, then, is what makes for a "good life." I believe this is true in life and business—you need to invest in relationships with people first.

Certainly the happiness I've felt through my professional career and the success I've enjoyed has been the direct result of the goodness—the support, guidance, and wisdom—of the people around me. Over the course of my career, I've committed to making people—over ideas, over products, over profits—my highest priority. This means evaluating decisions through the lens of what's in the best interest for the entirety of the people in an organization and making every effort to get there. Whether it involves a job opportunity or a potential idea, my questions have been: With whom will I be working? Whom will this impact? Does this honor my personal values and the values of the people in my organization? What does this decision say about our collective quest for truth, compassion, and wholeness? Consequently, I've helped to build two significant strategic advisory firms, arguably one of the most people-centric of businesses. Afterward, I worked with another mentor, Dick Harrington, who is a partner of mine today, to spearhead a massive cultural shift in a forty-five-thousand-person Fortune 500 business, now known as Thomson Reuters. In more recent years, I am very proud of cofounding and serving as chairman of a lifestyle retail service chain called MiniLuxe, a brand that is redefining the nail care services industry with technology and experience design, and in so doing, positively impacting hundreds of thousands of nail technicians and the clients they serve. Eight years ago, I cofounded the Boston-based investment firm Cue Ball with my college roommate, and I've served as the CEO ever since. At Cue Ball, we've been spreading a new model for venture capital based on that same people-first philosophy and being human-capital centric in everything that we do.

The common theme of my career and personal decisions in life has been the effort to work with good people. One of the things that has made me happiest about my career path is that I have had the chance to work with several of the same colleagues over many, many years—and in some cases, decades. I can truly say that I've enjoyed my work, and being with the right set of people is no small part of that equation. If you focus on the right people with the right values, the rest resolves itself. I also believe that if you are privileged to be in a position of leadership, you have a duty to try to do whatever you can to become the best version of yourself and to help others become the best versions of who they are.

Work is one of the strongest influences on our personal development. This endows business leaders with enormous responsibility and enormous opportunity to pay it forward. It makes me think deeply about my own duty to colleagues and stakeholders. There can be few greater joys in business than those times when younger colleagues achieve their goals in part because of your mentorship. We all have someone we're proud of, someone who perhaps we helped once, who has gone on to accomplish great things.

One example that comes to mind for me is a young woman named Stef Jay, who was a summer intern at my former digital and Internet strategy firm, ZEFER. I was in my first CEO role and still learning the ropes of leadership, so I did more things wrong than right. But no matter what I asked Stef or needed her to do, she always exuded a positive energy and optimism, as well as a genuine care for her colleagues.

She went on to have a successful fourteen-year career at Goldman Sachs and, as fate would have it, would marry another ZEFER alum. I've enjoyed staying in close touch with Stef over the years. From time to time she would call me for professional advice, and it has been a privilege to give a perspective on what might be in her best interests in those moments. I've remained steadfast in one piece of advice: nothing even comes close to the importance of the people who surround us, so we should always prioritize clan and culture—over competency, company name, and cash.

I believe that Stef has put people first in her decision making. Today, she is a senior executive of global e-commerce at Walmart and a super-mom to two children. Our relationship has evolved to *me* calling *her* for advice about contemporary trends in the digital and e-commerce space. I'm not just proud—I feel really *good* about seeing her and other mentees do so well and be happy in what they are doing. This is the reward and larger success that comes from being good that I've realized we should all chase after—the collective and larger happiness of others and the knowledge that we've tried our best to make that happen.

THE GOOD PEOPLE MANTRA

The pursuit of goodness and good people has become the central organizing principle of how I try to conduct my life, raise my children, build my businesses, and lead my firm in ways that meet our business objective of delivering superior returns while also positively influencing our partners, colleagues, entrepreneurs, investors, and all other stakeholders. But until recently, I wasn't able to define this feeling. You know how around certain people, you feel more inspired and elevated while simultaneously more grounded and confident? Each time I experienced this feeling in the presence of others, I tried to bottle it up so that later I could take it out and reexamine it in order to better understand what had just happened.

I vaguely began to understand that what I felt in the presence of good people was the result of someone helping me become a fuller version of myself. I wanted to learn how I could help others feel that way as well, and how I could turn it into a way of living, working, and leading. Which is why, three years ago, I resolved to reflect further on my own experiences while also researching what goodness means in leadership, philosophy, theology, history, and literature. In the end, I concluded that while there are many things that make good people tick, knowing a few meta-level choices, frameworks, and themes that most good people embody can help leaders and businesses speak the same language and come together to change the way we work. The result is this book.

Throughout, I have drawn from the wisdom of a fortuitous string of mentors, several great leaders, and everyday good people who have advanced my thinking on the topic of goodness. It's impossible to be comprehensive in listing the people who have shaped you, but this partial group of mentors represents some of that continuous chain that has positively influenced me and consequentially inspired me to mentor others. These people include business leaders like the late advertising creative icon, Jay Chiat; current Dean of the Harvard Business School, Nitin Nohria; legendary venture capitalist and chairman emeritus of Greylock, Henry McCance; the first person ever to invest behind me, Vernon Lobo; early ZEFER board member and former executive vice president of Condé Nast, Cathy Viscardi Johnson; a lifelong mentor, Tsun-yan Hsieh; and my colleagues Dick Harrington, who served for eleven years as CEO of Thomson, now known as Thomson Reuters, and Mats Lederhausen, who helped lead Chipotle and Redbox and first exposed me to the philosophy of being purposeful in business.

Leadership, however, is not something limited to business. In fact, speaking to as many people outside the world of business as possible was important because many are skeptical about how much good can or does exist in businesses and its for-profit world—especially on its investment side. In the end, I was searching not just for leadership of competency, but also for leadership of character and goodness. In this regard, it was key to dig deeper and wider. I have gained great perspective and inspiration from several extraordinarily good people outside of traditional business, but leaders in their own right, including: jazz artist Herbie Hancock, architect Moshe Safdie, MIT Media Lab interdisciplinary researcher and professor Neri Oxman, Tufts Medical Center oncologist Dr. Jack Erban, and General (Ret.) Stanley McChrystal.

In total, I benefitted from the insights from almost a hundred interviews for this book. It was key to get this diverse perspective because clearly the importance of goodness and good people is something that we all feel. Many people, not just those with recognizable names, have critical insights into goodness. Therefore, this book also draws from a large number of positive influences, many of whom were not necessarily formally interviewed but are instead unsung heroes in my own life and well-known personalities who have inspired me, both in person and on paper. These people include everyone from my parents and family, to my high school teacher turned family friend Valerie Pike, to Supreme Court Justice Sonia Sotomayor, for whom my wife clerked when she was a judge on the Second Circuit and with whom we have stayed in touch. The strength of character of all these people, together with their shared commitment to goodness, has been invaluable in shaping the ideas in this book. There is no question in my mind that the more perspectives you receive on a subject such as goodness, the more you are able to filter, see, and understand the essence of that idea.

Good people purposely and proactively *put people first* in their decision making. This is not done selectively; if you want to be good, then you need to do this consistently and over the long haul. Second, good people grow by continually seeking to improve themselves; this means that they not only pursue their own betterment, they also acknowledge a responsibility to help others feel and become *the fullest possible versions of themselves*. Third, while acknowledging the need for and the importance of competency, at the heart of goodness and good people is the premium they put on *values*—the values that underpin the very meaning of goodness beyond competency. Fourth, good people are realists. This means they understand that goodness requires hard work and a constant *balancing* of aspirations and real life. Fifth and finally, good people see goodness as something that must be put to work not only when tested in extraordinary situations, but also *whenever they are faced with the opportunity to do good.* Put simply, they step forward to do good whenever they can, not when they need to; their goodness becomes habitual.

When we see or experience goodness, these five dimensions are often in play—and we should continue to develop these qualities in ourselves, encourage these traits in the people we care about, and bring this ethos to our work. These qualities have become a "Good People Mantra" that I try to live my life and run my business by. We will discuss all five areas in more detail throughout the book, but for now, let's briefly explore each of these five mantra elements in turn.

GOOD PEOPLE MANTRA

BE
PEOPLE FIRST

HELP
OTHERS BECOME THE FULLEST VERSION OF THEMSELVES

COMMIT
BEYOND COMPETENCY TO THE VALUES OF GOODNESS

BALANCE
THE REALITIES AND TENSIONS OF GOODNESS

PRACTICE
GOODNESS WHENEVER POSSIBLE, NOT JUST WHEN TESTED

Good People Mantra Principle One: Be People-First, Proactively and in the Long Term

The premise of being people-first isn't remotely controversial, but it's not as simple as declaring, "It's all about people!" Making people a priority and the core of one's purpose is a proactive choice that good people maintain in the long term. It's a guiding principle of former Harvard Business School professor Georges Doriot, a founding father of venture capital and the founder of INSEAD. Doriot often proposed the following thought experiment: Given the choice between an A idea with a B team, and an A team with a C idea, which should you choose? Many of us would choose the better idea. But Doriot's answer? You should always go with the A team. Why? Because ideas and industries change far faster than people change. Good people who are As can adapt and evolve plans while motivating their teams to do the same. Furthermore, they can do this while staying true to their core organizational values.

So why don't we always go with the A team? Well, the truth is that most of us get more excited by ideas than we do by people and their values and characters. The danger of falling in love with ideas while compromising on people is that you can end up with a lot of mediocrity and execution risk. While As can attract As, the hard truth is that Bs tend to attract Cs and Ds. There is no question in my mind that Doriot had it right. Find the right people—the right As with strong, value-centered characters, who are also well regarded in their fields—and you are that much closer to building an extraordinary business.

The most admired leaders in business and life, then, are those who embody a people-first philosophy. As Doriot reminded us, it is people who create and execute on great ideas, and not the other way around. More to the point, only good people are able to imprint goodness onto others. In the end, it's good people who make good things happen. To be people-first is a very long-term pursuit—less a sprint than a journey, and one that lasts a lifetime. Do you have the attitude, inclination, and behaviors to make goodness a way of life? Can you cultivate this quality so that it spreads out to the conscious ways you think and behave?

Good People Mantra Principle Two: Help Others Become Fuller
Versions of Themselves

In his many years of inspiring and shaping goodness in others, Tsun-yan helped to make other people feel as though they were moving closer to their full potential and to the core of who they were. Think about the people in your life who are devoted to helping make others better. They recognize the most fundamental truth of all: we are all human. In recognizing our shared humanity, good people connect authentically with others and see beyond résumés, job roles, and professional titles to help others become better, fuller versions of themselves. They have the patience, integrity, self-confidence, and generosity of the woman who invited a precocious teenager selling picture frames to take a seat in her living room one hot summer afternoon in Toronto nearly three decades ago. The most compassionate and human moments occur when people are willing to break from their characters to focus on commonalities rather than differences—when a person gives us an unexpected hug or holds out a hand, when we experience a moment of connection with a stranger, or when a president bends down to look deeply into the eyes of a child visiting the White House.

When we look past job titles and ignore corporate hierarchy, we can harness the potential of an entire organization. Some of the greatest support I've ever received has come from administrative and junior colleagues, who have helped a lot more than just sharing a common workload. Their honesty and unexpected perspectives inspire me to become a better leader. For example, a young associate recently came into my office at the end of the day and asked if she could have a few moments. With obvious anxiety, she explained that the stress I'd expressed earlier that week in the face of a looming deadline was unproductive. "When you're stressed, it makes us feel like we have failed you," she said. "And it is upsetting because we know it is not what you intend, and that it's not who you are, either." Later, I wrote her an e-mail of gratitude for her openness and her courage. Mentorship should never be an exclusively top-down phenomenon. The people who surround us can mentor us, teach us, and help us become better versions of ourselves, and we can do the same for them.

What would happen if we cast aside our titles, lowered our guards, and focused instead on the things that make us just human? We all dream and love. We want to be accepted. We want to make a difference. We want to be secure. We want to be seen and heard. We fear mortality and contemplate our self-worth. We are just as strong as we are vulnerable. We have infinite love for our children. Many of us conceal these very human qualities at work. Somewhere along the line, we accepted the idea that being human means being unprofessional. No—it just means that we all share something profound.

If we can allow for a little more compassion in the workplace and reintroduce humanity into the practice of leadership, I believe we have the capacity to create more goodness without compromising any of our overall business goals.

Good People Mantra Principle Three: Commit to Values Before Competencies

When I speak of goodness, I consistently emphasize that I mean something much more than just competency. We need competency in business, but quite frankly, it's not enough. Goodness is deeper than competency; it's an expression of a person's purpose, nature, and fundamental values. And goodness is more valuable than competency, as General Norman Schwarzkopf once remarked: "Leadership is the potent combination of strategy and character. But if you must be without one, be without strategy."[9]

When I was an MBA student at Harvard Business School, the majority of my classmates and I felt that the most important courses the university offered taught hard skills like finance, technology, and operations management. Yet alumni and professors took pains to remind our class that we were more likely to remember the soft skill–oriented classes on subjects like leadership—and they were right. Most of my classmates can barely remember how to do any of the calculations or discounted cash flow models from our hard skill classes, but most of us now recognize how much more the soft stuff matters in our careers and lives than we could have ever imagined.

Our prejudice toward competency is apparent in other aspects of business, too. For many years, I assessed other people using a tacit shorthand: the schools they attended, their academic accolades, the number of years they trained in their professions, and the sales and/or results they generated for their previous employers. But that's no way to develop a vibrant and good culture. If all universities selected their incoming freshmen exclusively on the basis of applicants' SAT scores, it's doubtful these incoming classes would have the richness, diversity, character, and sheer potential that they do now. Résumés and conventional job interviews don't tell us anything about the more nuanced and elusive traits of goodness. Yes, grades, scores, and job titles are relevant and useful data points, but they're hardly predictive of anyone's future potential, character, and—most important—goodness.

I see this dynamic all the time in the business world. The best leaders today aren't just smart, shrewd, and strategic; they're also skilled or naturally gifted in conveying a quality that's more difficult to define. It's both soft and powerfully eloquent, and it affects the way they work, lead, and live. In his book *Superbosses*, management professor Sydney Finkelstein details how some admired leaders go above and beyond to lead by example, stay authentic to their values and culture, and achieve goals by being simultaneously hands-on, flexible, and creative.[10] For example, to test if people can fit in with their organization's values and culture, superbosses frequently develop unconventional hiring practices. Advertising legend Jay Chiat—who was also a mentor of mine—would ask something weird or do something shocking in interviews to see how prospective hires reacted to unexpected situations. World-renowned chef Alice Waters likes to discuss books on topics outside of the restaurant industry with prospective candidates at the beginning of interviews to assess their critical thinking.[11]

What iconoclastic leaders, superbosses, and good people do differently is place a premium on the goodness of character and on the human-centric values that go with it. These subtler, more complex, nonlinear qualities and values are ones we intuitively recognize and appreciate, but in practice, they often become secondary to competencies. This is in large part because it's so difficult to screen for them, which is why—as the examples of Chiat and Waters show and as we will discuss more deeply later—we need to think about different ways to become a better judge of good people. At the same time, these good-people traits and values are essential to the development of great leadership and great organizational culture. It is people, their values, and the cultures that come with them that become the secret to great long-term success. It is this that allows us to establish both common values and common standards.

Good People Mantra Principle Four: Find Balance in the Realities and Tensions of Goodness

We are in many ways born with the values that support and promote goodness—it is in our human nature to be good. But practicing goodness is an ongoing challenge thanks to real-world challenges. We often need to hold competing objectives in equilibrium. For example, I truly value idealists in my organizations for their optimism and positive energy. On the other hand, I also recognize that pragmatists who can develop and execute concrete ideas are crucial. It doesn't take too much imagination to conjure up possible scenarios where the two values of idealism and pragmatism might be at odds with one another. In business, it seems to happen every day as we navigate the time and space between our visions and the reality of their implementation. But good people realize that they need to seek a balance between competing priorities and tensions. One of the most admirable things that good people bring to the table is balance.

Part two of this book will explore the tensions we experience when practicing goodness. Understanding how to find balance in any set of tensions is key. Balance typically comes with time, counsel, and experience—it requires patience, good people, and wisdom. The good news is that balance is possible. The balance beam we need requires the will to be self-aware, the recognition that these tensions exist, and the time and perseverance to allow people to find the right equilibrium point and move forward with confidence.

Good People Mantra Principle Five: Practice Goodness Whenever You Can, Not Just When Tested

When I first heard Dean Nohria distinguish leadership of competency from leadership of character, I assumed he was attempting to dissuade businesspeople from the excess, greed, and temptation of which the business world has frequently been accused. Wasn't he simply reminding people to just "do the right thing"? After all, the past few decades haven't exactly seen the business world at its best. We've heard and read about far too many financial scandals and corruption cases, and there has been an overall decline in institutional trust among the general public. Moreover, increasing income disparity and volatility in domestic and international politics have sparked public outcries and demonstrations. I initially thought that Nohria meant that we could lower the overall balance sheet of what most people deem "bad" in the world if we find ways to increase the integrity and character of organizations.

But it turns out Nohria was saying something more. Crucially, goodness is not just about decreasing "badness." Goodness is a mandate to create more goodness in the world. It's not enough to be good in times of crisis; we need to *choose* to be good whenever we can, especially when we're in a position to influence positive change. Are we proactively seizing opportunities to create and drive positive change? Are we staying true to our values not just in the face of adversity but also when no one's looking?

Goodness is about practicing your values until they eventually become a default way of being. *Do good whenever you can.* By doing so, we can create real transformational change. After all, change begins with a single person with the will to foment change in others.

Another one of the good people I've been lucky to know and have as a mentor is Henry McCance, the chairman emeritus of the legendary venture capital firm Greylock. Henry spent forty-five years leading the firm that backed everything from Continental Cable to LinkedIn, Workday to Facebook. It was Henry who helped me see venture capital as an exercise in putting people first, because he sees it as his mission to help other people realize their visions. "Imagine," Henry said, "if throughout your life you are able to help change the lives of ten people, and they in turn change the lives of ten people, and those in turn do the same."

We all have our own "small world" of people who have helped us along the way. In whose small world can we participate and help shape for the better?

Our choices to do good have the potential to ignite positive change across industries around the world. This potential—and the hope that I can inspire you—motivated me to write this book. As you read, I hope you'll ask yourself: Are there ten people with whom I'd be willing to start up a relationship of goodness? To be a champion of their cause, an anchor in a time of need, a counselor or mentor in a time of dilemma, a cheerleader during times of success? When you're in a position to do good by these people, do you step forward and actually do it? Can you encourage these ten people to find their own ten?

SUMMARY OF KEY POINTS FROM CHAPTER 1

· · · · · · ·

- **Everything begins and ends with people.** What are we really saying when we claim we want to be good and be around good people? We should have a people-first attitude in decision making that is grounded in a set of human-centric values.

- **We are all connected, so we can help others become the fullest possible versions of themselves.** Our common humanity is revealed when we put aside our positional roles and hierarchies and sincerely seek to act in the best interests of others.

- **Competency is important, but character and values matter more.** Real goodness of leadership isn't just about having the requisite skills for a job or task. Leadership of competency is relatively easy to source, but people of character and goodness, who are rooted to a set of core values that explain who they are and what they stand for, are much rarer and more valuable.

- **Goodness requires finding a balance.** The realities and tensions that exist make the practice of goodness hard work. The key is to find the right balance points against the competing tensions that sometimes fight to override our goodness.

- **Goodness must be put to work not only when it is needed and tested in situations of moral choice, but whenever we're presented with the opportunity to do good.** This is what allows for a virtuous circle of goodness—we are positively influenced to imprint goodness on others who we in turn hope do the same.

2

———

A NEW FRAMEWORK AND
LANGUAGE FOR GOODNESS

From early in life, we learn to rely on references rather than specific criteria to describe good people. *That guy is like Atticus Finch. He reminds me of Ebenezer Scrooge.* As children, we're drawn to superheroes like Superman and Spider-Man, who allow us to roughly differentiate between good and evil, right and wrong. But as time goes on, we accumulate real-life experiences, encounters, and models. One of mine is the retired social worker in North York who unwittingly planted the seeds in my mind for what would become a lifelong preoccupation with goodness. Others draw moral rules from their faith, like the biblical Golden Rule of doing unto others as you would like others to do unto you. By the time we're in our thirties and forties, most of us share an intuitive sense of what it means to embody goodness.

The feelings that goodness so often inspires—feeling humanized, gaining inspiration, expanding one's own perspective—generally derive from a set of qualities, traits, and values most of us learned either implicitly or explicitly from our parents, teachers, and faiths. Only rarely are these same characteristics discussed or disseminated in a business setting. "Goodness" in the context of business has historically almost exclusively been used to refer to competency. Who is the best engineer to hire? Who has performed the best in the most elite schools, colleges, and universities? Who has created the most sales? It goes without saying that we want to surround ourselves with highly competent people who can get things done, but if we truly want to rise to a higher level of leadership and performance, it shouldn't be at the expense of how and why people do what they do. We need to have goodness be more holistic and incorporate character and values.

This more holistic goodness is what separates revered businesses and leaders from those who are merely competent. I believe that goodness and good people are integral to individual, business, and societal success and to creating the future we claim we want. Business leaders have been forces of change for a number of reasons. First, we spend an enormous amount of time at work—about half or more of our waking hours. Second, businesses have the potential to create innovative products and services that can impact large numbers of people. Third, our workplaces offer a huge opportunity to instill, build, and shape the mind-sets, attitudes, and practices of a future generation. In fact, some of the most respected and accomplished people we interviewed for this book—from a four-star general to one of the heads of Oncology at a major hospital—believed it was their *duty* to instill values over competencies within their organizations to help ensure strong leadership and culture in the future.

Goodness is the most important driver of genuine lasting value, but few people can agree upon a common vocabulary to define a good person, let alone practice, measure, and share how to become a better judge of people. The data points we tend to collect in the business world reflect only performance, since that's easier to measure. So how can we give equal attention to the intangibles that underlie character and the principles that motivate people's actions and behaviors?

To do so, we need to understand what goodness really means in everyday practice, separate from the teachings of philosophy, psychology, and religion. In the workplace, we need to help make this so-called soft stuff more concrete and applicable. That way, we can begin to value and even practice those things we know are good but find so challenging to define, let alone measure.

By analogy, consider how the vocabulary for wine has evolved over the years and created with it the contemporary wine industry. Without it, there would be no such thing as a sommelier. There is poetry, seduction, and grace in wine, especially when experts can distill its taste and character into its elemental ingredients using the right words, analogies, and metaphors. For centuries, wine was little more than a fortified drink, an alternative to possibly unsanitary drinking water. A *New York Times* article called "Drinking Wine, From a Chore to a Choice" noted that wine has evolved from a necessary evil to an indulgence.[1] Consequently, the market for wine evolved, and along with it the need to describe wine's attributes with a more precise vocabulary.

We've learned to analyze the character of a wine from its specific fruits, to discern its earth notes by teasing apart every steely mineral or wood characteristic down to the lees (the sediment of a wine's barrel). Complex wine terminology is quite new, however, at least in the United States. It wasn't until the 1930s and 1940s that the first sommeliers appeared in America.[2] With them came new frameworks for analyzing a wine's character, with categories like color, smell, and origin. Within each of those categories, sommeliers refined their language even further by using additional color descriptors like "light," "brick," "ruby," or "inky"; fragrance notes like "dark blackberry fruit," "moss," and "forest"; textural categories like "powerful," "heavy," "light," and "tannic" for taste; and terms like "terroir" to describe a wine's historical and geographical profile.

Surely we can also improve how we define and think about good people. As with wine, our capacity to intuit and recognize "goodness" and "good people" is instinctive, but we can ask a few keen questions to anchor our endeavor to go deeper into the subjects of goodness and good people. What, for example, is the difference between a decent leader and a great one, a good acquaintance and a true friend and anchor of support, a detached consultant and a trusted counselor? When we look beyond people's competencies to uncover what makes them tick, we're asking ourselves to go beyond the obvious and uncover the intangible qualities, values, and words that guide them.

I have thus found the need to extend my preliminary understanding of goodness and good people into a concrete framework—which I've structured as a pyramid—and lexicon, developing categories and definitions for an all-encompassing set of *values* that comprise goodness. In creating a framework and vocabulary, I've tried in this book to go from the general to the specific, using the building blocks of a pyramid to first understand what "good people" really means before discussing how to put goodness into practice.

This much I know: nothing can be put into practice without common definitions and language. But I am also aware that there are other frameworks that may work equally well for describing good people. I hope that mine will spur ideas and discussion on this subject and, most important, help you put much more goodness into practice.

DEFINITION, FRAMEWORK, AND LANGUAGE

Our general definition of "good people" is this: *those committed to continuously cultivating the values that help them and others become the fullest possible versions of who they are*. This definition serves as a North Star. However, we still require the details of a map to show us the markers along the way to our destination. This is where frameworks and language together can give us a more concrete understanding of what lies beneath the definition while also providing specifics that can help set the stage for what it means to practice goodness.

Sometimes we use the terms "definition," "framework," and "language" interchangeably without considering their nuances and differences in meaning. A definition is a high-level declarative statement of meaning, and a framework provides the structure to help us better understand that definition. Think of a framework as a mental model that provides anchor points to contextualize our understanding, like the cornerstones of a building. Language, on the other hand, fills in the spaces between these anchor points and adds dimension, hue, and layers, allowing us to explore the overall concept more deeply.

With this taxonomy in mind, consider the following for the breakdown of what we mean by good people and goodness.

General Definition of "Good People"—*Those committed to continuously cultivating the values that help them and others become the fullest possible versions of who they are*. This is our overall statement and description of meaning for good people and goodness.

The Framework: The Goodness Pyramid—Again, if we think of a framework as a kind of architecture, then there are three principal cornerstones that make up good people: *truth, compassion,* and *wholeness.* These three cornerstone qualities of goodness are our anchors in the pursuit of goodness.

In developing the Goodness Pyramid framework for goodness and good people, I was inspired by the American psychologist Abraham Maslow, who is renowned for his hierarchy of needs theory. At the base of Maslow's pyramid are our most basic physiological and safety needs. Next, we move to needs that help satisfy our *belonging and esteem* requirements. Only after that can we evolve toward *self-actualization.*

The Goodness Pyramid is structured similarly. First, it requires the foundational value of *truth*: honesty and congruency in your thoughts and actions. The next layer in our pyramid is *compassion*: selflessness made possible by understanding others' experiences. At the top of the Goodness Pyramid is *wholeness*: fulfillment and gratitude for the people we have around us and for our situation in life.

Frameworks allow us to easily analyze difficult concepts; in multiple fields, many have yielded crucial insights. Maslow's hierarchy of needs has been crucial to the field of psychological development. In the world of web development, Bootstrap, Foundation, and Semantic are frameworks for user-interface design. Some examples of frameworks in business are Boston Consulting Group's famous "stars and dogs" growth-share matrix and Michael Porter's five forces of competitive strategy. Each of these lenses helps people to develop their thinking into actions.

A *language* refers to the ways in which we delve, define, and add detail and nuance to our framework of goodness and good people. In our case, the language helps to describe the values within each layer of the Goodness Pyramid. If the architecture of the Goodness Pyramid serves as an organizing structure, then the language underneath is what fills in the personality, decor, and hues of its rooms to give it the fullness of its expression, tone, and life. We have established three values for each category—truth, compassion, and wholeness—that serve to further describe the *mind-sets, practices,* and *actions* that underpin each layer of the

Goodness Pyramid. The diagram of the Goodness Pyramid on the next page can help us understand this concept as well as the language behind goodness and good people.

Language matters much more than one might imagine, and the right language, used correctly, can illuminate any subject matter. Many studies have shown that how we speak and talk about a subject can alter our vision of the world. In the 1920s and 1930s, for example, the work of linguists Edward Sapir and Benjamin Whorf advanced the hypothesis that language and perception are inextricably linked. Many contemporary linguists, psychologists, and anthropologists stop short of saying that language determines *all* of our thoughts and cognitive processes, but there is little debate that language is highly correlated to how we perceive the world. Bottom line: a common language organizes and shapes our collective understanding of all concepts. We must unpack, in Minsky's words, the "suitcase" of goodness to establish a concrete foundation for the practice of goodness.

OUR FRAMEWORK AND LANGUAGE FOR GOODNESS

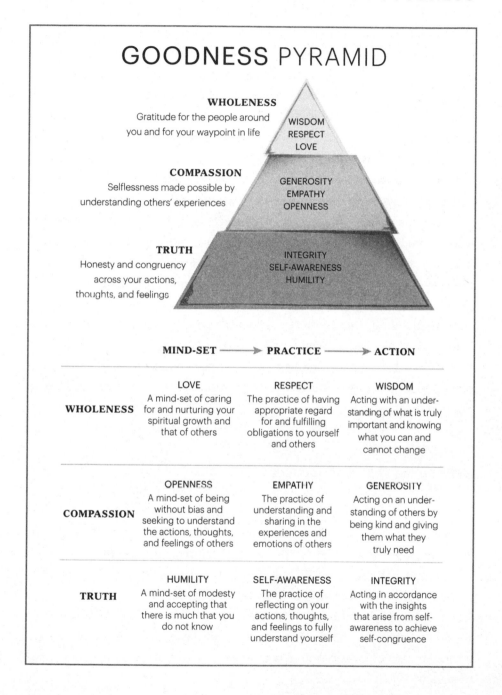

GOODNESS PYRAMID

WHOLENESS
Gratitude for the people around you and for your waypoint in life

WISDOM
RESPECT
LOVE

COMPASSION
Selflessness made possible by understanding others' experiences

GENEROSITY
EMPATHY
OPENNESS

TRUTH
Honesty and congruency across your actions, thoughts, and feelings

INTEGRITY
SELF-AWARENESS
HUMILITY

MIND-SET ⟶ PRACTICE ⟶ ACTION

	MIND-SET	PRACTICE	ACTION
WHOLENESS	**LOVE** A mind-set of caring for and nurturing your spiritual growth and that of others	**RESPECT** The practice of having appropriate regard for and fulfilling obligations to yourself and others	**WISDOM** Acting with an understanding of what is truly important and knowing what you can and cannot change
COMPASSION	**OPENNESS** A mind-set of being without bias and seeking to understand the actions, thoughts, and feelings of others	**EMPATHY** The practice of understanding and sharing in the experiences and emotions of others	**GENEROSITY** Acting on an understanding of others by being kind and giving them what they truly need
TRUTH	**HUMILITY** A mind-set of modesty and accepting that there is much that you do not know	**SELF-AWARENESS** The practice of reflecting on your actions, thoughts, and feelings to fully understand yourself	**INTEGRITY** Acting in accordance with the insights that arise from self-awareness to achieve self-congruence

Why Use These Categories and Words?

We can use any number of adjectives to describe "good people." But it is the three cornerstone categories of truth, compassion, and wholeness that mattered the most when my colleagues and I pondered the following points. First, what words best encapsulate the overall end state for a given category or dimension of goodness? Second, do the words intuitively resonate with people? And third, do these categories reflect a temporal, longitudinal path of progression? We're setting forth a hierarchy that begins with the foundation of truth, moves to the human factor of compassion, and ultimately culminates in a state of wholeness.

Over the course of my career interacting with dozens of respected leaders, and interviewing nearly one hundred people for this book (and many others for my last book), it's become clear to me that for those who are most respected and admired for their leadership, the journey toward goodness is a long-term—even lifelong—commitment that involves the continuous pursuit and practice of our three qualities of truth, compassion, and wholeness, as well as the values that underpin them. Think of truth, compassion, and wholeness as the major notes of a triad that when played together form a musical chord, similar to the harmony we seek in good people.

Defining the Values of Goodness

The heady concepts of truth, compassion, and wholeness can be made more accessible by conceptualizing each one as the combination of specific *mind-set*, *practice*, and *action* values. For example, what is the right *mind-set* for truth? What values help us better *practice* that truth each day? And ultimately how does truth manifest itself in the way we *act*? We will share many examples for each in subsequent chapters, as we have dedicated an individual chapter to each of the three major layers in the Goodness Pyramid: truth, compassion, and wholeness. In the interim, here's a quick overview.

TRUTH

Truth is our foundation, and humility, self-awareness, and integrity are the *mind-set*, *practice*, and *action* values of truth. Together, they suggest a trait much more layered and nuanced than simple honesty. If we aren't true to ourselves and true to others, our foundation is hollow. It is our honesty and congruency across all our thoughts and actions, and it is our authenticity, consistency, and credibility. When we think about the experiences of our everyday lives, such as shopping for a particular brand or frequenting a particular restaurant, our decisions are driven by a set of consistent expectations about what we're going to get. The same is true of the leaders we admire. Today, there's widespread focus on how to best increase employee engagement, but truth still flows from the top; people trust their leader if she is true to herself and true to others. To be truthful, we must be consistent in our words, actions, and values.

Like the other layers of the Goodness Pyramid, truth begins with the right mind-set—that is to say, a predisposition that allows for the expression of truth. The *mind-set* value of truth is humility. Humility requires that we acknowledge that we are often far from perfect, and that now and again even the best of us veer off course. One paragon of humility and self-awareness is Frank Blake, the retired chairman and former CEO of Home Depot. He once explained to his board why he might not be the right person for his job. After all, his experience in retail was minimal.[3] While he may have been less competent than others at the outset of his eight-year tenure, Blake's humility and self-awareness were integral to his successful leadership of the chain.

The *practice of self-awareness*, the second value of truth, is key to leadership success. It is the intellectual honesty to understand your strengths, your weaknesses, and the biases that influence your decision making. There are areas where each of us is more naturally passionate or capable, and there are also areas where we are less so. We need to have objective standards we aspire toward, and we need to measure ourselves according to those standards. The right mind-set, practice, and actions allow us to aspire to our full potential in a way that makes us satisfied that we did our best. With the mind-set of humility and the practice of self-awareness, there is the opportunity to *act with integrity*—to behave consistently so that there is congruency between our actions, thoughts, and feelings. Integrity is the third value in the truth level. It is the ultimate act and expression of our truth and our character.

COMPASSION

The second major category or dimension of the Goodness Pyramid is compassion, which in many ways is the human side of goodness. Compassion is about selflessness made possible through the understanding of others; it is composed of the *mind-set*, *practice*, and *action* values of openness, empathy, and generosity.

Openness is a mind-set. It is about reducing bias and expanding our viewpoints. The *practice of empathy* describes our ability to see and feel ourselves in other people's shoes. We practice empathy by developing better listening skills, for example. Generosity is *compassion in action*, and it denotes our willingness to act upon the empathy we feel. It can be as simple as giving a person a hug, advocating for a colleague, or volunteering for a cause—but in all cases, generosity translates the compassion values into tangible actions. By being open in our mind-sets, empathetic in our practices, and generous in our actions, we can attain a state where we care enough to act with generosity.

Good people humanize us because of their compassion. This "goodness feeling" stems from their selflessness, which comes from their deep understanding of others' experiences. People cannot be good in and of themselves. From experience, I can state unequivocally that it is the leaders who show genuine care and concern for their employees—whether it's by recognizing their unique contributions or taking the time to learn who they are—who engender the greatest degree of loyalty and engagement. Compassion is palpable; we feel like fuller versions of ourselves in the presence of the right good people. It is an intuitive litmus test for goodness that is worth remembering. One of the questions I later pose as a way to judge goodness is whether someone is a net energy giver or taker. Do you feel more optimistic, neutral, or pessimistic in the presence of this particular person?

WHOLENESS

Love, respect, and wisdom are the *mind-set*, *practice*, and *action* values of wholeness. If compassion engenders caring, then wholeness allows us to feel satisfaction and gratitude for the people around us and our situation in life—gratitude for "having existence, and being content with that existence," as Deepak Chopra once shared with me.[4] John Wooden, the late UCLA basketball coach, was once quoted as saying, "Success is peace of mind, which is a direct result of self-satisfaction in knowing you made the effort to become the best of which you are capable."[5] It's useful to try this thought exercise: Does someone in your close circle come across as complete or integrated? Wholeness derives from knowing you have sought to live your life truthfully and compassionately and thereby gained the contentment born of integration and fullness.

Love, the *mind-set* of wholeness, elevates the conditional care of compassion to the unconditional. It is more than practicing generosity toward others in given situations. Instead, it is about attaining the permanent *mind-set* that our own satisfaction and ultimate fulfillment results from supporting the fulfillment and success of others.

It is imperative that we practice goodness not only when we are asked or tested but whenever we have the opportunity to do so. To do so, we *practice* respect. Wholeness requires us to respect ourselves while equally respecting the interconnectedness of all humanity. Respect is not about obedience or submissiveness; it's about fulfilling our commitments and understanding our responsibilities and obligations to one another.

Then, when we *act with wisdom*, we demonstrate good judgment with regard both to the people with whom we associate and to the balanced decisions we need to make, knowing and accepting the things we can and cannot control. While we may never entirely achieve wholeness, we must commit to vigorously and continuously pursuing goodness in order to see the full potential in ourselves and others.

THE GOODNESS PYRAMID IS AN IDEAL— INTENTIONS MATTER

When you're trying to gain a sense of why you feel the way you do about another person or when you want to gain perspective on how you might improve a situation, consider truth, compassion, and wholeness as an entry point into assessing and understanding the problem in front of you. We are all born with the capacity to be and do more in each of these three categories—to be more truthful, more compassionate, and more whole— while influencing others to do the same.

That said, goodness isn't an absolute. It has no concrete perimeters or measurable metrics. Goodness is more than that; it is a clear-eyed pursuit of an ideal while having humility enough to recognize the inevitable tensions and challenges that complicate our desire to "be good." (I discuss these tensions in more detail in part two.) By its very nature, goodness is fluid and organic. There are no check boxes involved. Intention matters— the continuous, purpose-driven pursuit of goodness.

Next, we'll continue our exploration of goodness by digging deeper into the most foundational elements of goodness and the foundation of the Goodness Pyramid: truth.

SUMMARY OF KEY POINTS FROM CHAPTER 2

• • • • • • • •

• **Defining goodness and good people, especially in business, is challenging.** Goodness is something we all intuitively sense but nonetheless have trouble describing clearly or tangibly.

• **The core components and cornerstones of the Goodness Pyramid are truth, compassion, and wholeness.** The best way to define goodness is by creating a structured, consistent, and common architecture and vocabulary to guide us. The Goodness Pyramid has three levels: the foundation of truth; the center of compassion; and finally, the peak we strive to attain, the values of wholeness.

• **The language and values of good people are built on an underlying set of mind-set, practice, and action values.** Truth, compassion, and wholeness are the anchoring pillars of the Goodness Pyramid. The language we use to describe each of these pillars is based on underpinning values that help us fill in the spaces between the cornerstones of truth, compassion, and wholeness.

• **The pursuit of goodness is an aspirational lifelong journey.** The hardest part of developing a framework for good people is understanding that it is a continuous lifelong journey that begins with truth, moves toward compassion, and ultimately seeks wholeness. This iterative path is as much about the intention and the effort as it is any particular end state.

3

———

THE FOUNDATION: TRUTH

At the center of your being
you have the answer;
you know who you are
and you know what you want.

LAO TZU[1]

The foundation of goodness is truth, and the bedrock of truth is humility. Poorly set or misplaced expectations are a fail-safe way to come face-to-face with humility. The most humbling moment of my career happened to coincide with one of the most dizzying aberrations of the modern economic era: the heyday of the dot-com boom.

I was fortunate enough to be among a group of people who early on glimpsed the future commercialization of the Internet. In 1994, I landed my first real job, as a business analyst at the strategy consulting firm McKinsey. There I met my first-ever business partner in the most unlikely of circumstances. Despite working for the same firm, we played vastly different roles there. In those days, before analysts made their own presentations, they would bring their hand-drawn slides to a graphics and production department, where a team of specialists would then produce them. It was in McKinsey's Toronto office's production department that I first met Kaming Ng, a creative graphics specialist who was brilliant at structuring information and programming interactive presentations.

Whenever possible, I tried hard to get my slides assigned to Kaming. He was faster, smarter, and just plain better at understanding and visually expressing my chaotic-looking data charts. We loved talking about information design, and after several late-night conversations, I think both of us sensed that we could complement each other and that we had the potential to create a really special business.

A few months later, Kaming and I began moonlighting, creating multimedia presentations under the working name Zephyr, which we changed later to ZEFER. Our work caught the attention of some partners at McKinsey, and we soon had an overflowing docket of work. In 1996, when I was on the verge of entering Harvard Business School, Kaming and I brought in new team members to help evolve ZEFER's strategy and positioning on the Internet. Today, the number of real commercial sites globally is more than one billion, but in those days the Internet was in its infancy; when I first met Kaming in 1994, there were an estimated 2,700 websites in the world. The following year, that number jumped to around 20,000, and it became clear that something big was happening with the commercialization of the Internet.[2] Little could we imagine that there would be close to one billion websites today. Back then, Kaming and I were content with believing that we could become a "McKinsey of the Internet," offering both the creative and technical chops to become a one-stop shop for large-scale web applications, before most people (including the two of us) really knew what that meant.

But we thought we had everything figured out! Which is why, in 1996, we formally founded ZEFER, one of the country's first Internet advisory and web application development groups. What happened after that was mind-boggling. Before we knew it, we had a few dozen employees, then one hundred, and by late 1999 we were on pace for one thousand employees, and well over $100 million in revenue. The name ZEFER was the phonetic spelling of "zephyr" and was meant to evoke a gentle breeze blowing in from the west. The logo was originally conceived with a reverse second "E" to convey the bridging of left- and right-brain thinking— the crux of the founding philosophy and partnership that Kaming and I shared. Our timing was good, too. There was a seemingly insatiable demand for this new medium known as the Internet, and ZEFER's dazzling upward trajectory was the kind most Silicon Valley start-ups can only dream of. At the same time, I began making some angel investments in other Internet start-ups that also bore great fruit. *This is all so easy!* I remember thinking.

It was a crazy, exhilarating time. New start-ups with no revenue to speak of and no rational business model were receiving exaggerated valuations, fear and greed were rampant, and many of the world's best-known businesses worried that they'd be the next to get "dot-com'd." It was a modern-day Henry Ford moment: good-bye horses-and-buggies, hello automobiles—much like how the taxi industry feels today about Uber and Lyft, and how the traditional hotel hospitality industry feels about Airbnb. ZEFER rode high on this wave, selling the picks, pans, and shovels to the people chasing a gold rush. We were building large-scale Internet sites and applications before our clients even knew what they were.

But I started to lose some sense of self, and the externalities of ZEFER's success waged war against my own humility and self-awareness. By now, ZEFER was an industry darling, and I'd become one of the poster boys for the Internet's hysteria. Some of that definitely went to my head. After all, I'd only just graduated from Harvard Business School, where my colleagues and I had won the business plan competition and inspired two business school case studies. Two of the most popular technology publications at the time—the *Red Herring* and the *Industry Standard*—regularly referenced us, and one asked me to become a regular contributor. By then, ZEFER had raised record amounts of money: $1.2 million at the end of my first year of business school and $100 million the year after graduation—and we continued to gain new clients hand over fist. We started to believe our own hype, and to confuse positive PR and dollars raised with business success, which is always a dangerous thing.

Still, we pushed ahead, setting the groundwork to take ZEFER public in 2000. We spent days completing what in the finance world is called an S-1 filing—in effect, a prospectus of disclosures and key business information that has to be filed with the SEC and given to potential investors before any company goes public. It's the entrepreneur's engagement ring, so to speak, before the dream IPO day, when logo banners hang down in front of the stock exchange on Wall Street.

How could we have known what lay ahead when every indicator pointed in the right direction—toward the sky? Each one of us secretly, and sometimes not so secretly, calculated the winnings we would take from a range of different IPO values. One day while visiting our New York offices, I remember literally pinching myself as I ran my own numbers—the minimum won in almost any scenario was in the tens of millions, or so I thought. But our IPO road show hit a wall in March 2000 as the market began to show its first signs of turbulence. We watched the NASDAQ drop lower and lower, eventually losing one third of its value. Our brief window of opportunity had slammed shut. One moment we'd been front and center of the dot-com boom, and the next we were front and center of the dot-com bust. It was the most surreal experience imaginable.

We had planned to show up at the NASDAQ the next morning to take the company public—to ring the bell, an initiation of sorts into the exclusive club of other public companies—but instead we pulled our offering at the last minute. A professional victory very quickly became a cringeworthy and extremely public embarrassment. The very same press that revered us in the weeks leading up to the IPO targeted us as a black-eyed symbol of the crash. In fact, the day ZEFER intended to go public was the largest NASDAQ drop in its history to date, a slide that would only continue over the next few months.

In the short term, our disappointment came from not going through with the IPO. Even more deeply dismaying was the realization that our perspective was fundamentally flawed. We'd defined our success by what an initial public offering could bring us, rather than by any of the meaningful roles or innovations we had created, or their impact on the world. We had deviated from our purpose and focused more on growth than on what we were growing. There was more. We had overly managed and grown ZEFER into what we believed the market wanted, rather than who and what we actually were. We had veered away from a truthful and authentic purpose. We had spent time figuring out how to become a public company at the expense of growing into a great company that could dictate its own future (public or not). The aftermath was predictably dispiriting. We restructured, filed for protection, and had three rounds of layoffs before the business stabilized. Eventually it was acquired, but for nowhere close to what we had hoped.

The failed IPO was humbling—truly humbling, where you feel everything inside you sink to your toes. But if there was a silver lining, it was that it took us back to our founding purpose, and I was fortunate that the lesson occurred at a more youthful stage of my career. ZEFER was a crash course in the importance of goodness to business that otherwise might have taken me much longer to absorb. I learned to be unwavering in the integrity of the *purpose* of a business; to seek to be people-centric in everything; to prioritize the inputs of what makes for a great business over any financial outputs; to learn ways to better communicate with true understanding; and to focus on the intrinsic rather than the extrinsic rewards. The final lesson was the most important: to maintain perspective and gain clarity on the people who really matter around you.

This last lesson was eye-opening. Who is there for you when it counts, and who isn't? Missed financial transactions are one thing—a bruising of the ego and wallet—but it stings to discover that some of the loving, trusting relationships you had with people turned out to be merely transactional. In those moments, you learn a lot about yourself, and a lot about truth, friendship, goodness, and expectations.

Whenever a company files an S-1 in preparation for going public, there is a mandatory quiet period during which the principals are forbidden to talk about the company. During that time, they also have the opportunity to allocate shares to friends and family so that they can buy in at the IPO price. Well, as it turns out, when friends and family believe there is something to gain, a lot of them come running to line up. Some did everything they could to make me feel guilty for not allocating them enough shares. And when things did not turn out as we expected, there were also those who felt bitter and entitled to something that had never belonged to any of us in the first place. And some blamed me. I was anxious, confused, frustrated, and unhappy during a time in my life that should have been a celebration.

Experience is a cruel teacher. First it gives us the test, then it gives us the lesson. The market crash had permanent consequences for ZEFER's future. That said, along the way I gained numerous lifelong lessons early on in my professional career that many people take decades to learn, if they ever do. I learned that businesses should never compromise truth in purpose, humility and self-awareness in leadership, or integrity in values.

BEGIN WITH THE MIND-SET OF HUMILITY

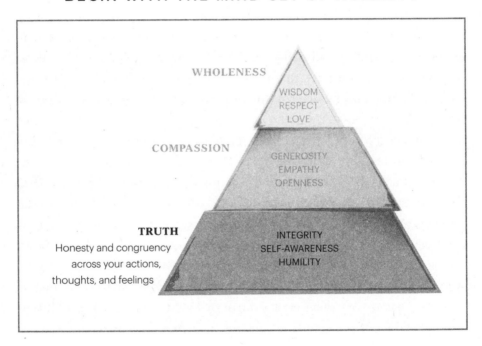

"There is nothing noble in being superior to your fellow man," Hemingway once said. "True nobility is being superior to your former self."[3] Hemingway's words demonstrate that truth begins in yourself and your purpose. As I learned through my early experience with ZEFER, it is impossible to be truthful without humility, and being humbled has a curious way of reminding you of the core purpose underlying everything you do. In *Start with Why*, Simon Sinek shows that the "what" of a business matters far less than the "how" and the "why."[4] Don't let distractions cloud your "why," your purpose.

Humility in Leadership

In 2001, *Good to Great* author Jim Collins popularized what he dubbed the "triumph of humility" as the core critical trait of his "Level 5" leaders— those men and women who have created and steered the highest perform- ing organizations.[5] Many who read his article in *Harvard Business Review* found Collins's conclusion puzzling and counterintuitive, and in the years since then, I'm not sure how much his recommendations have been prac- ticed in the business world. Why? Because this critical component of goodness—being humble or having humility—is seldom among the first set of traits typically identified as key for leadership success, let alone singled out as an essential trait for elevated leadership, as Collins ar- gued. Many people in business take a desire for truth and integrity for granted, but the various preconditions of truth—including self-awareness and humility—are more modern phenomena of business practice and lead- ership.

Collins was among the first to argue that it's the softer factors that make for great leadership. He maintained that larger-than-life results are less likely to come from larger-than-life personalities than they are to come from leaders who exhibit authenticity and humility in mindful, deeply self-aware ways. This may seem strange. After all, the media fo- cuses on tough, swashbuckling CEOs. In many public and private compa- nies, the extrinsic rewards of money and positional power are so great that some high-ranking executives feel they have "arrived" even if they are performing and behaving at a mediocre level—or even poorly. Actor Mike Myers once noted, "Fame can be the industrial disease of creativ- ity."[6] For whatever goodness we may have innate within us, and whatever goodness we may desire, there are externalities—and as we will discuss in the next section, tensions—that look to either tempt us or override our goodness.

Only by maintaining genuine humility can one foster a lifelong intel- lectual curiosity and the openness required for even greater possibility, creativity, and humanity. Humility allows us to rethink and reframe our definitions of success and failure. At WD-40, for example, they don't think of speed bumps as mistakes but as learning moments. The word "mistake" has been erased from WD-40's vocabulary. At its core, humility needs to differentiate between factors within our control and those external forces, variables, and learnings beyond our control or reach.

Today, thanks in no small part to Collins, humility is widely seen as a "must-have" value of business leadership. Before humility took its rightful place in business leadership, the worlds of religion and psychology both embraced it as a desirable core teaching, just as many iconic historical figures have done. In his autobiography, Benjamin Franklin identified humility as the last of his thirteen must-practice virtues, which he described as the ability to "imitate Jesus or Socrates"—a nearly impossible standard, but still a worthy ambition.[7] Indeed, most of us have a lot of ground to cover in the humility department, but recognizing the gap is critical and part of the practice of self-awareness.

Humility as a Mind-set

Many mistranslate humility as the belief that you think very little of yourself, but that's not what humility is at all. Being moderate and unpretentious in your perspective on your own capabilities does not equate to poor self-esteem. Rather, humility is thinking somewhat *less*, rather than *little*, of yourself. Do we consider ourselves to be important? Are we convinced we are more right than wrong? Humility serves as a powerful counterbalance.

Peter Georgescu has an extraordinary background story that has doubtlessly helped shape his leadership principles and views on the importance of humility. Born in Bucharest, Romania, on the eve of World War II and left to survive in a labor camp at age nine, he eventually immigrated to the United States with little schooling or English language skills. Yet Georgescu persevered, attending both Princeton and Stanford before joining the advertising firm Young and Rubicam, where he spent thirty-seven years of his career and served as the chairman and CEO.

Georgescu attributes much of his success to leading with integrity and fidelity to his own values. He argues that humility does not have to come at the expense of other important business traits and values so long as leaders are still able to push things into action. As he wrote in his book *The Source of Success: Five Enduring Principles at the Heart of Real Leadership,* "a leader who has no doubts is a fanatic. A leader whose convictions are strong despite doubts is humble, willing to learn and listen, but with a strong bias for action."[8]

This begs the question: Is it possible through time or practice to develop the right mind-set for humility? And if we can develop humility, what is it that slows us from doing so—what makes it difficult for humility to be a more natural element of our lives and leadership?

Robert Roberts, the distinguished professor of ethics at Baylor University, has produced one of the clearest explanations of how our emotions interact with virtues as well as vices. Along the way, not surprisingly, he quotes Benjamin Franklin, who wrote in his autobiography:

> *In reality, there is, perhaps, not one of our natural passions so hard to subdue as pride. Disguise it, struggle with it, beat it down, stifle it, mortify it as much as one pleases, it is still alive, and will every now and then peep out and show itself.*[9]

Ultimately, Roberts defines humility as the absence of pride, quite a change in thinking from some perceptions of leadership. He then challenges us to recognize that it is pride's negative side—envy, arrogance, or self-righteousness versus the more positive traits of pride, like self-respect or even patriotism—that is the true enemy of humility.[10] This theory is helpful because it makes us more aware of what pulls us away from being more naturally humble. Indeed, the best way to understand and develop the mind-set for humility may be to understand its darker qualities, which are the risks that come with positional authority. If we're arrogant, envious, snobbish, or self-righteous—or have ever been accused of such—it's useful to reflect on our actions, behaviors, and decisions. Have we used our status to help us gain an advantage? Have we taken smug pleasure in winning a negotiation or debate? By continuously reflecting on your actions, behaviors, and words, you can develop self-awareness and increased sensitivity to the relationship that exists between your pride and your humility.

THE PRACTICE OF SELF-AWARENESS

I think self-awareness is probably the most important thing towards being a champion.

BILLIE JEAN KING[11]

If asked to pick out one desirable trait above all others within the foundation of truth, I would always opt for self-awareness. More than any other quality or value, self-awareness helps us better understand the successes and failures of our lives as they relate to other people—both good and bad. Practicing self-awareness allows us to be rigorously honest about our actions, as well as the results derived from those actions. In the end, the consistent practice of self-awareness is the path to elevated leadership. Self-awareness helps us build stronger integrity and congruence between what we say, think, do, and feel.

My first book, *Heart, Smarts, Guts, and Luck*, explored self-awareness by analyzing the four core traits common to successful entrepreneurs that drive decision making. Practicing self-awareness of the traits of heart, smarts, guts, and luck increases our chances not only of achieving professional success but also of living a life congruent with our true selves. By knowing and managing our tendencies toward some of these traits more than others, we can better identify the strengths and weaknesses that ultimately shape and inform our decisions. Specifically, the past research and work that I did with my coauthors demonstrated that we tend to be biased toward one or more of the four traits of heart, smarts, guts, and luck. If we know our bias, we can increase our awareness of the best ways to complement our teams and thinking, and where our strengths help or hinder us.

We have similar biases in how we think about good people, too. Take a moment to reflect on past relationships, failed partnerships, or hiring mistakes you've made over the years. What biases contributed to those decisions? Were you truly self-aware? Self-awareness has its own symbiotic, mutually reinforcing mechanism; when you are better able to judge, find, and associate with good people, they will help you reach a higher level of self-awareness. It's little wonder that people ultimately seek a dynamic where a partner or team together makes its participants better as a whole than a single person could be working independently.

Sometimes it seems that businesses put practices in place that actively demote self-awareness. Processes, policies, and the adherence to "norms" can have the unintended consequence of encouraging mindless behavior— the complete counterobjective of self-awareness. Ellen Langer is a psychology professor at Harvard and the author of the classic 1989 book *Mindfulness*. As a bellwether of the mindfulness movement, Langer has long argued that self-awareness and truthfulness cannot help but bring greater depth and meaning to both our professional and personal lives.[12] In 2014, I moderated a Boston Book Festival session with Professor Langer, where I was once again reminded of the importance of self-awareness and consciousness. Langer used one of her favorite examples to illustrate how easily we can slip into mindlessness.

A cashier once noticed that Dr. Langer had forgotten to sign her new credit card, so she asked her to sign it before ringing up her purchase. Dr. Langer obliged and signed the new credit card right in front of the cashier. After ringing up the last of the goods, the cashier handed Langer the credit card slip to sign, which Langer also did quickly. This is where things got interesting and, unfortunately for Dr. Langer, a little frustrating. Mindlessly following the store's standard operating procedures, the cashier asked if she could have Dr. Langer's credit card again. When Dr. Langer asked why, the cashier said she needed to check that the signatures matched. *But I just signed both in front of you!* Dr. Langer must have been screaming in her head. Still, Langer acquiesced, handed back her new credit card, and watched—a little stunned—as the cashier took the credit card and turned it over to see where Dr. Langer had just signed it, holding the credit card and credit card slip side by side to make sure the signature was the same. The process had overwhelmed its purpose, which was to ensure that the person making the purchase was the real owner of the given credit card. But clearly, in this case it was the same person. There was no evidence of self-awareness.

As Langer's anecdote shows, it's easy to slip into standard operating procedures and routines without thinking about them and to follow processes that distract us from our own self-awareness. It takes very little external conditioning for us to lose sight of who we are and to behave in ways we could never imagine. We all too often mindlessly and automatically conform to the roles that we are told to play. This is because we are often taught to follow rules and processes rather than to cultivate good judgment. In business, we ought to be cautious of implementing best practices and standard operating procedures that unwittingly reduce our own self-awareness. Just as breaking from character allows people's goodness to come out, we sometimes need to break from the rules when exceptions are warranted. Leaders must give permission to their teams to be more reflective, expressive, and human.

This is one way good people help us preserve our own inner truth and self-awareness—to not lose the truth of who we are. Good people beget other good people. In other words, positive peer pressure is the antidote to negative peer pressure. When we are around good people, we are positively influenced by our peer set to become the fullest and truest versions of who we are. In so doing, we become more aware of how our behavior and actions measure up in that group. Good people who are willing to break from their character and shed their titles and roles help others become truer and better versions of who they are.

The opposite can be true. There are plenty of situations in which the people around us do not necessarily foster our best interests. Positional authority can often lead to an innate bias to fit perceived expectations of that role, even though this might be against one's own intrinsic values. In the end, we are motivated by the behaviors—positive or negative—of those people around us. This is why the practice of self-awareness is so critical to understanding our biases and to recognizing that biases serve as an internal warning system that flags when we go against the principles we stand for or believe in. But are we really that easily influenced by those around us? Absolutely. As research has shown, we can be negatively influenced to the point that we act completely inconsistently with our values, and in some situations, to the point where we no longer even recognize who we are.

Consider the well-known 1971 Stanford prisoner experiment, in which Stanford psychology professor Philip Zimbardo split twenty-four randomly selected men into two groups and asked them to play either prisoners or guards in the basement of the Stanford psychology building.[13] Much to Zimbardo's amazement, the "guards" proceeded to exhibit extreme authoritarian behavior, while the "prisoners" became uncharacteristically subservient. As the experiment continued, the lines between fantasy and reality became blurred, and "prisoners" began to break down emotionally, which forced Zimbardo to abruptly end the experiment early. Zimbardo's classic experiment may have taken place four decades ago, but its lessons endure: if we don't focus vigilantly on self-awareness and trust the people around us, our own behavior can quickly become unrecognizable. Being in the company of the right people who provide positive peer pressure is the best way to avoid falling into the trap of wearing a mask or playing an unnatural role.

Deepening our knowledge of ourselves, and doing everything to acknowledge and appreciate the real human bonds that connect us to one another, is the key to solving the problems that taint business and the larger world. While most of us do not inhabit a world of prisoners and guards, our lives run an equivalent gamut: from enhanced or exaggerated social media personas, to fraudulent businessmen running Ponzi schemes, to extreme radical groups actively recruiting new membership. All of these externalities are negative influencers on our inner goodness—to say nothing of the potential negative unintended consequences that success may bring along with fame, power, and money. Truth, including both humility and self-awareness, is the foundation of strong leadership and authentic collegiality in business, and it is what we need to preserve and promote the goodness that is within us all.

Practices for Self-Awareness

So the question becomes: How do we cultivate a level of self-awareness that ultimately leads to greater truthfulness and integrity of behavior? Below are five practical techniques.

1. Meditate and stay mindful. Meditation is the simple practice of finding an inner place of calm where you can achieve moment-by-moment awareness. It's an easy place to start if you need help centering yourself. Most forms of meditation focus on the breath, calling attention to the simple acts of inhaling and exhaling. Periodically during a meditation, I ask myself a set of questions, among them: What am I trying to achieve? What am I doing that is working? What am I doing that is slowing me down? And what can I do to change?

That said, all that meditation requires is attention to your thoughts, feelings, and environment. It means being aware of context and ultimately drawing on that context to improve your understanding of yourself. The most frequent form of meditation I practice is informal. My best moments of reflection take place while I carry out seemingly mundane tasks, including washing dishes, working in my garden, or spending a Saturday morning writing in the Art of the Americas Wing of Boston's Museum of Fine Arts. Putting thoughts to paper in the right setting can be extraordinarily meditative. These quiet moments create windows for self-reflection and increase the clarity of my self-awareness.

2. Write down your key plans and priorities. One of the best ways to increase self-awareness is to write down what you want to do and then track your progress. Warren Buffett, for example, is known for carefully articulating his reasons for making a particular investment at a particular time. His journal entries serve as a historical marker and reminder for assessing whether he can attribute future outcomes to his own sound judgment and analysis or just plain luck.

It is impossible to gain self-awareness if you're unable to define what success means or if you lack a scorecard or metrics that can tell you if you are winning. This is especially true in business, where all too often people set priorities by defining goals without ways to measure how they will judge their own future success. Consider writing down your goals in a transparent manner for all to see. Think of it as your own institutional self-awareness check. At Cue Ball, we ask each of our CEOs to write down their top five priorities on one simple page at the beginning of the year so that they can share this touchstone document with their board and employees and refer back to it throughout the year. Codification is an extraordinarily powerful tool for the practice of self-awareness and for integrity.

3. *Psychometric tests.* In my previous book, my coauthors and I present a simple psychometric entrepreneurial aptitude test we developed (www.hsgl.com) that forces people to answer trade-off questions, which ultimately helps them gain greater self-awareness of their own true characters and inborn biases. For example: Are you more driven by intellectual reasoning or gut feeling? Do you think you are driven more by passion or action? Do you care more about the details or the big picture? Our goal was to emphasize that there were no right or wrong answers and to help readers understand which traits they were biased toward both in business and in life. Other well-known psychometric tests include the Myers-Briggs test and Predictive Index.

4. *Ask trusted friends and colleagues and be vigilant about holding them to a standard of goodness.* None of us is altogether aware of how we come across to others, which is why a selection of peers, friends, and mentors can often serve as honest mirrors of your actions and behaviors. If you are vigilant about becoming a better judge of the people around you, consider whether they have the qualities of truth, compassion, and wholeness. A good way to start is by letting

friends know when you are seeking candid, critical, and objective answers and perspectives. I recently received the following e-mail from a venture capital colleague: "Please tell me as a friend: do you think that I currently hold any beliefs or assumptions that you think are incorrect and that will lead me to act in a way that is not ideal? I just want an honest check on myself." Another strategy is to ask friends to call you out when you are behaving in a way you'd like to change. For example, "Look, I know I have a tendency to be a 'story-topper' who needs to one-up people in conversations, but do me a favor and let me know when I do it—preferably discreetly—so I can learn to stop." Have a few good people you can rely upon to give it to you straight. We all need this from time to time.

5. *Regular formal feedback.* In addition to friends and family, use the feedback processes and mechanisms at your workplace. If there are none, see if you can implement some regular feedback loops. Provided that it's done well, constructive, formalized feedback allows us to better identify our own strengths and weaknesses, as well as the places we could stand to improve. At Cue Ball, we encourage founders to formalize some level of regular feedback where peers—both supervisors and direct reports—have access to a safe, professionally mediated format for providing feedback across multiple areas, including values, competencies, and work styles. The practice of collecting formal, written, or even surveyed feedback may feel like an outdated corporate tradition, but it is surprising how many organizations, both small and large, say they want to do this but don't. Feedback is just a means of having an honest conversation with the aim of getting a better picture of an individual or the overall health of an organization. One simple way of doing this—which we do with our own team—is to have employees write and update their own goals for self-evaluation. Other means of collecting feedback include engagement surveys, 360 coaches and facilitators, and online sources like Yelp and Glassdoor. You may not

get a perfectly accurate picture, but you should get an approximate sense of how people are feeling.

ACT WITH INTEGRITY TO EMBODY TRUTH

Truth is ultimately expressed in terms of how we act, especially if we act with integrity. Integrity means one's behavior is consistent with one's values. Integrity is complete self-congruence, so that:

What you do is what you say
What you say is what you think
What you think is how you feel
And understanding how you feel is who you are.

Seeking the truth of who you are today and who—and where—you want to be in the future has much to do with the larger concept of integrity. Here we see the interconnectivity of doing, saying, thinking, and feeling. How we feel is who we are. How we feel is the by-product of our internal values. If our thinking, saying, and doing is consistent with these values, we've reached the purest form of integrity. It is this level of self-congruent integrity that allows the best leaders to earn trust. Stated simply: values espoused must be values expressed.

Most of us can intuitively sense whether the people around us live and breathe their values. Any manager, leader, or organization that merits respect needs to strive for this same consistency of behavior and do so in an authentic, human-centric, and transparent manner. At every organizational level, there must be clarity of a purpose backed by actionable principles and unwavering values; this is what gives an organization its soul, meaning, and purpose. We should discuss integrity not only in terms of individual leadership but also with respect to a company's purpose or a brand's soul. It's relatively easy for most leaders and organizations to codify the values, mission, and purpose for which they stand. It's much harder to practice the self-awareness that demands that we acknowledge when we are straying from our purpose and values.

More challenging still is reaching a personal or organizational state in which values and culture are *a way of being.* You cannot fake values or force a culture. These come from accumulated daily behaviors, experiences, and memories. Being around and having relationships with the good people is what guides us the right way along this journey. Leslie Brunner, former COO and head of People and Process at athenahealth and now president of Mini-Luxe, shared a similar sentiment with me. She emphasized the following:

> *For me it came down to a couple of things. It's one thing to be a company that values integrity, lives by a code of conduct, etc. But most companies expect individuals to hold up their end of the bargain. I believe a way of being isn't just doing those things but bringing others along. It's not enough just to want to be a good corporate citizen. A way of being means you ensure others are set up to be the best version of themselves too. And you consider that charge a core part of your responsibility.*[14]

Brunner recognizes and promotes those who are good at "bringing others along." This philosophy is completely consistent with our definition of goodness: *those committed to continuously cultivating the values that help them and others become the fullest possible versions of who they are.* It is a mind-set and attitude that looks hard at values, principles, and culture rather than merely evaluating individual competencies and numbers.

But something else has stood out to me when I've spoken with Brunner about how to promote stronger personal and organizational integrity: the importance of seeing the "power in failure." As my partners at Cue Ball and Brunner emphasize, our daily work is often messy. We need to be okay with that and to celebrate it rather than exposing those who take a leap and try something different or bold. The important thing here is transparency. Athena is still led by its original cofounder, Jonathan Bush, who strives for a radical level of transparency. Bush encourages openness throughout the organization, about both the good and the bad. One way to promote a culture of risk taking and learning is to put those who "failed big" in public, transparent, and accessible positions. This transparency, which demonstrates integrity of values, is what gives organizations credibility and trustworthiness among its employees.

Practical Strategies to Achieve Integrity

The starting and ending point for goodness is consistency in your truth—uncovering it through self-awareness and consistently evolving and enhancing it through humility. Li Lu, a coleader of the Tiananmen Square student demonstrations, who today is a highly respected investor, once told me about an exercise that he and other top leaders practice for their own truth-seeking development, one originally inspired by Benjamin Franklin. One of life's most interesting balance sheets has nothing to do with finances, Li told me. Instead, it records your own personal accounting of your assets and liabilities. Franklin recorded any new strength he believed he could learn from someone else and marked down any self-perceived weaknesses in order to better assess how the net worth of his character grew over time.

At age twenty, Franklin's personal mission was to become more virtuous—to become the best "good person" possible. "It was about this time I conceived the bold and arduous project of arriving at moral perfection," Franklin writes in his biography. "I wished to live without committing any fault at any time; I would conquer all that either natural inclination, custom, or company might lead me into."[15] To accomplish this, he wrote down the traits he deemed to be thirteen of life's most critical virtues and defined them for himself. It's an even more ambitious list than what I have put forth as the values of good people! Here are Franklin's thirteen virtues[16]:

1. **Temperance**—Eat not to dullness; drink not to elevation.

2. **Silence**—Speak not but what may benefit others or yourself; avoid trifling conversation.

3. **Order**—Let all your things have their places; let each part of your business have its time.

4. **Resolution**—Resolve to perform what you ought; perform without fail what you resolve.

5. **Frugality**—Make no expense but to do good to others or yourself; that is, waste nothing.

6. **Industry**—Lose no time; be always employed in something useful; cut off all unnecessary actions.

7. **Sincerity**—Use no hurtful deceit; think innocently and justly, and, if you speak, speak accordingly.

8. **Justice**—Wrong none by doing injuries, or omitting the benefits that are your duty.

9. **Moderation**—Avoid extremes; forbear resenting injuries so much as you think they deserve.

10. **Cleanliness**—Tolerate no uncleanliness in body, clothes, or habitation.

11. **Tranquillity**—Be not disturbed at trifles, or at accidents common or unavoidable.

12. **Chastity**—Rarely use venery but for health or offspring, never to dullness, weakness, or the injury of your own or another's peace or reputation.

13. **Humility**—Imitate Jesus and Socrates.

Franklin placed these thirteen virtues in a column against a datebook. In this way, he could mark the days when he violated any one of these virtues and reflect on his record, which also served as a broader trend report for monthly and annual reviews of his progress. For each virtue, Franklin developed crystal-clear definitions. My personal favorite is his definition of industry: "Lose no time; be always employed in something useful; cut off all unnecessary actions." To this end, Franklin was careful to have a systematic schedule that would help ensure that he practiced his virtues and always reflected on which of his activities helped generate greater goodness. A few pages from Franklin's diary are reproduced on the following pages[17]:

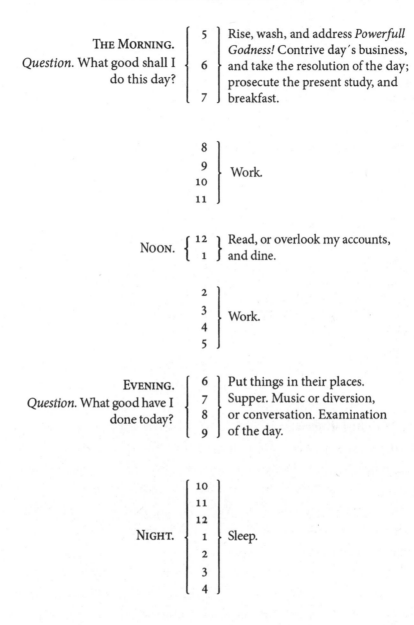

The Morning.
Question. What good shall I do this day?

5 | Rise, wash, and address *Powerfull Godness!* Contrive day's business,
6 | and take the resolution of the day;
7 | prosecute the present study, and breakfast.

8
9
10
11 } Work.

Noon. { 12 } Read, or overlook my accounts,
1 } and dine.

2
3
4
5 } Work.

Evening.
Question. What good have I done today?

6 | Put things in their places.
7 | Supper. Music or diversion,
8 | or conversation. Examination
9 | of the day.

10
11
12
Night. 1 } Sleep.
2
3
4

Franklin possessed the unusual ability to appreciate and pursue self-awareness using a disciplined and orderly process to ensure he lived with integrity. (The third of his thirteen virtues was, in fact, "order.") As you can see from the pages reproduced from Franklin's autobiography, there

FORM OF THE PAGES

	Sun.	M.	T.	W.	Th.	F.	S.
Tem.							
Sil.	*		*	*		*	
Ord.	*	*			*	*	*
Res.		*				*	
Fru.		*				*	
Ind.			*				
Sinc.							
Jus.							
Mod.							
Clea.							
Tran.							
Chas.							
Hum.							

is an almost militaristic structure to his entries, and a check-box mind-set to ensure he remembered to ask himself what acts of goodness he achieved each day. Annie Dillard, author of *The Writing Life*, seems to be a kindred spirit of Franklin's. She writes: "How we spend our days is, of course, how we spend our lives. What we do with this hour, and that one, is what we are doing. A schedule defends from chaos and whim. It is a net for catching days."[18]

I strongly believe in a similar orderliness in my own workplace. Every day, I do my best to follow an AM/DB (a morning debrief) of the key upcoming items of the day and week that addresses objectives of meetings we have scheduled, follow-ups from previous meetings, and gaps we need to fill. Following an order and a sequence to ensure we optimize the time we have to accomplish our tasks is my own workplace's version of Franklin's diary. Inspired by Franklin's habit of creating checklists and tables, I've created a laminated card of the sequence I follow in these AM/DB meetings. It includes the following prompts: What are the biggest upcoming priorities? What have I committed to do today? What are the follow-ups that were promised? When do I have gaps in my schedule? This may sound overly choreographed, but it offers a degree of efficacy and efficiency I never had before I began the practice. The goal for me now is to elevate this checklist beyond competencies and "to-dos," and to have a values-centric version that helps me ascertain whether progress is being made.

What Franklin grasped and mastered was his own version of an R & R—not rest and relaxation, mind you, but rather routine and reflection. More precisely, he combined mindful reflection with the order and discipline of routine. Together, this makes for a lifelong learner and, not unrelatedly, a lifelong leader. The best leaders in my experience are students first and teachers second. By combining Franklin's routine and reflection with the disposition for lifelong learning, you enhance the likelihood of maintaining both consistency and integrity in your behavior.

As Benjamin Franklin's example shows, the journey toward integrity and self-congruence takes a lifetime. Franklin's mission to achieve moral perfection was nothing short of noble, but it was also unobtainable, considering that we can always do more, and more consistently, too. But sometimes, fulfillment can come from the consistency of a habit that routinely prompts a question relevant to a current or future goal. As Franklin himself wondered aloud every morning: "What good shall I do today?"[19]

TRUTH AND VALUES AS OUR RIVERBANK

While truth is a virtue we should all aspire to attain personally, truth is also critical to the businesses and brands that we connect deepest with as consumers—companies like Patagonia, Trader Joe's, Southwest, Soul-Cycle, IKEA, Hermès, and Chanel. All companies share a relentless drive to live by and protect the integrity of their brand, whether it's socially conscious, quirky, lifestyle, or ultra-luxury. At first, we may think of this as mostly a marketing or PR tactic. Although this is true on one level, these brands are strong because there is something pure and honest underneath. Put simply, their values, whether stated explicitly or not, lead to the expression of an authentic brand.

Truth and its concomitant values of humility, self-awareness, and integrity can form the foundational guiding principles for a company to become one of those brands that really connects deeply and emotionally with consumers. It is truth that allows many businesses to separate themselves from the pack. Truth is also needed during the business-building stages to filter what is core and essential from the things that can be shed or evolved to help a business move to the next level. Goodness can be a transformative force in businesses because what starts at an individual level of leadership can propagate to other members of the organization and ultimately become a defining part of a firm's cultural fabric.

When leaders need to make important or difficult decisions, they come back to the committable, guiding truths and values of their organizations. If an organization holds "people-first" as one of its values and truths, then in a moment of challenging decision making a leader should ask himself or herself, "To what extent does this further help or hurt our value of being 'people-first'?" Garry Ridge of WD-40 describes the importance of organizational and individual truths and values as a riverbank of sorts. Day to day we may ebb and flow with great freedom through the activities of our work, but when a challenging decision comes our way, it is the riverbank of one's values that shapes and guides our actions. Truth—and humility, self-awareness, and integrity—is that riverbank for all of us. Without being true to ourselves, without our organizations being true to themselves, we can't know what we stand for. And what goodness is there in that?

SUMMARY OF KEY POINTS FROM CHAPTER 3

• • • • • • • •

- **Truth and the values of humility, self-awareness, and integrity are at the core of great leaders and great organizations.** Being a truth seeker is foundational for people to lead with consistency and for businesses and brands to have authentic connectivity. People, whether they are colleagues, followers, or consumers, can easily feel and sense the presence or absence of truth.

- **Humility is best understood through its opposite—pride, especially negative pride.** By assessing whether your behaviors are more representative of the vices of pride or the virtues of humility, you will gain in modesty. The mind-set of humility is the basis for truth.

- **With self-awareness, practice makes approximately perfect.** Self-awareness is about having the intellectual honesty to hold a mirror up to yourself and know your strengths, weaknesses, and biases. The good news is that self-awareness is a practice that can be perfected through meditation, writing, psychometric testing, and both peer and formal feedback.

- **True integrity comes when we attain a state of self-congruence, where what we do is what we say, what we say is what we think, and what we think is what we feel.** To act with integrity means the values we espouse are the values we express. Ultimately, when we consistently behave according to our purpose and values, integrity becomes just a way of being and living both at an individual and organizational level.

4

THE HUMAN FACTOR: COMPASSION

Compassion is a beautiful flower born of understanding.

THICH NHAT HANH[1]

In the United States alone, approximately 10,000 oncologists care for the roughly 1.7 million people who are newly diagnosed with cancer each year. Roughly 1,600 men and women succumb to the disease every day. A staggering 40 to 50 percent of us will contract cancer in our lifetimes.[2] It's safe to say we all know someone close to us who has been touched by cancer. And you never forget when you first learned the news.

I certainly don't. It was the summer of 2001, a time of immense change in my life. I had just left ZEFER to begin a new chapter in my career. I was consumed with the complexities of transitioning jobs, planning my upcoming wedding, and moving into a new home. I wasn't at all prepared for the call I received one morning as I was walking off the tarmac after a shuttle flight into New York. "We have bad news," my father told me over the phone. My then twenty-two-year-old brother, James, had been diagnosed with a rare form of cancer, and the prognosis wasn't good. I was stunned. Had I heard my father right? I asked him to repeat himself, but a blur of confusion and denial had overwhelmed me. James was young and in such good health—how was this even possible? James himself had no idea. He told me he felt perfectly normal and could hardly believe that doctors had found a non-seminoma germ cell tumor about the size of a tennis ball lodged between his lungs.

It's in my nature to solve problems. Over the next few weeks, I reached out to my personal and professional networks and spent days poring over scientific literature until I had produced a short list of the world's best oncologists and cancer institutions. My parents and brother flew in from Canada to Boston, where I was living at the time, and together we began our medical tour. I was positive we would end up at one of Boston's top hospitals, very likely a globally renowned cancer institute that was at the top of our list.

After weeks of trying, we finally managed to schedule a meeting with a top oncologist who specialized in the type of tumor that James had. But after we arrived at the hospital, we sat patiently in the waiting area for more than an hour before a resident beckoned us in. When the oncology physician finally saw us, there were few pleasantries. He went straight to the business at hand and hastily informed us that James indeed had a rare type of cancer, that he might be the right surgeon for the job, and that James ought to consider participating in his research study. In hindsight, I'm sure his intentions were good. But at the time, the physician's blunt and unfeeling execution of what for him was obviously an everyday routine—telling patients they have cancer, offering trite condolences, asking whether they'd like to participate in a study—made me feel sick. Leaving the hospital that day, all of us felt as if some of the hope had been sucked out of us.

The physician was impeccably competent and boasted impressive credentials, but there was indubitably something missing. A good number of the other doctors we met with that week were also missing this indescribable "thing." It was almost as if because they dealt with these diseases on a daily basis, they had become more focused on the cancer than on the *person* with the cancer. It felt like these doctors had become immune to their patients. They made little effort to connect with us on a human level, and they seemed more interested in securing participants in their clinical research trials than helping heal actual people.

In his posthumously released memoir, *When Breath Becomes Air*, neurosurgeon Dr. Paul Kalanithi chronicles his own experience being diagnosed with terminal lung cancer. Suddenly a cancer patient himself, he poignantly recognizes the crucial importance of remaining human when with his patients, of never allowing patients to become mere paperwork. He writes:

> *The call to protect life—and not merely life but another's identity; it is perhaps not too much to say another's soul—was obvious in its sacredness. Before operating on a patient's brain, I realized, I must first understand his mind: his identity, his values, what makes his life worth living, and what devastation makes it reasonable to let that life end. The cost of my dedication to succeed was high, and the ineluctable failures brought me nearly unbearable guilt. Those burdens are what make medicine holy and wholly impossible: in taking up another's cross, one must sometimes get crushed by the weight.*[3]

Had he survived, Dr. Kalanithi would have become an even more gifted, humanizing physician. My family was lucky. With a stroke of good luck and plenty of persistence, we eventually found a physician who was the best of both worlds, both a brilliant medical practitioner and one of the most compassionate human beings I have ever met: Dr. Jack Erban. My brother, sister, parents, and I were tired, frightened, upset, and shell-shocked, but Dr. Erban of the New England Medical Center was ultimately able to bring us back to some semblance of calm and spark renewed optimism.

With quiet confidence, openness, humility, and focus, Dr. Erban patiently walked us through James's options. Other doctors had given us ten or fifteen minutes, at most. Some of these conversations had taken place in waiting or examination rooms, and we were always aware that the doctor was eager to move on to the next patient waiting her turn to be seen. But when Dr. Erban spoke, his voice was gentle, warm, empathetic, and caring. He was an expert in his field and occupied a top position at the hospital—no doubt he too had other patients to see that day—but he was more than generous with his time. After putting James through various tests, he assured us he would be available at the end of the day for another hour-long discussion so that he could carefully talk us through what was happening, counsel us on what we needed to think about, and tell us about our various options. My family walked into Dr. Erban's consultation room feeling anxious, scared, and uncertain, but that evening—after spending nearly two hours at the hospital—we walked out feeling cared for and, dare I say it, even optimistic. There was no question in anyone's mind that Dr. Erban was the right physician for James.

Subsequent visits and meetings with Dr. Erban only reinforced this impression. When we told Dr. Erban we had exhaustively researched James's diagnosis online and consulted with other top experts whose perspectives in some cases differed from Dr. Erban's, he didn't get defensive, brush us away, or act offended. Instead he applauded our efforts and set up a conference call with the other doctors to better understand James's condition, exchange perspectives, and uncover the best answers and approaches in the field.

Over the years of my brother's illness, Dr. Erban tracked every single one of James's blood lab tests, MRIs, CT scans, radiology reports, and physical examinations. He administered countless rounds of highly aggressive chemo treatments and oversaw three critical surgeries, including one in which James's rib cage was split and butterflied so that surgeons could remove any post-chemo cancer remnants. At each step of the way, Dr. Erban visited, counseled, and consoled us; he made us feel as if we mattered and that he *felt* what we felt, too. I've spoken with several of Dr. Erban's other patients, and every single one of them has expressed profound gratitude for Dr. Erban's authenticity, openness, empathy, and compassion. It's just who Dr. Erban is.

My family credits Dr. Erban with saving James's life, and I think he is one of the best models from my own life of what it means to be "good." When I interviewed Dr. Erban for this book, he spoke extensively about how he feels it is an honor to serve others, even going so far as to say that we all have a "duty to serve and a duty to care," and that this duty is both our gift and our privilege. "I was raised in a family where everyone was treated equally," Jack told me later, "and it left a mark that led to a sense of equity being important to me. Medicine is very hierarchical, and equity can suffer easily. I bring to the patient the same level of care and attention I'd want for myself."[4]

In *The Soul of Medicine*, the late neuroscientist and Yale professor Sherwin Nuland recounts nearly two dozen inspirational stories of doctors whose real gift was their compassion—not their clinical competency, training, or expertise.[5] Nuland himself spent much of his career studying the importance of the doctor-patient relationship and the profound impact a physician's bedside manner can have on healing. He was critical of contemporary medicine, claiming it failed to treat patients as human beings first and medical studies second—might something similar be said of business, which treats people as employees first and people second? Nuland argued that the medical education system's preferential teaching of technique and protocol effectively rendered the emotional and psychological side of the patient equation an afterthought. His advocacy for a more holistic view of medicine and patient care, in which physicians step off their pedestals so that they can treat patients with mutual respect at the moments when they are most vulnerable, is reminiscent of a lesson I learned from Nitin Nohria: leadership on a personal and institutional level is more about character and compassion than competency.

Some fifteen years after my brother's illness, it's my privilege to call Jack a good family friend. We've enjoyed each other's company at various social gatherings outside of the hospital, but whenever I learn that a family member, friend, or acquaintance has received that dreaded diagnosis, I pick up the phone to put them in touch with Jack. He's always there, ready as ever to fulfill a duty to serve, a duty to care. Cancer still afflicts far too many people, but I'm thankful that Jack has been there, an anchor for all those who have been fortunate enough to know him.

Jack's exemplary compassion—his openness, empathy, and generosity—has confirmed my belief that true leadership transcends competency. I firmly believe that the only way to inspire authentic, positive engagement and to add enduring value to an organization is to bring the human factor back into business and leadership. In all fields of work—from medicine to business, academia, and the arts—compassion is an essential component of work that can connect with and engage others.

COUNTERCULTURAL COMPASSION IN BUSINESS

A very successful businessperson once told me that the best way to make the world a better place was to make a lot of money. His words have never sat well with me, because they imply that compassion and business don't mix. Indeed, compassion seems absent from the average businessperson's training. We learn or are conditioned to think early on that business is an impersonal and competitive endeavor, and that success can only be measured using hard performance metrics. Standard operating procedures and "best" practices—like "weed out the bottom," "up or out," and "hire slow, fire fast"—actively discourage compassion in the workplace. Human resource policies are frequently designed solely to tick off the boxes in a compliance checklist, rather than to actively foster belonging, growth, and engagement. Company values, if they exist, are customer-first and outside-in. We are taught that to win in business, we need to be smarter and more competitive than everyone else.

Of course, traditional business processes, practices, and philosophies do have something to teach us. Workplaces require some means of ensuring accountability, measuring productivity, and managing risk. But these policies are often carried out at the expense of compassion, so that the "what" of the business overwhelms the "how." Put another way, businesspeople are often trained like the doctors my family met with before we found Dr. Jack Erban—all graphs, poor bedside manner. What would the business world look like if we designed our policies to reward and encourage self-awareness, self-improvement, and overall goodness? If we built a compassionate culture upon a shared purpose, mission, and values? If we did so, we might frequently ask ourselves a new set of questions, like: How do my actions affect others? Can I be more collaborative or empathetic? How would I feel if I were the person receiving this review or that feedback? Could I be more generous?

The second layer of the Goodness Pyramid is all about compassion, defined as the selflessness that allows us to fully understand the experiences of others. The three values we use to describe compassion—openness, empathy, and generosity—are deliberately sequenced. Just as with truth and wholeness, the values of compassion progress from a mind-set to a practice to an action. Compassion begins with the mind-set of openness, which is the capacity to be present, unbiased, and non-judgmental. From there it moves to the practice of empathy, meaning being able to place ourselves in the place of another. And finally, it is the act of generosity that represents the manifestation of one's compassion in the most tangible of ways.

It's important to understand that compassion and competency are not mutually exclusive. In fact, compassion can amplify organizational objectives and performance. While some business leaders have quickly scaled the corporate ladder by stepping on their peers, the best of the best succeed precisely because compassion is a key part of their purpose—because they care about the well-being of other people and creating a culture to foster them.

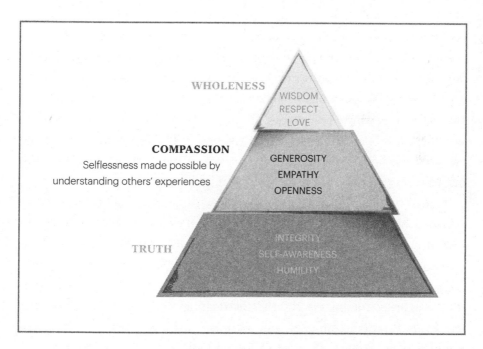

DEVELOPING AN OPEN MIND-SET: THE 24 X 3 RULE AND DISTRIBUTED NETWORKS

A full-page advertisement by Apple featuring a photograph of Jay Chiat, a mentor of mine who was an extraordinary leader in his field, hangs on the wall in my office. The ad appeared in the *New York Times* the day after the paper ran an obituary announcing Jay's death, and contains only two words of copy: *Think Different.* At Apple, Jay and his business partner, Lee Clow, created some of the most iconic and breakthrough advertising campaigns of all time. I learned many lessons from Jay, but the one I've tried to live by most over the years is to fall in love with *possibility* and keep an open mind.

Jay always sought out the good before analyzing the bad. After his memorial service, I began talking with a friend of Jay's about what we missed the most about my old mentor. We both agreed that it was his openness to new ideas and types of thinking, and his commitment to giving every idea, even the so-so ones, a full and fair chance before finding fault with it. This conversation led me to develop the 24 x 3 rule. Here's how it works: when someone tells you about their new idea, try to wait twenty-four seconds before responding with any criticisms. Next, try waiting twenty-four minutes. If you want to be truly open-minded, spend twenty-four hours identifying every conceivable reason why the idea might work before you consider why it might not.

Banishing our conscious and unconscious biases and adopting a mind-set of openness expands, enriches, and diversifies our point of view. Openness allows for inquiry, too. Recall how Dr. Jack Erban listened to the other doctors' opinions and welcomed their input, even though they might contradict his own recommendations. By contrast, those who are stubborn and arrogant exist in tightly closed circles of ignorance and negativity. There can be no empathy and optimism without openness. Openness removes prejudice and therefore allows goodness to shine through.

How does openness operate on an organizational level? At Zappos, CEO Tony Hsieh has created one of the most open business cultures I have ever encountered. In fact, a core value at Zappos is "Be adventurous, creative, and open-minded." Another is "Build open and honest relationships with communications." Hsieh's open press policy demonstrates how much he lives by these values. Press and guests are free to ask any and all questions, and employees are encouraged to answer truthfully and openly. Once when I attended an all-hands meeting at Zappos as an invited speaker, someone raised their hand to express concern that the local press had criticized the company's downtown development. Hsieh replied calmly, "Well, the press is a good source of valuable feedback and public perceptions."

You might be surprised to learn that for many years, the key military leader in charge of America's war on terror was a strong proponent of open, distributed leadership. When now-retired four-star general Stanley McChrystal took the leadership of the Joint Special Operations Command in 2003, he quickly saw that the military's traditional, hierarchical, highly centralized command-and-control model would fail to defeat al-Qaeda in Iraq. The only way to beat al-Qaeda would be to transform the military into an open, collaborative network that moved power out from the center to enable people in the field to engage in autonomous decision making.[6] So in the midst of the war, McChrystal dismantled existing decision-making structures and implemented a faster, flatter, and more agile organizational model. In McChrystal's "team of teams" approach, transparent communication of information became more important because each person was empowered to be a potential decision maker. It wasn't delegation— it was truly equally distributed decision making that required soldiers to open up and trust their colleagues to make the right decision at the right time. No wonder high-ranking military personnel like McChrystal identify "soft" values—like humility, empathy, openness, and compassion—as critical predictors of soldiers' success.

Our ability to think openly and react flexibly rests on the foundational layer of the Goodness Pyramid: truth and, within truth, self-awareness. Perhaps an example can help us see how these values build on each other, such that greater truth and self-awareness enable greater openness and compassion. Remember when the cashier asked Ellen Langer to sign both her credit card and receipt slip in front of her, but then asked for Ellen's card once more so she could check it was the same signature? I've also witnessed non-mindful, non-self-aware behavior driven not by lack of goodness, but by senseless, bureaucratic rules and processes.

This past summer, I was working on this book at an outdoor bar at a nice resort. A woman had just ordered drinks for herself and some friends, but when she produced two twenty-dollar bills to pay for the drinks, the bartender told her they didn't take cash. The woman told him that she was here attending a wedding, that she'd lost her wallet earlier that day, that this forty dollars was the sum total of her emergency backup cash, and that she only wanted to buy her hosts a thank-you drink. The bartender repeated that house rules prohibited him from accepting cash, and finally the woman and her friends walked away. I then watched incredulously as the bartender proceeded to take the drinks that had been made for the woman's order and pour them down the sink, one by one. It would've been one thing to set the drinks aside—the woman might come back with a credit card, after all—but if he was going to discard the drinks anyway, why not simply give them to the woman? I was tempted to tell the bartender to confer with his manager. Cash might not be accepted at this particular bar, but weren't there exceptions?

Some rules just don't make sense. Of course, businesses need processes in place as guardrails to prevent unwanted behavior. This particular bar's no-cash policy was probably originally implemented to minimize "shrinkage"—when sales proceeds are lost or stolen by dishonest employees. In U.S. retail services, shrinkage is estimated to amount to 2 percent of total sales,[7] about $200 billion annually.[8] This is not a small number, so business owners are justified in seeking ways to protect themselves. But how much emphasis should be placed on process and controls rather than on principles and values? If you know that the majority of your employees are good and honest people, should you design your systems to control the few bad actors or to instill, cultivate, and reward values such as openness, generosity, honesty, and common sense?

The problem I see in business is that we are too often *over-ruled and under-valued*—pun intended. We burden employees with rules and in the process undervalue and underestimate their desire and ability to do the right thing. A values-based open mind-set is based on the belief that good people will come to the right decision if your organization's values are clear to them. Process and rules-based systems should only be designed for and applied to unfortunate exceptions. A colleague of mine says it best: "Just because we have one bad person doesn't mean I should treat everyone in the organization less well." Overly onerous and rigid processes, policies, and controls frequently produce negative unintended consequences that damage everyday customer interactions and overall organizational culture.

Think just how different that woman's experience at the no-cash resort would have been if the bartender was empowered—along the lines of McChrystal's distributed decision-making approach—to remain open to the possibility of saying, "I'm really sorry you've had a hard day, and I hope you get your wallet back soon. Here, the drinks are on us." This small act of generosity would likely have cost less than a couple of dollars (if that) and generated a significant return as measured in employee engagement and customer retention.

Creating a more open mind-set and culture at an organizational level helps us become more receptive to new ideas and possibilities. While there are many ways to show your employees you care about them, it's easy to begin by listening carefully to their perspectives, expressing optimism when they come to you with new ideas, and empowering them to make significant decisions in areas they find meaningful. But to do this well, we need to be able to see the world from the eyes of another. This brings us to the practice of empathy.

THE PRACTICE OF EMPATHY

The second value trait of compassion is empathy, which can be defined as "the imaginative projection into another's feelings, a state of total identification with another's situation, condition, and thoughts. The action of understanding, being aware of, being sensitive to, and vicariously experiencing the feelings, thoughts, and experience of another of either the past or present without explicitly articulating these feelings."[9]

One of the twentieth century's most influential American psychologists, Carl Rogers, pioneered a holistic and humanistic understanding of people and relationships. Rogers believed that empathetic listening requires understanding both the nuance and the feeling behind what another person is saying. Leaders should practice paying attention to the motivations and emotions expressed by their employees, customers, colleagues, and mentors. Indeed, during a 1974 lecture for the American Personnel and Guidance Association, Rogers noted, "Over the years the research evidence keeps piling up and it keeps pointing to the conclusion that a high degree of empathy in a relationship is possibly the most potent factor, and certainly one of the most important factors in bringing about change in learning."[10] We'll discuss how to be an effective mentor in chapter 11, but for now, suffice it to say that a shared baseline of genuine empathy is a key ingredient in all meaningful relationships, mentorship included.

I have found that the best good people are also gifted with high levels of inborn empathy, which motivates them to effect positive change in the workplace and even the world. Empathetic team leaders like Leslie Brunner of Athena and Garry Ridge of WD-40 demonstrate an ability and a desire to develop and care for others, even placing their employees' interests over their own. These leaders are modern-day incarnations of an ancient archetype of leader, the servant leader. They believe that superior performance and engagement is achieved by developing and empowering others, not by harnessing power and knowledge at the top. Robert Greenleaf, the father of modern servant leadership, argued that leaders should continually strive to share power by pushing it out from the center of an organization. He proposed that servant leaders ask themselves the following questions: "Do those served grow as persons? Do they, while being *served*, become healthier, wiser, freer, more autonomous, more likely themselves to become servants?"[11]

Best-selling author and management guru Ken Blanchard has also written extensively on servant leadership. He emphasizes that servant leaders do not become subservient to employees, nor do they abdicate responsibility for driving their organizations' visions, values, and goals—some things need to come from the "top" of an organization. True servant leaders balance their responsibility and accountability to the larger company with policies that empower employees to make meaningful, productive decisions. They embody the Good People principle: our duty in our lives and work is to help others become fuller versions of themselves.

In its purest form, empathy demands that we put aside our own vanity and biases in order to feel as others feel. Over the years, I've learned to deal with conflicts and disagreements by recognizing effort and offering validation before voicing my own point of view or recommendation. Acknowledging another person's frustration or anger is the first step of dissipating negativity. Next, try to understand his emotions by uncovering what aggravated him. We often forget that we get to choose how we respond to other people's anger. Rather than playing dumb or writing someone's anger off as irrational, acknowledge his or her frustration and try to empathize. So rather than saying, "Look, I have no idea why you're so upset," consider saying something along the lines of "Look, I know and want to acknowledge that you are upset, and I'm sorry. Perhaps it might have been something that I did—I know I disagreed with the point you made in the meeting—but if it's something else, I'd like to try to understand so we can clear the air." Make a genuine effort to understand why someone feels the way he does. Practice empathetic listening, and don't be selective; frequently we hear what we want to believe without having fully heard or understood the entirety of what the other person said.

Ask Questions to Learn

"Phatic" language describes words and phrases we regularly use in our everyday social interactions that have become procedural. They are shorthand at the service of convenience and convention rather than genuine expressions of inquiry. "How are you?" is a classic phatic question. We don't really listen to the answers of phatic questions; we are merely being polite.

One way to become a better, more authentic listener is to steer clear of phatic questions. Instead, genuinely ask a few simple questions. Below are five of the most important non-phatic questions to ask anyone you'd like to know better. While these questions can of course be pulled out during interviews, mentor meetings, or formal feedback sessions, they are powerful ways to kick off a conversation with anyone you'd like to know, perhaps at an impromptu "no-agenda lunch."

1. How are you, really? Authentic, non-phatic inquiry is about caring enough to listen like you mean it even if the question asked and answered is profoundly simple. One of the people I interviewed for this book, Mark Tatum—deputy commissioner and COO of the NBA—grew up in a poor neighborhood in Brooklyn, where his mother cleaned schools for a living. Because he remembers just how many of his mother's employers ignored her or acted as if she were invisible, Mark to this day makes a point of learning as much as possible about everyone he meets. He has reminded me more than once, "When you ask 'How are you?' you should *really* mean, 'How are you?'"[12]

2. Tell me something about your background that I don't know. I'm always surprised by the stories I hear from our portfolio companies' employees when I ask this question. One is a working mother who takes care of her children and her ailing husband, another once worked as a pastry chef, and a third tried four times to get a job at the company. Learn where your people come from and what interests them. Their answers will often surprise you and, more important, help establish a genuine relationship.

3. What would you love to be doing a few years from now? Ask someone about their current role at their organization, then ask how what they're doing now helps them reach their goals or full potential. It is important to know where someone aspires to go, whether that's inside or outside the firm.

4. Are you happy working here? Leslie Brunner, whom we've introduced, worked for seven years as Athena's chief people officer. It was Leslie who taught me to ask people this question. It's simple, but it can solicit unexpected answers. Ask, listen, and learn.

5. *Is there anything I can do for you?* The CEO of the LEGO Group, Jørgen Vig Knudstorp, was once quoted as saying, "Blame is not for failure, it is for failing to help or ask for help."[13] I recently asked the leadership team at one of our businesses to ask their employees this same question. Consider framing it more specifically and in the context of your business. What company policy frustrates you the most? What would you do if you had an extra $500? Is there anything special you would do if you had the day off?

These questions may seem commonsensical, but you'd be surprised how rarely they're actually asked. All too often we say the right thing without the right mind-set, and so we hear without listening or understanding.

THE ACT OF GENEROSITY

This next lesson will come as no surprise to students of evolution. In *On the Origin of Species*, Charles Darwin theorized that evolution is driven by heritable variation and natural selection. If in fact only the "fittest" survive, you might justifiably assume that our ancestors who held tight their resources and refused to share them were far likelier to survive and reproduce. But pioneering biologist E. O. Wilson argued that there was an exception to this rule. Wilson presented evidence that humans and ants are among only a handful of species that will sacrifice individual resources for the good of the group. But critically, this only occurred when humans or ants felt abundantly secure in their resources or lived in communities with robust norms of justice and fairness.[14]

On the one hand, humans are preprogrammed to acquire, hoard, and guard resources. On the other, we're predisposed to share with and give to others, provided our own lives aren't at risk and there is a culture that values fairness and justice. Herein lies the solution to reconciling competition and compassion. This dynamic explains why companies that reward employees based both on merit (i.e., quantifiable performance metrics) and on ability to develop and care for others receive high marks in employee engagement and job satisfaction.

A growing body of research supports the conclusion that *practitioners* of kindness also benefit when they act generously. Plainly put, helping others makes *us* feel good. Ironically, altruism can at times be self-rewarding. My own personal experience has shown me that people are happier—even healthier—when their activities are invested with a purpose and meaning larger than themselves. *Pro-social behavior* is defined as any behavior that is intended to benefit someone or something other than oneself. But pro-social behavior can also have powerful reciprocal benefits for the practitioner.

Michael Norton, a Harvard Business School professor and member of its Behavior Insights Group, has observed that people both rich and poor experience greater pleasure spending money on others than on themselves. I once had the pleasure of moderating a panel with Professor Norton in which we discussed whether giving to others increases our own self-fulfillment and well-being. Norton described one experiment where he measured how much satisfaction and happiness research participants reported when they were forced to choose between giving a five-dollar gift card away or keeping it for themselves. Across the board, the people who surrendered their gift cards reported greater levels of happiness.

But that's only five dollars, you might say. What happens when you increase the dollar value, or if you explicitly direct participants to give the money away? It makes no difference. Norton and his two colleagues, Elizabeth Dunn and Lara Aknin, found that happiness levels of participants stay the same even when they are told to be kind, when kindness is doled out randomly, and when the dollar amount in question varies. In fact, the only significant intervening variable Norton and his colleagues found was whether or not the money given away ended up being spent pro-socially.[15] While it's true income and happiness are correlated (up to

a certain threshold), *how* we spend our money seems to be just as important as how *much* money we earn.

Generous people feel a duty to help others. People who tithe give away
a percentage (typically 10 percent) of their incomes because they believe
that giving back is an essential part of being a good person and creating
more good in the world. The Giving Pledge is a campaign started by
Warren Buffett and Bill and Melinda Gates in 2010 that encourages the
world's wealthiest people to step it up much more and give away the majority of their wealth. All Giving Pledge participants compose and sign
their own pledge letter, in which they vow to donate at least half of their
wealth to charity and to foster discourse on how the group's collective
resources and capabilities can be put to use solving critical global issues.
A mere six years later, nearly two hundred individuals have signed the
pledge, including David Rockefeller, Elon Musk, and Tim Cook. I can't
help but wonder when these givers felt more fulfilled: when they were
creating their extraordinary wealth, or when they were pledging to give
it away? My guess is the latter.

Consider the example of the artist Al Hirschfeld. During a chance
encounter with Charlie Chaplin, Chaplin asked Hirschfeld what it would
take for him to commit to his artistic talents and pursue his dreams in art.
When Hirschfeld responded with confusion, Chaplin reframed the question: How much money would it take for Hirschfeld to continue capturing
the character of personalities like Chaplin using his signature graceful,
minimalist, "art of the line" style? The young Hirschfeld answered with a
sizable sum. Without further discussion, Chaplin wrote out a check,
handed it to Hirschfeld, and told him to do what he was meant to do.
Chaplin's generosity not only offered Hirschfeld the opportunity to realize his artistic calling—he also provided millions of other people with the
privilege and opportunity to appreciate Hirschfeld's art.

But generosity also can be exhibited through the gift of time and opportunity. In Adam Grant's best-selling book *Give and Take*, the Wharton
professor presents evidence that givers, "those who contribute without
expecting anything in return," almost always end up doing better because
they end up getting the best of both worlds: doing well and doing good.

He shows, for example, that the most collaborative and giving students at American medical schools also tend to achieve the most success after graduation.[16] Pro-social behavior has a multitude of benefits. Acknowledging, recognizing, and helping employees can be just as effective as offering them monetary rewards.

One "compassion practice" that we can adopt to shape our ongoing goodness and cultivate our instinct for generosity is an annual "perspective journey." We all should periodically appraise and acknowledge where we stand in terms of our own self-awareness, and gauge to what extent we've taken it upon ourselves to act as "Good Samaritans" when we've had opportunities to do so. An annual perspective activity doesn't have to be like a pilgrimage to Mecca; something as simple as volunteering— either individually or with a group—or simply devoting a day every year to a personal self-reflection trip, or getting some perspective from an off-site retreat for work can help us become more compassionate both in business and in life. One of my firm's most special annual events is our holiday gathering with families, but this year we decided to replace the event with a day of volunteering. Goodness, after all, has a lot to do with giving back, whether this is time, money, or some other type of "gift." There is no exact formula for how much we should give back; the habit of giving is far more important than the quantity.

In businesses, generosity is all too often boiled down to paychecks, bonuses, equity, and promotions. Extrinsic rewards are certainly important, but if these are the only means an organization has to express compassion for and genuine interest in its employees, then something essential is missing. Jim Goodnight has led SAS for nearly four decades, during which time the analytics software company has consistently been identified as one of the country's most admired workplaces. By providing benefits such as subsidized childcare, work-life balance counseling, health professionals, and on-site recreational activity centers, SAS signals that it cares about its employees' health and happiness. In fact, Goodnight had been focused on creating a company culture built on employee trust and respect long before SAS rolled out these perks; for decades, SAS has offered employees meaningful flexibility and independence in their day-to-day work. The most powerful demonstration of the company's "generosity" occurred during the 2008 global recession, when Goodnight made a commitment not to lay off a single employee. That year, SAS also hit record profits.

But generosity does not need to be precipitated by an event such as a downturn to be regularly practiced. Some people who rise "to the top" make a habit of acknowledging—not forgetting, and not neglecting—the people around them who made their achievements possible. To me, it's become crystal clear that good people remember those who helped them along the way. Sometimes all it takes is a simple thank-you note, while other times it may mean gathering people together. Generosity need not be complex, but it must be authentic. Over the twenty-plus years of my professional career, I have observed how different people behave when they reach new pinnacles of success. I believe there is no finer exemplar of humility, compassion, and generosity than Supreme Court Justice Sonia Sotomayor.

My wife was a clerk for Justice Sotomayor when she was a federal judge in New York's Second Circuit. Justice Sotomayor's approachability and genuine interest in each clerk as a person was obvious back then, and she is no different today. What is remarkable is how consistently Justice Sotomayor *chooses* to show her gratitude. For example, our family recently sent Justice Sotomayor a holiday photo featuring our children, and she replied with a thank-you note in which she commented on the children and sent her well wishes. I have no doubt Justice Sotomayor does this as a regular practice with many other families. Moreover, I've personally experienced Justice Sotomayor's gratitude and generosity through her efforts to annually reunite her past clerks and their families. One year, Justice Sotomayor's reunion weekend fell near Halloween, so she hosted a large Sunday brunch that was attended by at least 150 family members of her past clerks. Over several hours, I noticed how Justice Sotomayor made a deliberate point to spend time with each and every child, giving candy to each of them out of a large bag she carried around with her the entire morning. And there are countless other examples of Justice Sotomayor's kindness and generosity, like when she arranged a very special send-off for her assistant of many years who was retiring. For me, she's been an inspiration. Other leaders should learn from her example and aspire to act in much the same way when they reach the greatest heights of achievement.

• • • •

Goodness and character are complicated to understand, and to define, as is humanized character. I don't know if it can come down to a singular word. But if there is only one word, the one that comes to mind is: children.

DR. STEPHEN PORTER, CLINICAL PSYCHOLOGIST

Almost daily, children remind us of the essence of goodness—that it is instinctual, even impulsive, with vast potential to change lives. When my oldest son turned ten, my family decided to celebrate at a neighborhood family-friendly hibachi restaurant. At one point, the chef—who was also trained in balloon art—pulled out some balloons as a treat for the kids at the table. One by one, he asked each child for his or her favorite color and then twisted and tied together a special balloon animal. But by the time the chef got to my twin daughters—who were five at the time—he had begun to run out of colors. My first daughter received the orange balloon animal she requested, but when my second daughter asked for pink and was told there were no pink balloons left, her eyes welled with tears. Eventually the chef managed to convince her to accept a red balloon—"It's like a darker version of pink," he explained—but, as Murphy's Law would have it, the red balloon burst a mere second after the chef put it to his lips. My daughter started to cry. After a few more tearful minutes, my wife and I finally convinced her to choose a blue balloon, just like the one a little boy across the table had received. We turned to the chef. "I'm so sorry," he said as gently as possible, "we are all out of blue balloons, too."

My daughter burst into tears yet again, but my gaze was caught by the expression on the face of the little boy holding the blue balloon. Slowly he rose and came over to our side of the table. As he came closer, my daughter's crying slowed, and she wiped her tears on her sleeve. The boy stood there for a few moments, and at last took a final step forward, gripping his blue balloon dog. Shyly he said to her, "Would you like mine?"

Ask yourself: What are *you* willing to do to help another person? In his preface to Piero Ferrucci's book *The Power of Kindness*, His Holiness, the Dalai Lama, writes, "I believe that if we stop to think, it is very clear that our very survival, even today, depends upon the acts and kindness of so many people."[17] The Dalai Lama's wisdom makes me wonder: How many of us would consistently pass a "blue balloon" test? How regularly do we commit actual *acts* of kindness?

THE HUMAN FACTOR— HOW COMPASSION TRANSLATES

Our self-awareness and compassion are what separate us from all other species. And there are some of us who seem to exude this brilliant "human factor" more than others. For me, Herbie Hancock—whom many regard as one of the greatest musicians of all time—is one of these people. Over a five-decade-long career, Herbie has altered the face of jazz and indelibly influenced many other musical genres, from hip-hop to funk to classical. Herbie has inspired me to think differently about the human origins of goodness and virtuosity.

When interviewers ask Herbie how he has managed to maintain his musical relevance for as long as he has, he always gives the same answer: "First and foremost," he says, "I remember that I am a human being; second, I am a human being who happens to play music." Music is simply the vehicle Herbie uses to express his innate humanness and insatiable desire to become the best person he can possibly be.

In short, by combining his own humanness with his natural gifts, skills, and drive, Herbie has attained extraordinary heights in the world of music. Herbie sets a world-class example for his field. Authentic, engaged leaders must have a foundation of truth and compassion, and they must manifest these values in consistent acts of open-mindedness, empathy, and generosity. When we genuinely care for others—whether by getting to know them better as people or helping them develop professionally—we become better doctors, who combine competency with compassion; better musicians, who combine technical proficiency with soul-bearing emotion; better entrepreneurs, who lead with both head and heart; and better overall leaders, who strive for the highest level of performance while also building relationships with employees. And it all begins at the top, with leaders who are unafraid to show compassion in their leadership approach. These leaders understand that only by working as hard to realize others' potential as they work to realize their own can they transform entire industries, cultivate vibrant cultures, and produce enduring value.

SUMMARY OF KEY POINTS FROM CHAPTER 4

· · · · · · ·

- **Compassion is composed of three underlying traits: openness, empathy, and generosity.** Openness asks that we eliminate biases, empathy demands that we push for a more genuine understanding of one another, and generosity requires that we perform an actual act of kindness.

- **An open mind-set allows us to be receptive to and optimistic about new ideas.** Organizations with clear, commonly held values can empower their employees to make significant decisions and trust they will do the right thing.

- **We practice empathy when we try to genuinely understand another person's situation, often by asking non-phatic questions.** When you ask someone, "How are you?" you should genuinely care about the answer.

- **Generosity benefits the giver as much as the recipient and is a powerful source of transformative change.** In the end, compassionate leadership is all about saying that we care—and that you matter.

- **Compassion is ultimately at the heart of the "human factor" of goodness.** The starting point for compassionate leadership is remembering that we are all humans linked through shared values. When organizations act compassionately, everyone becomes more engaged through a sense of shared connectedness and purpose. We want to be among good people and leaders not only whom we respect, but also with whom we feel a connection.

5

THE ULTIMATE QUEST: WHOLENESS

*I cannot pretend I am without fear. But my predominant
feeling is one of gratitude. I have loved and been loved;
I have been given much and I have given something in
return; I have read and traveled and thought and written.
I have had an intercourse with the world.*

OLIVER SACKS[1]

Photograph by George Tames/*The New York Times*/Redux.

A framed photograph by George Tames titled *The Loneliest Job* hangs in both my home and work offices.[2] It shows President John F. Kennedy looking out the south window of the Oval Office, his shoulders hunched and arms outspread, both hands pressing against his desk. Even with his back to us, the president looks exhausted and burdened. The photo is a valuable reminder of the stark reality of leadership: alongside the periodic joys that attend influence and success, there are also speed bumps, mistakes, and solitary, far-reaching decisions.

The Cuban missile crisis of October 1962—the moment in history when the Cold War reached its fever pitch and our country came closest to nuclear war—forced President Kennedy to make a set of difficult decisions. The central issue at hand, of course, was how to force the removal of Russian missiles that had been placed in Cuba following secret meetings between Fidel Castro and then Soviet leader Nikita Khrushchev. In another leader's hands, the crisis could have resulted in cataclysmic destruction beyond any of our imaginations. How was it possible for a leader like John F. Kennedy, during his presidency and foreshortened life, to achieve a sense of *wholeness*? Did he ever?

The pursuit of wholeness—a state within which love, respect, and wisdom combine and mutually reinforce each other—helps to guide us during stressful moments. The good people who surround us bolster our likelihood of achieving wholeness. These anchors provide counsel and support that goes beyond casual compassion. Much has been written about the pivotal role played by Robert Kennedy, JFK's brother and close advisor, during the Cuban missile crisis. JFK leaned heavily on Bobby's advice and judgment when choosing between the two options put forward by the Executive Committee of the National Security Council, which were to either form a blockade—thereby preventing further missiles from entering the island—or initiate immediate military action with air strikes on Cuba. In the end, JFK elected to go forward with the blockade. The tense and lengthy negotiations that followed ultimately convinced Russia to withdraw its missiles from Cuba.

It is impossible for us to fully appreciate the inner turmoil JFK must have faced when considering the profound consequences his decision would have on the lives of millions. The Cuban missile crisis forced JFK to make some of the most difficult decisions ever put before a modern-day leader. In his seminal book on the crisis, renowned political scientist Graham Allison appropriately labeled the challenge the "Essence of Decision."[3]

. . . .

All of our lives are filled with trials and tribulations, successes and failures, periods of light and dark. But leaders experience many more of these
moments when they are left alone to reflect on and execute impossibly
difficult choices. It is in these times when leaders are most acutely aware
of the altitude of their highs, the depth of their lows, and the heavy burden
of their own resilience and stoicism.

Leadership, especially great leadership, is a lonely job. As Shakespeare
wrote in *King Henry IV,* "Uneasy lies the head that wears a crown."[4] Proper
leadership requires sacrifice so that others are shielded from this same
loneliness and uncertainty. Leaders privately manage their doubts and
work hard to control their emotional responses. Yes, many leaders *choose*
to be lonely.

Leadership is a lonely business, but leaders can remedy that by seeking
wholeness. Becoming whole doesn't happen all at once. It requires great
patience and courage. Even those who are predisposed toward wholeness
and peace find the journey can take many slow and painful years. The
pursuit of wholeness is less a 100-yard dash than it is a slow, loping run;
we never fully reach the finish line of wholeness, but we gain peace of
mind and being as we asymptotically approach wholeness, coming closer
and closer. Wholeness is the highest expression of someone's goodness. It
is the melding of love, respect, and wisdom, the three traits that sit at the
top of the Goodness Pyramid. Together, the mind-set of love, the practice
of respect, and acts informed by wisdom orient us toward a larger concept
of success: the realization that one's best efforts have contributed to a
greater whole.

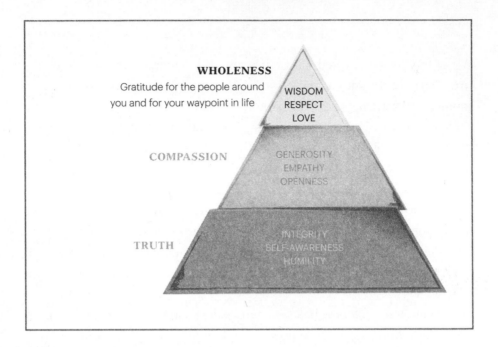

We feel whole when we are at peace with the realities of the roles we play. Wholeness is a state of satisfaction with and appreciation for the people and circumstances that define us and for our "waypoint" in life. It is the knowledge that we have done our best to help others become fuller versions of themselves. Have we reached a point in our work and lives where our natural disposition is to root for others' happiness? Do we practice respect for ourselves and others? And have we accrued sufficient wisdom and experience to be able to distinguish between good and bad judgment, and to act appropriately?

JFK's decisions affected the entire country, and indeed, the entire world. Precious few people make decisions so momentous, but we should not underestimate our own capability to serve the greater good. Whatever our position in life, our goodness can be judged by whether we have done all we are capable of to help make others better. Large-scale transformations can begin with just a few people dedicated to creating positive change—everything starts with one, then a few, before it touches many. For a business leader, this can mean holding a company and its people to a standard of success that goes beyond short-term financial results, a standard that includes the sustainability of performance and the business's impact on the entire stakeholder community, as John Mackey has done at Whole Foods. So the question for each of us during the waypoints of our journey is: Have we added something to the overall community, not just financial wealth as it is measured on the balance sheet, but also a greater level of prosperity measured by goodness? The best leaders recognize this truth—that we must be more than just numbers, that we must work toward the durability of something institutionally good in the character and culture of our organizations and the people we touch.

Perhaps you think these aspirations—leadership guided by wholeness and success measured in goodness—are too idealistic. How can anyone possibly achieve wholeness in leadership roles that seem almost custom-made to produce stress and solitude? Can leaders appreciate that their authority is a privilege, and then accept the duty to help others become the fullest versions of themselves as their highest calling? This is possible so long as we understand the real challenges leaders face, adjust our expectations to match those realities, and practice steadfast patience with the good people who surround us. Yes, the path to wholeness is an ongoing endeavor. Yes, this endeavor requires bringing good people together to realize their potential to act as agents of change and creators of enduring value. But this is all possible, and it begins with embracing the most universal value and powerful emotion we know in life: love.

A MIND-SET FOR LOVE—LOVEMARKS AND INSIDE-OUT LOVE

To experience wholeness, one must allow oneself both to *be* loved and also to find more love in others. People who put themselves entirely in the service of others act out the highest form of love. It may seem odd to discuss love in a business context, but the truth is, the most admirable business leaders are purpose-driven and place themselves in the service of others. "This is also what true leadership is," my business partner, Mats

Lederhausen, has said. "And not to be corny about it, but this is love." This is Mats's favorite definition of love:

> *Love is the will to extend one's self for the purpose of*
> *nurturing one's own or another's spiritual growth . . .*
> *Love is as love does. Love is an act of will—namely,*
> *both an intention and an action. Will also implies choice.*
> *We do not have to love. We choose to love.*
>
> M. SCOTT PECK[5]

To love and be loved means you consciously wish and work for someone else's happiness—you love with an intentional mind-set. The value of love is ultimately deeper, more emotional, and more intense than any of the values of compassion we discussed in the previous chapter. In this case, love is not synonymous with desire and romance; rather, love is something more strongly nurturing, widely practical, and deeply service oriented.

Why does speaking of love in the context of business make so many people uneasy? I think it is because love seems too intense an emotion for the professional world. If the word "love" is simply too grandiose and personal for you to use in a business setting, try "affection" or perhaps even "care." But aren't businesses obsessed with getting consumers to "love" their brands and products? And isn't employee engagement just another word for "love"? Leaders claim they aspire to this kind of culture, but more often than not they seem afraid to practice what they preach. Therein lies the irony: for employees to genuinely love the company for which they work, their leaders must give them implicit permission to love their jobs and embrace a higher purpose.

The first time I heard the word "love" used in a business context was when I read the book *Lovemarks* by Kevin Roberts, former chairman of the advertising firm Saatchi & Saatchi. Roberts was intent on bringing love into the conversation that was occurring between brands and their consumers, and he argued that companies should aspire to create not trademarks but "lovemarks." "The idealism of love is the new realism of business," Roberts wrote. "By building respect and inspiring love, business can move the world."[6]

The response to Roberts's book was strong and immediate. Consumer brands moved quickly to adopt Roberts's philosophy that the best global brands built emotional authentic conversations with their customers. Roberts argued that to accomplish this, brands had to score high among consumers on two separate axes: respect and love. Companies with low respect and low love effectively sell commodities. And companies with renowned brands haven't automatically succeeded in creating "lovemarks," either. High respect for and trust in a brand can coexist with little to no emotional connectivity—that's the definition of a "brandmark." The question for many businesses became how to move from being a "brandmark" to a "lovemark." Recall the truth section of this book where I called out some examples of companies that hold their values dearly and use them as a filter for all their decisions—those companies, ranging from luxury brands like Hermès or Chanel to conscious consumer brands like Patagonia or Trader Joe's to lifestyle brands like SoulCycle or IKEA, connect authentically with their consumers through consistent practices and actions that amplify their brand values.

It actually does not matter whether you are a value brand like Trader Joe's or a luxury brand like Hermès—it's about living those values fully and consistently. I've had the chance to spend time with both the former president of Trader Joe's, Doug Rauch, and the current U.S. president of Hermès, Bob Chavez. It is so immediately and abundantly clear how both have lived the values of their respective brands. The Trader Joe's company story is all about delivering great value: "value is a concept we take very seriously" and "we keep our costs low because every penny we save is a penny you save." Being a product-driven company to Trader Joe's means providing great products at outstanding prices.[7] All of this thinking is embedded into the culture of Trader Joe's. As Rauch has said, "It turns out that culture is the real power of an organization, that's the ability for a business to create real magic with a customer. . . . And for retailers that means really serving that customer authentically."[8]

Now think of a very different company, Hermès—it would seem that it is a brand and product from another planet—but the two businesses overlap in a deeper way in the respect that they have for their respective values. Hermès is one of the last independent luxury brands as well as one of the world's most iconic and valuable. The key for Hermès has been a fierce and steadfast commitment to time-honored traditions of artisanal craftsmanship. Nothing is spared in the quality of any product and the company pays homage to its heritage—hand making horse harnesses—by refusing to use any form of mass production.[9] It has significantly expanded its product lines, but like Trader Joe's, it has stayed true to its core values and identity. It is not surprising that Chavez's thoughts on what has helped the Hermès brand endure for 180 years are similar to Rauch's: "For Hermès it is about keeping consistency and authenticity, it was built on the culture and simple commitment to uncompromising quality and craftsmanship."[10] Both Trader Joe's and Hermès are relentless about their products—an expression of the two companies' deep commitment to being consistently authentic to who they are.

Since 2000, Roberts's theory has been at the core of Saatchi & Saatchi's approach to advertising. Consumers and online social media communities have also shared their opinions on other brands they perceive as true lovemarks, including the likes of Guinness, Ben and Jerry's, Google, Warby Parker, and Moleskine.[11] How do these and other brands inspire love while others do not? Early on in my career, I believed that the best way to build a brand was to focus single-mindedly on inspiring the consumer to love the brand, service, and product as much as possible. As a consultant, I had learned to research a customer segment and then built the competencies required to deliver customers the product they wanted. This is an outside-in approach, and while it's had its successes, I've found it frequently fails to establish an emotional connection with end consumers. Today, I've reversed course. I believe that the strongest businesses and brands have an inside-out philosophy. They establish a culture of self-care among the leadership and throughout the organization, and then they invest in building emotional connections with customers. Think about your own experiences with love; wholeness and self-love are prerequisites for sharing love with others. Think about all of the "lovemark" companies mentioned above and others

you feel a deeper affinity toward. Organizations with consistent growth and success are grounded by a deeply rooted set of common values that ultimately inspires both trust and emotional connectivity with their consumer bases.

Fabian Pfortmüller—the cofounder of Holstee, a Brooklyn-based company that produces and sells environmentally conscious products—helped to influence and frame my own thinking about "inside-out" love. Fabian once told me to imagine concentric circles: the smallest circle is self-love, the second circle spreads our love outward to others, and the third contains love and appreciation for the interconnectedness of all humanity. The outward reach of love, spreading from one concentric circle to the next, allows us to experience a deep joy and sincere desire for others to achieve fulfillment, even ahead of ourselves. I know this is easier to conceptualize than it is to internalize, but the point is that in business and in life, we must begin with a baseline of care and love for ourselves before moving outward to care and love for others.

Generally, you can either feel the love of a business or you can't, short and simple. Whenever I evaluate businesses for investment, I always try to visit their workplace to see if I can literally "feel the love." For example, I recently came across a business with financial and user metrics that were doubling month over month—soon to reach the tens of millions—but when I visited the business, people were quiet, desks were empty, and something was just off. So I passed. You don't always need to measure quantifiable metrics like employee turnover, tenure length, and manager reviews to know when something feels inauthentic.

That said, one way to practically measure an organization's love for itself is through employee-engagement surveys. In contemporary management theory, workplace engagement has been in vogue for the past decade. Studies of workplace engagement ask what workplace conditions are required for people to love their work and feel both committed to and motivated by their roles. Recall WD-40, where 98 percent of employees report that they love to tell others they work for the company.[12] When people feel happy at work, they extend this happiness outward to customers and other stakeholders. Happy employees who love their companies manifest this love

in their work, product, and service—and customers can just sense that. In my mind, a happy employee means a happy customer. Your employees are your key stakeholders, so if they are engaged and impassioned about your purpose and brand—in short, if they love what they're doing—your business will be poised to grow in strength and influence.

So what should business leaders do to establish an emotional connection, a lovemark, with their employees? Leaders need to connect the vision and values of their organizations to a set of meaningful roles for employees. The intrinsic reward of seeing how one's job fits into the larger picture and thus owning a part of the business's vision is more powerful than any extrinsic reward put on the table. Leaders should ask themselves the following questions: Have we clearly communicated our vision and values? How can I know that employees genuinely wish to engage in conversation? What can I do to more effectively prioritize other people's success? How do I empower my employees in the field to make self-directed decisions? Is there a way to ensure their voices are genuinely heard? Answering each one of these questions will open up more opportunities for love.

Defining What Love Really Means in the Context of Leadership and Business

In *Heart, Smarts, Guts, and Luck,* my coauthors and I found that a full 70 percent of successful entrepreneurial endeavors are primarily "heart" driven. Most people identify a passionate founder as the heart of any given business, but there are actually many different types of "love" that are relevant to business. The ancient Greeks produced sophisticated, nuanced, and granular definitions for the different classes of love. C. S. Lewis's 1960 book, *The Four Loves,* is also largely based on these ancient Greek definitions.[13] How can we apply these varieties of love in the context of business and leadership?

- *Eros* is erotic desire, which the Greeks believed could be dangerous if not tempered. Eros is intoxicating and addictive, and might

even make us behave irrationally. In a business context, eros is the "fire in the belly" that helps inspire founders to get their sometimes "crazy" but good ideas started. However, this passion must eventually be reined in and productively channeled so the business can get to the next level without growing too fast or lacking a sustainable business model.

• *Philia* is loyalty, friendship, camaraderie, affection, and companionship. In the workplace, philia is the basis of the caring and collegial relationships we seek to establish with our colleagues.

• *Storge,* which C. S. Lewis referred to as the "empathy bond," recalls our earlier discussion on compassion. Storge means placing yourself completely into the shoes of another and is essential for establishing mutual understanding with others.

• *Agape* is unconditional and sacrificial love, like that of a mother for her children. Saint Thomas of Aquinas described agape as "willing the good of another," and C. S. Lewis believed agape was the greatest and most virtuous of the four types of love. In writing *Heart, Smarts, Guts, and Luck*, my coauthors and I really wanted to think about the meaning of love in life and business. All four types of love come into play in both of these arenas, but by far the most interesting one we explored in that book—and the one that I feel is most critical to wholeness—is agape. Indeed, both servant leadership and goodness—which we've defined as putting people first— require agape, or love strong enough to convince us to sacrifice for the good of a greater whole.

We all make sacrifices each and every day for work, whether we're leaders, managers, or line-level employees. After all, most of us spend at least half of our waking hours working, in no small part because we are usually paid for our work. But we would all do well to remember what Confucius professed: "Choose a job you love, you will never have to work a day in your life." We can find joy in our work by owning meaningful roles that contribute to a firm's vision and help others become fuller versions of themselves.

Leaders who want to heighten their employees' emotional engagement must choose to create a culture that's worthy of love. As Casey Gerald, founder of MBAs Across America, once summed it up for me: "I don't know that I, or anybody else, can be whole without engaging in the very dangerous exercise of trying to love oneself and love other people. Love isn't mush, hugs, or butterflies. It's very serious business."[14]

PRACTICING RESPECT: TREATING PEOPLE RIGHT, SAYING SORRY, AND SHOWING UP

I'm not concerned with your liking or disliking me. . . . All I ask is that you respect me as a human being.

JACKIE ROBINSON[15]

The second value of wholeness is the practice of respect, both toward yourself and toward others. How do you treat complete strangers? How does the person you're with treat the coat check attendant, the Uber driver, or the waitress at your table? Does he treat that person with openness and respect, or with indifference, arrogance, and even rudeness? It seems like in every workplace there's at least one person who feigns affability to their superiors but shows profound disrespect to those below them.

You can learn a lot about another person simply by observing how they treat children. I once attended a New Year's Eve party with my young nieces, and as I walked around the room introducing the girls, I observed that the party guests could be partitioned into two distinct groups. The first treated the girls with genuine respect and interest. The second politely shook their hands and were clearly eager to move on to other guests and new conversations. For his part, the host couldn't have been happier that our nieces had accompanied us. He warmly welcomed them and asked them questions about themselves. The host seemed genuinely interested in what they did, where they went to school, and what they thought about our hometown of Boston. This stood in stark contrast to the behavior of some of the other guests, who treated the girls like an inconvenience. In moments like this, good people are strikingly "human"—they break from character, tear down the social hierarchy, and treat others as people who deserve their respect.

Respect means consistently behaving in a way that is consistent with one's values, exhibiting the same integrity and self-congruence we discussed in our chapter on truth. You may not agree with another person's values, but you should respect people who are true to who they are and do what they say. I would rather do business with someone who is straight and true to their values, even if they differ significantly from mine, than someone who fickly changes their position to suit whoever's in the room. My partner at Cue Ball, John Hamel, has an expression for people who are less upfront about who they are and hide behind false personas, "people you need to keep swimming through to figure out who they are." Well, those types of people should generally be avoided. Simply put, it's much easier to respect people who are comfortable in their own skin.

Respect is a close cousin of compassion, but the practice of respect also demands that we defer to others, observe proper decorum, recognize our mistakes, and follow through on our commitments. In this sense, respect can be practiced on a small scale through simple, everyday habits, like being on time, being fully present during meetings, apologizing quickly, and avoiding pettiness. Consider the three simple rules Coach John Wooden set for his players, all of which concern respect for oneself and one's peers:

1. *Never be late*—Respect the value of time and other people's commitments. Wooden held a very strict line when it came to attendance and punctuality; players who showed up late or missed parts of practice risked getting thrown off the team.

2. *Neat and clean, and no profanity*—Wooden required his players to observe proper decorum for the culture and context. Respect the occasion you find yourself in: being neat and clean underscored the

seriousness of each and every practice and game. When basketball star Bill Walton showed up at practice one day sporting a beard, Coach Wooden immediately told him to go home to clean himself up. When Walton insisted it was his right to have a beard, Coach Wooden replied, "That's good, Bill. I admire people who have strong beliefs and stick by them, I really do. We're going to miss you." Walton immediately went home to shave his beard.[16] Even to this day, I live by the old-school rule that it's always better to be overdressed than underdressed.

3. *Never criticize a teammate*—To Wooden, success was about more than winning; it was about how the collective whole felt and performed. Wooden believed the best games were those where both teams left the court and neither could tell who had won. He taught his boys to never criticize another player, never score without acknowledging another person's contributions, and never treat the other team with anything less than full respect.

People in positions of power often assume they deserve respect without having fully earned it. It does not matter if you are the captain of a team or the CEO of a business; deference can only be won by earning the genuine admiration of another person, typically for either the consistency of your character or the caliber of your competence. Ultimately, genuine respect accrues to those who respect other people. Respect is a two-way street. When someone you admire makes a misstep, are they willing to step forward and openly admit it? Leaders are fallible, and mistakes happen. The question is, are they transparent about their errors and do they hold themselves accountable?

On Valentine's Day in 2007, an ice storm in the Northeast caused a series of cancellations and massive delays for JetBlue Airways. Public outcry was sharp; people were stranded for up to a week, luggage was lost, and rebooking hundreds of flights posed a logistical nightmare for JetBlue's stressed staff. David Neeleman, the founder and CEO of JetBlue, called it the worst operational week on record for the seven-year-old airline. Immediately after the storm, Neeleman delivered a sincere and humanizing apology in which he took full accountability for the hardships JetBlue travelers were experiencing. Neeleman's apology appeared in an online video, on JetBlue's website, and in full-page advertisements in national newspapers. Built on the old adage "the customer is always right," the apology signaled authentic respect for passengers. Neeleman did not blame the weather for the cancellations or delays; rather, he issued a textbook mea culpa that acknowledged the problem, empathized with those affected, explained what went wrong, and laid out what they would do differently in the future, including issuing a new JetBlue Customer Bill of Rights. Here is an excerpt from Neeleman's apology:

> *Words cannot express how truly sorry we are for the anxiety, frustration and inconvenience that you, your family, friends and colleagues experienced. . . . JetBlue was founded on the promise of bringing humanity back to air travel, and making the experience of flying happier. . . . We know we failed to deliver on this promise last week. . . . You deserved better—a lot better . . . and we let you down.*[17]

Neeleman could have blamed extenuating circumstances and uncontrollable weather conditions, but he chose instead to do the right thing—to respect how his passengers felt and apologize. Neeleman's apology connected with passengers on an emotional level. In a moment of truth, when the airline's reputation was on the line, Neeleman managed to win even deeper trust from JetBlue's passengers.

Some of the most powerful moments of leadership I've observed in my career have involved a senior person apologizing to lower-level staff members. One of Dr. Wayne Dyer's most well-known quotes is "When given a choice between being right and being kind, choose kind."[18] It's difficult to practice respect and pursue wholeness if the workplace is a battle between coworkers each insisting they're right. We commend children for their maturity if they learn from difficult moments rather than pointing fingers and avoiding blame. As adults, we would do well to remember this lesson. Ultimately, what really matters is whether a person's actions support or detract from the organization's larger purpose and core values.

Dick Harrington has been my friend and colleague for nearly twenty years. I respect his success—he rose from humble origins in the plumbing business to eventually run the largest information services company in the world—as well as his strong values. When I was at Thomson working for Dick, there were frequently times when Dick would resist pressure from others to execute more quickly on business strategy and operations. At the time, I did not fully understand Dick's reasoning—why not hit the "go" button? But over the years, I learned from Dick just how important it is to provide stakeholders with opportunities to voice their input so they can arrive at the conclusion for themselves.

Another part of Dick's leadership model is to separate *individual contributors* from *team leaders*. Dick believes that even the smartest individual contributors—especially those suffering from "Smartest Person in the Room Syndrome" (SPRS)—are less valuable to the overall organization than "skill-poor" team leaders who excel at making other people better. To Dick, the collective whole is more important than any one individual. People with SPRS have difficulty respecting those who are less competent than them, and they tend to demand respect before they've necessarily earned it. They frequently end up alienating their colleagues and unraveling the fabric of trust and respect teams need to work effectively. In the end, this bias for competency over character can stunt SPRSers' quest for wholeness and cut short their career progression. I've learned to seek out those who have earned respect for their values and actions and to avoid as much as possible those who ask us to command positional respect from perches of power.

Have faith that people will respect you if they see that you behave in a manner consistent with your values, that you follow through on your promises, and that you do what you say you will do. For example, Trader Joe's consistently receives high Net Promoter Scores (NPS)—a measure of consumers' willingness to recommend a company to others—by consistently "showing up" to deliver on the promises they've made to consumers and going above and beyond the call of duty when it really matters. The number one core value at Trader Joe's is the golden rule—"Treat others as you would like to be treated."[19] One December evening in

Pennsylvania, inclement weather "snowed in" an eighty-nine-year-old re-tired naval officer. When the man's concerned daughter called around to some grocery stores in the area hoping one would be able to deliver some food to her father, she came up empty. Finally she reached out to Trader Joe's. The representative on the phone explained that they didn't normally deliver, but not to worry, they would make an exception. Thirty minutes later, some bags of groceries were delivered to the man's home, along with some other items the representative thought the man might need to last out the storm for a few more days. But the real kicker is that there was no charge. The representative simply said, "Merry Christmas."[20]

In this situation, Trader Joe's helped someone who was in need, demonstrating in spades all the values of truth and compassion contained in the Goodness Pyramid. By living up to its first value—treating others as you would want to be treated—Trader Joe's amplified all of its other company values, including "Create wow experience" and "No bureau-cracy." Unlike the bartender at the resort who poured a guest's drinks down the drain because she didn't have a credit card, the Trader Joe's representative was empowered to make frontline decisions based on the company's values rather than rigid rules and standard operating proce-dures. Trader Joe's believes in "no bureaucracy" because it believes its employees will do the right thing, including making exceptions if the situation is right. Trader Joe's literally showed up to deliver groceries to an eighty-nine-year-old retired naval officer in a snow storm and symbol-ically showed up to live out its core values.

Author and scholar Brené Brown has said that "courage starts with showing up and letting ourselves be seen."[21] The world's most respected companies and leaders match consistent financial performance with con-sistent moral action—they show up and they follow through. It sounds easy enough to do, but showing up and following through on what you say you will do is anything but easy. We always have competing priorities—things come up—but, as Brown suggests, we also sometimes break commitments because we feel embarrassed or unprepared for diffi-cult conversations. But you need to treat others with the same respect you would want if the roles were reversed. You would want people to be there who said they'd be there. And you'd want people always to follow through till the end. Who are the people you can most depend upon? People respect organizations that show respect for them, show up, and follow through on their values whenever the opportunity presents itself for them to do so. This is true leadership.

New York Times columnist and best-selling author Adam Bryant teaches a leadership class at Columbia University and lectures throughout the country on leadership. In his lectures, he likes to ask the audience how many of them have had a boss they respect. Typically, less than half the class raise their hands. Another survey has estimated that 65 percent of working Americans would prefer a new boss to a pay raise.[22] When I heard this, I was reminded of something a colleague once told me, which he in turn had learned from a Silicon Valley venture investor. When considering whether to take a new job, he had said, there are really only a handful of questions you need to ask yourself: Do you have affection for these people? Can you imagine yourself caring for them and them caring for you? Do you respect the boss's leadership style, and do you think she will respect you? And finally, would you be proud to talk with other people about your colleagues, your boss, and your workplace?

Really good managers and leaders respect the truth and expectations that stem from the answers to these questions. This brings us to our next section on wholeness: acting with wisdom.

ACTING WITH WISDOM

She hoped to be wise and reasonable in time; but alas! Alas! She must confess to herself that she was not wise yet.

JANE AUSTEN, *PERSUASION*[23]

If you see a whole thing—it seems that it's always beautiful. Planets, lives. . . . But close up a world's all dirt and rocks. And day to day, life's a hard job, you get tired, you lose the pattern.

URSULA K. LE GUIN, *THE DISPOSSESSED*[24]

We develop wisdom when we experience the world and learn good judgment alongside good people. Wisdom is wholeness in action. It allows us to discern what's important and what's not, what's passing and what's permanent, what's right and what's wrong, what's naïve and what's well considered. Wisdom helps us make better decisions when we are stuck in the gray ambiguity of tough questions. It helps us distinguish between those things that are inside our control or those that are outside our control. Acting with wisdom demands we acknowledge that there are rarely perfect black-or-white interpretations of or solutions to any of life's problems.

Wisdom Begins with Truth in Expectations and Balance

> God, grant me the serenity to accept the things
>   I cannot change
> The courage to change the things I can
> And the wisdom to know the difference.

REINHOLD NIEBUHR[25]

When things don't work out as expected, a helpful exercise is to consider—with brutal honesty—what things in our control would have led to a different and more positive outcome. This allows us to separate out the uncontrollable externalities that may have caused the situation to go in a different direction than expected. Niebuhr's prayer is as close to a perfect definition of wisdom as there is. It provides us with another layer of nuance to define "success" in the context of wholeness: as the self-satisfaction of knowing we have done everything in our capability to make ourselves and others better and fuller versions of who we are. The key detail here is *everything in our capability*, meaning everything that was in our control.

To understand what is inside and outside of our control, we must reconcile the truth with our expectations. Our appreciation of our own success is a function of the expectations we have set for ourselves and others. We are more in control of our happiness if we can be realistic about what "line" we should strive for. If we expect we should always be the absolute best at everything, we will constantly disappoint ourselves, even if we're truly great by any other measure.

A famous study on the relative happiness felt by Olympic athletes who win bronze, silver, and gold medals helps to illustrate this point. In 1995, Cornell University psychologists Victoria Medvec and Thomas Gilovich and Scott Madey of the University of Toledo found that Olympic athletes who win bronze are often happier than those who win silver.[26] Olympic silver medalists experience the greatest disappointment because they dwell on what might have been and how close they were to winning the gold. But for the bronze medal winner, the counterfactual is having no medal at all.

Counterfactual thinking involves the recasting of "what if" questions as "what might have been" scenarios. Our self-realization and wholeness is a direct result of the expectations we set for ourselves, be they around anticipated promotions or bonuses, planned budgets of record, or expectations for people. Of course, we're always happy when we get upside surprises, but downside outcomes that are misaligned with our expectations—especially in near-miss cases—can deeply affect our state of mind, confidence, and sense of wholeness.

It's therefore important for our own expectations of others to be truthful and realistic. Realistic expectations help us to be more compassionate to others and more forgiving of their blind spots, as well as our own. Even more important, realistic expectations help us avoid disappointment from "reality gaps" that sow disdain and frustration. Admittedly, setting the right expectations is a careful balancing act. On the one hand, we want to help people stretch to realize their potential. On the other, we want to support them if they stumble and fail to reach high-performance thresholds.

In the business of venture investing, truth and expectations are most relevant when setting goals and planning budgets. When we work with CEOs, we have them set their own top priorities and provide concrete metrics by which the board can measure their success. Closely related to their priorities are, of course, the implied financial outcomes set each year as a plan of record. My goal on both these fronts has always been to push CEOs to the point where they are just making or exceeding their goals.

It's an almost impossible task, but each year we learn how to do it better. By my own estimation, we only meet or exceed our targets about 75 percent of the time. This isn't all bad—believing you can do more than you are actually capable of can push you to deliver extraordinary results—but repeated misses are more demoralizing than motivating. I have learned that most people can deal with bad news or subpar outcomes if they set realistic expectations early and are given a chance to course correct.

More often than not, wisdom is about finding equilibrium and balancing the tensions we encounter when we pursue goodness. We will fully explore these tensions in the next section of the book, but for now, it is worth just acknowledging that we face a considerable range of irreconcilable trade-offs every day. For example, what is the best balance between pragmatism and idealism? What do we need in the short term, and what should be considered a longer-term endeavor? As we attempt to reach wholeness as leaders, we will need to settle on balance points that allow us to feel grateful, at peace, and satisfied with our decisions, achievements, and overall goals.

The search for balance raises an interesting question: When should we follow our ambitions, and when should we make compromises? Wisdom, after all, should help us discern between those situations where satisficing will suffice and those that warrant pushing for the extra mile. The work of Nobel laureate and political scientist Herbert A. Simon on the concept of "satisficing" versus "maximizing" is relevant to this very question.[27] Psychology has since co-opted these terms as metrics for measuring happiness (which, in this case, I use as a proxy for wholeness). Simon's concept is relatively straightforward. He argues there are only two types of decision makers: satisficers and maximizers. To better appreciate their differences, imagine you need to find a particular sewing machine needle that ideally runs 3.55 inches in length. Unfortunately, that needle is an unusual dimension, and worse, it's also buried in a pile of hundreds of needles anywhere from one to five inches in length. A satisficer would paw hurriedly through the needles until he found one that was adequate (close to 3.55 inches, perhaps 3.25 or 3.75 inches), whereas a maximizer would comb through the pile for hours, if necessary, until he found the precise needle.

Neither the satisficer nor the maximizer is the be-all and end-all decision maker. In some cases, good enough makes perfect sense. Seamstresses, for instance, follow the classic 80/20 rule that says that a 3-inch needle can fix almost any garment. In other situations, however—like designing the engineering specifications for a suspension bridge—precision, accuracy, and optimization are essential. The key, as Niebuhr's serenity prayer reminds us, is having the wisdom to know the difference. That said, it's fair to say that most of the problems we have to solve don't involve suspension bridges. They may feel that way sometimes, but in truth, most are 80/20 problems that can be addressed using a needle of approximate length.

Here's where things get sticky: ambitious, type A personalities—and I include myself in this group—often feel compelled to maximize the outcome of *everything*. From experience, I know too well that this often ends in frustration. Research shows that satisficers are happier people than maximizers, and that they report feeling more "whole." Knowing there's always more to be done, perfectionists and maximizers are never satisfied. As ever, the key is finding the appropriate balance, judgment, and disposition to accept compromise when it doesn't really matter but go the extra mile when it does.

One way to help us better navigate satisficing and maximizing situations is to simply reduce choice. In their research, Barry Schwartz, the author of *The Paradox of Choice*, and his colleague Andrew Ward have found that when it comes to happiness, less can indeed be more.[28] As our options increase, so, too, does our threshold for what makes us happy. The key to experiencing happiness, gratitude, and wholeness, Schwartz and Ward discovered, is realizing when good enough really *is* good enough. Imagine how you might shop for a new laptop. Almost every month, it seems, there is a new model that's faster or more powerful with sharper optics or longer battery life, and so on. Rather than agonizing over every single spec, Schwartz suggests you call one of your "maximizer" friends, ask them the model of the laptop they bought most recently, and buy the same one. Forget evaluating any other choices. Perfect? Probably not. Good enough? Absolutely.

Wisdom is also a function of time and people. Patience and time bring experience, perspective, and, ideally, a circle of people who can serve as our guides, mentors, and anchors in times of reflection or need. There is no doubt that the right individuals and partners, like JFK and RFK, can serve as invaluable guides, mentors, and supporters during our most challenging times. We should all cultivate a personal panel of people to provide us with support, complementary capabilities, and trusted counsel. Still, it bears repeating: the pursuit of wholeness and wisdom is a lifelong journey. To reap the full benefits of wholeness, we need to patiently hone our wisdom and allow it to mature. Wisdom is ultimately our wholeness in action, and the foundation of our judgment.

THE QUEST FOR WHOLENESS: HOW CAN WE GET THERE?

The term "ego-integrity" was coined by psychologist Erik Erikson to describe the final stage of human psychological development. Later in life, after age sixty-five, we are better able to accept life in its complete form, with all its successes and failures. But why should we have to wait until age sixty-five to achieve some semblance of ego-integrity? Is there a way to reach this stage earlier in life? If you can practice the values that drive ego-integrity—the same underlying values that help us build toward wholeness—there is no reason why you should not be able to accelerate your path toward wisdom. After all, most of us have a friend who is an "old soul."

I have two life goals. The first is to become as wise as I can as early as I can. Why wait for wisdom until I'm in my seventies, eighties, or nineties? If you feel like I do, study philosophy and the great spiritual traditions as early as you can; even if you don't believe in a higher power, there is still beauty and learning to be had in these teachings. For that matter, study whatever you can, wherever you can, whenever you can! My second life goal is to remember to experience the happiness, awe, gratitude, and curiosity common among children, especially as I grow older. It's almost as if we understand everything during our first and final five years of life, and in between lie all of life's struggles.

Still, it is possible to build toward wholeness earlier in life. During an interview for this book, I asked Deepak Chopra what he was most grateful for. He answered, simply, "Existence." As Chopra himself once said:

Be happy for no reason, like a child. If you are happy for a reason, you're in trouble, because that reason can be taken from you.[29]

Chopra reminds us that we have all been given the gift of existence, relationships, experiences, and belongings, and we should be grateful for these gifts, in that order. What are some of the practical ways we can achieve greater happiness and wholeness? I've taken a cue from Bobby McFerrin and his song "Don't Worry, Be Happy" to add just a touch of levity to this weighty subject. Below is my "Bobby List" of things that get us closer to wholeness.

Getting Closer to Wholeness: The "Bobby List"

1. *Be around good, happy, whole people.* Good people beget good people, just as happy people help others feel happier and more fulfilled. When you're in the presence of good people, their positivity is contagious.

2. *Focus on the intrinsic more than the extrinsic.* Concentrate on meaningful roles, experiences, learning, and development. At work, focus on the meaningful role you play and what you're learning instead of focusing on how much money your peers might be making elsewhere. *New York Times* columnist David Brooks says as much in his book *The Road to Character*, in which he argues that our competitive, credential-oriented world places too much emphasis on "résumé virtues" and not nearly enough time on those intrinsic qualities—our "eulogy virtues"—that would be worth commemorating at the end of our lives.[30]

3. *Don't focus on what you lack.* Optimism is an outsize trait of the most effective leaders I know. Ask yourself whether you're acting more like an energy giver or an energy taker. Try passing the 24 x 3 rule of optimism, and wait a day before criticizing new ideas.

The best leaders enumerate the possibilities before considering the obstacles.

4. Random and conscious acts of kindness. Can you deliver more happiness or positivity to someone else? Can you give a stranger a hug, have a real conversation with someone who is lonely, or help a colleague who is in obvious need of support? There is a role for both random and conscious acts of kindness. To accomplish the latter, we should be attuned to those who need our support. At any given time, can you name the colleagues whom you are helping to bring along?

5. Read and write about what inspires you. If nothing else, writing down your thoughts is a good reminder of the power of self-reflection. Then there's reading. Read as many books as you can. Dog-ear pages and scribble down notes. One especially easy exercise is to keep a log of themes and quotations that have inspired you.

In Abraham Maslow's hierarchy of needs, the top of the pyramid is self-actualization, a state in which people experience intense and transcendent "peak experiences."[31] In our quest for wholeness, self-actualization is the ultimate aspiration, but it has less to do with what we can do for ourselves, and more to do with what we can do for others. According to Maslow, self-actualized people accept the reality around them and feel driven by a sense of personal responsibility to help others and participate in solving larger problems.

Wholeness, love, and self-actualization are subjects more commonly found in the fields of philosophy and psychology than in business. Most of us keep our business and personal lives separate, in the same way we distinguish between the "soft" and "hard" qualities of leadership. But in fact, they are intertwined. So why should Maslow's hierarchy of needs—which begins with our basic needs for survival and safety and ascends to the human need for love, esteem, and self-actualization—bypass the worlds of business and leadership? In the business world, words like "love" frequently get coded as "engagement" or "culture," and self-actualization becomes "personal and professional development." But here's the secret: it's all the same thing! When we use politically correct business terms and euphemisms to make these concepts more palatable in professional contexts, we dilute their essence. The same common needs and values exist in both business and personal contexts; if we can talk about these needs and values in the business world using truly human terms, then we can create more businesses with the potential for great change.

WHOLENESS: WHEN DOES IT END? HOW DO I KNOW IT'S FINISHED?

The inescapable conclusion is that goodness is good for business and critical to organizational success. The path to wholeness is a progression toward a nonjudgmental, non-defensive state not only toward others, but also toward ourselves. Along the way, we become grateful for what we have and for the people we've become.

But if the journey toward wholeness is lifelong, how do we know when enough is enough? Will we be satisfied with the work we have done? To answer this question, I'll return to my favorite jazz artist, Herbie Hancock. Herbie once described how he struggled to find a way to end and resolve his song "Maiden Voyage," which he recorded in 1965 with Miles Davis, Ron Carter, Tony Williams, Freddie Hubbard, and George Coleman. The melody, he said, kept returning to the song's beginning, and at some point Herbie realized the beginning *was* the ending. I can't think of a better explanation of what it means to be whole and at ease with what is right in front of you. Wholeness means we've come full circle. To be whole is to value and practice truth and compassion. This is the heart of our humanity. This is the thing that binds and connects us and allows us to ignite change together. It is a never-ending quest that we can never finish, but we can pass on to the good people we inspire.

SUMMARY OF KEY POINTS FROM CHAPTER 5

• • • • • • • •

• **Leadership is a lonely business.** Leaders can achieve balance and a sense of wholeness if they remind themselves of their duty to serve others.

• **Like the overall pursuit of goodness, the pursuit of wholeness is an intentional, lifelong pursuit that never truly ends.** Wholeness is the highest level of the Goodness Pyramid. It is defined by the underlying values of love, respect, and wisdom. To achieve wholeness, one must feel love, practice respect, and act with wisdom. The choice must be proactive, and the journey will surely be long and asymptotic.

• **Love in the context of business and leadership is mostly about service.** Happy employees equal happy customers. We need to believe that a mindset of love is critical to the work we do and that the people we work with are worth sacrificing for.

• **Respect is the practice and habit of deference toward others, decorum in particular situations, and commitment to one's promises.** Respect is also about the principle of equality—we all have the right to feel there is meaning in what we do and to act in ways that are consistent with our values.

• **Wisdom is wholeness in action; it is an accumulation of experiences and knowledge that allows us to discern between the things we can control and the things we cannot control.** Wisdom empowers us in times of ambiguity. With wisdom, we are better able to grasp the truth of any given situation and to manage our expectations. Our truth helps us balance life's tensions and appreciate when satisficing is good enough.

• **Self-actualization and wholeness complement business and define great leadership.** Abraham Maslow put forth one of psychology's best-known frameworks. There are many parallels between this quest for personal self-actualization and the pursuit of more humanized, whole, and effective leadership in business. When we are at our best in business, we experience peak leadership—human-centric, self-actualized, and whole.

· · · · · · ·

PART TWO

BALANCING TENSIONS TO ACHIEVE GOODNESS

Are human beings intrinsically good but corruptible by the forces of evil, or the reverse, innately sinful yet redeemable by the force of good? . . . Scientific evidence, a good part of it accumulated during the past twenty years, suggests that we are both of these things simultaneously. Each of us is inherently conflicted.

E. O. WILSON, *THE MEANING OF HUMAN EXISTENCE*[1]

A few years ago, I traveled to Buenos Aires, where I witnessed the beauty of tango dancing—everywhere from the streets to tacky made-for-tourist exhibitions to "real-deal" dance halls known as "milongas," packed with local enthusiasts. Regardless of the dancers' skill level, tango is a peerless medium for expressing shared tensions and passions: the discordances and harmonies of an intense pair moving as one, giving and receiving each other's intentions; the intimate flow, punctuated by bursts of passions, all contained within the structure of the dance's steps. Two people familiar with each other's touch and embrace—controlled and tense one moment, poetic and flirtatious the next—start moving to the rhythm of that signature staccato and then seamlessly slip into the *slow, slow, quick, quick, slow* pattern of four synchronized feet making that tender first curve of the tango walk.

At its heart, the tango is a duel. The tensions between persuasion and dissuasion, restraint and acceptance, and right versus wrong remind us of how our strengths and weaknesses can be one and the same. The dance is a perfect illustration of the tensions most of us face daily and the realities that make the quest for goodness and good people so challenging.

Overlaying the framework of the Goodness Pyramid are five pairs of "tensions," or countervailing forces, perennially at work within all of us, that require balance and vigilance. The five tensions in our Goodness Pyramid add color to the tapestry of our human character and goodness and help us explain why being good and pursuing goodness require steadfast intention and resolve.

In part one of this book, I provided a framework, language, and process for discussing goodness and for becoming a better person. Now we are ready to discuss how this plays out in the real world. When you seek to put goodness into action yet immediately come up against life's inherent challenges, the world suddenly becomes far less simple. Imagine, for example, that you want to be truthful not only to your personal purpose but also to the distinct purposes of your company and your colleagues. Practically, how do you reconcile finite resources, competing priorities, and limited time?

The first part of this book explored a common language and process for goodness and good people. Parts two and three put goodness and good people into practice. Like any business plan, budget, or architectural blueprint, things get more complicated and a lot messier when they're put into action to be carried out in the real world. You can't manage or operate a business from only models and spreadsheets. Life is much more gray than either black or white, and it is filled with tensions and challenges.

I use the word "tensions" to describe the most common trade-offs we face when attempting to reconcile our ideals with the common roadblocks and setbacks that arise when we try to make the abstract real. Putting goodness into practice can feel much more difficult than it did in theory. The good news? With the help of an overarching approach and some daily habits and practices, like Benjamin Franklin's, we can uncover a better balance between the five core tensions that challenge our ongoing pursuit of goodness and good people. The five tensions we must balance as we attempt to live out the values embedded in our Good People Mantra and Goodness Pyramid are:

1. Pragmatism Versus Idealism. If our dreams are heady, far-flung, and ambitious, they often confront realities like time constraints and inadequate resources. *(tension against truth)*

2. Short-termism Versus Long-termism. In a world that can seem wed to short-term gains, solutions, and satisfactions, taking a long-term perspective requires patience. *(tension against truth and wholeness)*

3. Vulnerability Versus Conviction. Our confidence in our endeavors and ourselves often has to be balanced with the vulnerability that everything worth doing carries a measure of risk. *(tension against truth and compassion)*

4. Idiosyncrasy Versus Connectedness. We must learn to balance our shared humanity with the quirkiness, imperfections, and idiosyncrasies of our own characters and behaviors. *(tension against truth, compassion, and wholeness)*

5. Grit Versus Acceptance. Where is the line between stick-with-it-ness and self-awareness? When should resilience give way to the humility necessary to acknowledge when it makes sense to embrace failure and move forward? *(tension against wholeness)*

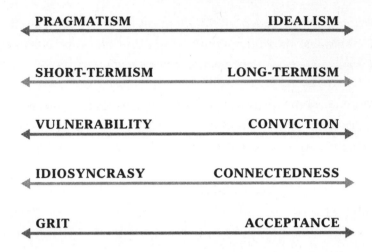

When we assess goodness and reconcile the tug-of-war of these tensions in the real world, the key element is *balance*. Are you torn between pragmatism and idealism? Then seek to be a pragmatic idealist. Resolve the pull of short-termism versus long-termism, and become a patient opportunist who is impatiently patient. Do you swing back and forth between vulnerability and conviction? Experience will show you where a comfortable middle ground lies. Find a midpoint between idiosyncrasy and connectedness where others will perceive you either as a multidimensional thinker or as a quirky, beautiful bird who can still manage to connect with others. Last but not least, the conflict warring between grit and acceptance should help us evolve into people who are both wise and whole.

Simple awareness of these five tensions can begin to help us make better choices.

R.I.S.E.—AN APPROACH FOR BALANCED DECISION MAKING

You've now learned the importance of incorporating goodness at work as a leader and you have a framework to develop goodness in yourself and others. And we've just walked through the tensions you'll face when you attempt to put the Good People Mantra and Goodness Pyramid into practice in the real world. Now to better equip you as you learn how to manage these tensions that can often pull us in opposite directions, we'll start by discussing a decision-making process to help balance these tensions.

First, it is worth stressing the point again: what you are striving to achieve is not a singular answer, but rather balance when confronting these tensions. Balance can be defined as:

An even distribution enabling someone or something to remain steady.[2]

A condition in which different elements are equal or in the correct proportions.[3]

While no one-size-fits-all answer exists to reconcile these tensions, developing a consistent approach to these dilemmas encourages better, balanced decisions. I've established a solid, repeatable approach for finding thoughtful, clearheaded, and consistent resolutions to thorny problems. First, remember you must start with yourself and be self-aware enough to recognize and internalize the issue at hand. Share your thinking with one or more of your mentors or most trusted confidants only after you have recognized and internalized the situation. Then it's decision time. Execute with conviction and confidence that your awareness of these tensions, your base of values, and your decision-making process have collectively helped you make a fundamentally *good* decision. I call this R.I.S.E., which stands for *recognizing, internalizing, sharing,* and *executing* on the inputs for effective and balanced decision making.

R̲ECOGNIZE

First, begin by recognizing the situation you're in and seeing it for what it is. Assess the real risks and consequences, and set realistic expectations. Recognize that it's normal to feel vulnerable at the outset of difficult decisions. Focus on finding an answer that is approximately correct and balanced; don't expend energy seeking a nonexistent perfect answer.

I̲NTERNALIZE

Recognizing and sizing up a situation is not the same as fully internalizing it. To internalize something means to have it come naturally to you, almost with an intuitive, unconscious, and innate ability to understand the information at hand. To do this, mentally play out the decision steps and explore potential "if/then" outcomes as if you were in a movie. Then view the movie forward and backward so you can more clearly see the decision steps that will lead to the desired outcome. Give yourself time and space to reflect on and internalize the situation.

S̲HARE

Once you've internalized a problem and its context, share the situation with a small group of good people: your mentors, confidants, and anchors. This will allow you to discover what you may have overlooked and gain greater insight by looking at the problem through a different lens. While some decisions require immediate action, the biggest decisions deserve deliberate and careful contemplation, with input and counsel from people you respect and trust.

E̲XECUTE

Time to execute with conviction! Once you've made your decision, write down why you made the decision you did, and include the key points behind your rationale and process. This will serve as a key reference for future self-awareness and learning. Do what you said you'd do, recalibrate as required, and as the results play out, see what you might do differently next time.

In the next five chapters, we'll explore these five tensions with the goal of finding balance. While a decision-making process doesn't guarantee success, it increases your probability of success. If the R.I.S.E. framework for balanced decision making is intuitive to you, use it. Whether it is this process or another, a structured approach can serve as a system of checks and balances against your own gut. When a stressful situation occurs, especially one that seems to challenge your values of goodness, having a go-to method will help ease the emotional weight and give you an initial guide toward balance. With all this said, this decision-making approach should be thought of not as a rigid recipe but as a set of principles sequenced in a logical manner to help you better frame thinking on how to put goodness into practice. If the Good People Mantra and Goodness Pyramid help ground us on what it really means to be good, this next section of the book is committed to sharing vignettes, case studies, and applications of R.I.S.E. that better illustrate goodness in action—how do we find balance and practically make all of this goodness happen?

If all of this seems a little overwhelming, there is also something else that we have discovered: good people reconcile most if not all of these tensions by finding an answer that already resides within them through deep self-reflection on their values. The frameworks provided here in this book and others that you may know are all meant to serve as a guide, a set of principles that can reinforce and magnify innate and developing goodness values. Outside of listening to the values they know and using some common frameworks and approaches, good people also seek counsel from trusted peers, advisors, and mentors in moments of key decision making (the share component of R.I.S.E.). Gathering a depth of perspectives from a small set of authentic relationships is far more important than casting a wide and thin net for votes among many. The people and cases in the following chapters will show you ways you can achieve balance by successfully managing the five tensions that conflict with everyday goodness. In so doing, you can become better at dancing your own seamless tango of tensions.

6

PRAGMATISM VERSUS IDEALISM

Idealism detached from action is just a dream. But idealism allied with pragmatism, with rolling up your sleeves and making the world bend a bit, is very exciting. It's very real. It's very strong.

BONO[1]

I was twenty-four years old, in my third year serving as an intern at the World Economic Forum (WEF) in Davos, Switzerland. Since the World Economic Forum attracts so many dignitaries every year, the conference relies on temporary staff to serve the needs of VIPs and other attendees during its famous annual confab in the Swiss Alps. When I was assigned to act as a temporary internal junior "body man" and WEF representative for the senior minister of Singapore, Lee Kuan Yew, I thought I had landed the assignment of a lifetime. The opportunity was particularly exciting to me because I had studied the case study of Singapore in depth as part of a course I took at Harvard, and one of my most important mentors, Tsun-yan, was from the region. I knew and respected the senior minister's work because I believed even his more controversial policies came from a place of good intentions and had led to modern Singapore's status as an Asian economic powerhouse. What I appreciated less at the time was how effectively he had balanced the tension between pragmatism and idealism.

For three days while the senior minister attended WEF events, I would be on standby for all of his needs, serving as his extra arms, legs, and—I hoped—brains. I knew my place: I would be the deckhand and serve as a temp administrative coordinator for one of the senior minister's aide-de-camps. My job directions were simple: *make it happen.*

Many regard Lee Kuan Yew as one of the greatest public servants in recent political history. He is widely credited with transforming the tiny city-state of Singapore—which has a land mass of only 277 square miles—into a major global shipping port and one of Asia's tiger economies. I got a strong sense of the senior minister's close attention to detail early on in my assignment when I fielded a peculiar request from one of his aides: I was to order the local Swiss telecommunications service to set up two secure phone lines—one with a flashing light option—that could ring simultaneously, at precisely the same time, in two separate hotel rooms. I was also advised to take note of the senior minister's morning swimming routine and to expect a briefing package replete with his travel preferences and protocols.

Having worked at WEF for the previous two summers, I was no stranger to the detailed protocol binders and itineraries, but the senior minister's attention to detail floored me. His materials included information on the number of steps and meters from his car to the hotel door, his preferred room temperatures, his exacting food preferences, his security protocol, and a series of sophisticated contingency plans. I was able to ride alongside the senior minister on some of these short trips, during which I was often struck by his infinite curiosity. "Tony," he would say, "do you know what those sticks are for at the top of the mountains? Do they have something to do with avalanches?" Or, "How are the cars managed for this World Economic Forum meeting, and how many are being dispatched each day?" Another was, "How many staff are working here at Davos?" I didn't know a lot of the answers to his many questions, and as much as I wanted to come across as smart and well-informed, I knew that giving him a wrong answer would be a terrible mistake.

The late senior minister balanced pragmatism and idealism better than anyone else I've ever met. When he died in 2015, many obituaries and tributes described Lee as the ultimate benevolent dictator, or as the *Guardian* put it, an "authoritarian pragmatist." One facet of this "authoritarianism" was Lee's dream to transform Singapore into global city-state, with meritocracy, multiculturalism, multiracialism, and financial independence for all. To attain these ideals, Lee wielded great power, control, and influence. He was critical and often unforgiving of those who failed to follow his guiding principle and broke Singapore's laws. "We in the West may quarrel with the way Singapore's prosperity was achieved," wrote Tom Plate, an American journalist, "but the achievement somehow seems to dwarf the critique."[2]

Lee's accomplishments are irrefutable. He helped create a municipality with virtually no crime, zero unemployment, and one of the highest savings rates in the world. In fact, Singapore is now frequently identified as a case study on how to achieve sustained GDP and economic growth. Lee believed it was his responsibility to ensure individuals fit into the society, and not the other way around. He faced harsh criticism for penalizing littering and prostitution with corporal punishment and handing down death sentences for the possession of illegal drugs. Yet at the center of these policies was a supremely self-confident and self-aware leader guided by a set of Confucian values and ideals. Lee believed society should respect and celebrate individual rights, but not at the expense of society itself. It was Lee's own version of John F. Kennedy's dictum "Ask not what your country can do for you, ask what you can do for your country."

Over the several days I spent with the senior minister, I marveled at how inextricably his disposition and practical philosophy were linked to his values and ideals, from his commitment to healthy living and exacting exercise routines to his team's flawlessly executed logistical planning. I still feel privileged to have had a brief but illuminating glimpse into the life of this highly pragmatic leader, guided at all times by deeply held values, and a true exemplar of pragmatic idealism.

ENEMIES OR COLLABORATORS IN WAITING?

The first of our five tensions is pragmatism versus idealism. Idealism encompasses our values, morals, and principles, as well as our heady, far-flung, and ambitious dreams, all of which we hope to embed in our businesses and relationships. This pair challenges our truth values and complicates our desire to achieve congruence between what we feel, what we know, and what we say we'll do. We know we ideally want to be good people, but there are practical constraints that can get in the way of our accomplishing something truly meaningful and significant.

This tension pushes and pulls across the cornerstone values that make up the Goodness Pyramid. Most of us want to practice truth and compassion and to attain wholeness, but reality is strewn with roadblocks and speed bumps. We need to get things done, often with scarce resources, while executing our visions and surviving the ups and downs of relationships. Idealism and pragmatism can resemble a pair of battling spouses, each one fighting for attention and dominance—and each with little left to give.

When does this tension most commonly emerge? In business, we experience it when trying to scale a company's vision, making a critical hire, mulling over a job offer, or whenever we feel fear that we may be settling on our ideals. Trade-offs like these occur often in business because of the reality of time constraints: "We have our ideal candidate profile for CEO and know he or she is out there; we just don't have the time to wait to find the right candidate." This tension can also show up in non-people decisions. In product development, for example, the ideal design specifications or user experience may be in place, but time or budget constraints may force us to fall short of our ideal. In each case, it's important to ask: At what point does the trade-off between pragmatism and idealism compromise our principles and values?

But as Lee Kuan Yew showed, pragmatism and idealism can actually complement each other in a productive tension. Rather than viewing idealism and pragmatism as a frustrating tension, recognize that a healthy opposition can ultimately lead to balance, positive cooperation, and coexistence. Seeking equilibrium and balance is very different from surrendering to compromise. While compromising and seeking balance may lead us to the same place eventually, the connotation of each word is different: compromise implies a painful trade-off, a concession, whereas balance suggests the ability to reach a productive equilibrium.

We can live our lives and serve others in a way that is consistent with our morals and ideals. The pragmatic idealist is aware of the intricate tension and balance between vision and implementation and is ultimately able to see that idealism versus pragmatism is a false dichotomy. In fact, this is a productive tension. Idealism and pragmatism aren't enemies squabbling in the ring; they are collaborators-in-waiting.

Balancing Quixotic Vision with Reality

There is a long-standing joke in philosophy:

The first law of philosophy: For every philosopher there is an equal and opposite philosopher.
The second law of philosophy: They are both wrong.

Vision and reality are two sides of the same coin. To create value, this coin must be balanced on its edge. Every initiative begins with a dream or vision, and breakthrough ideas continue to be a top priority in all companies. But how can we implement that vision, continuously innovate, and push for altogether new visions while also managing and executing on what we already have in place? In this case, the vision represents idealism, while the reality of implementation represents pragmatism. This may be the universal tension of business building, especially during the early stages.

So how to best balance vision with reality? First, to return to our tango metaphor, vision must take the lead. Ideally, any plan to execute on behalf of a vision should be guided by its values. Heart, vision, soul, purpose, values, idealism—or whatever you want to call the starting point that allows for extraordinary things to happen—always begins with a dream. Few great things come about as a result of someone saying, "Let's design our vision to look like everything we have around us." Invariably, people have an ideal, a dream; then, they figure out how to get the ball rolling. This point was strongly affirmed in the research my coauthors and I carried out for my last book, through which we found that approximately 70 percent of all successful businesses—those that eventually culminated in an IPO or successful sale—began as heart-driven initiatives equipped with strong direction, vision, and values, but no formal business plan.

Still, what about those times when a heart-led plan failed? After all, you can't be so far ahead and so idealistic that no one can join you on the journey. This is where balance comes in. As Rosalynn Carter, the former first lady of the United States, once said, "A leader takes people where they want to go. A great leader takes people where they don't necessarily want to go, but ought to be."[3] Carter's insight is balanced by this insight from Benjamin Hooks, former director of the NAACP: "If you think you are leading and turn around to see no one following, then you are just taking a walk."[4]

Take a moment to consider the people in your life who are driven by an insatiable desire to conquer insurmountable problems and carry out their visions. They have the courage to reimagine the world as they want it to be. Next, they do everything in their power and resources to create the best conditions for success, and they are patient as they bring others around to their goals and vision. We want people like this to help us embrace the big questions that go well beyond business: If every child had equal access to resources and education, could we reverse widening wealth inequality? Are there alternatives to locking people up in prison? How could business and business schools have a more positive impact on society? How do you help people do more than they believe they are capable of? The people who inspire us, the people whom we love and respect, have a strong sense of purpose and conviction. They earn our respect because they figure out how to help us get to a new reality.

In Eleanor Roosevelt's words, "The future belongs to those who believe in the beauty of their dreams."[5] This quotation is one of my favorites because it illustrates the symbiosis between a dream and its realization. It reminds us that all visions begin with a belief in something bigger that inspires you, and others, into practical action. We should always dream bigger if we want big things to happen. How do we discover our idealism and uncover our dreams?

DISCOVERING THE DREAM AND PURPOSE STATEMENT

Have a grand vision—then lead with purpose. It's much simpler in theory than it is in practice. The foundation of any great company lies in a founder's vision for what that company should be. What do you want to change? What do you want to create? What does your own ideal world look like? With that vision in place, it is imperative to understand your sense of purpose. Learn to communicate the *why* behind your vision.

In Australian Aboriginal culture, young boys spend six months in the wilderness as a rite of passage. This trek, known as a "walkabout," not only helps the boys discover what they're made of, it also helps them honor and reconnect with their own ancestry. The walkabout endures today in the Australian outback, allowing new generations of Aboriginal boys to experience deep reflection while developing practical skills for survival.

I first learned of walkabouts when a speaker I was on an entrepreneurship panel with suggested we uncover our dreams via an internal walkabout. Self-awareness can help entrepreneurs bring to light a vision that is usually already inside them, in a place where passion, capability, aptitude, and opportunity align to create purpose and significance. Good people should embark on a similar type of journey, somewhere they cannot be distracted or biased, to discover what it is that really matters to them and why.

Nick Craig and Scott Snook's 2014 *Harvard Business Review* article "From Purpose to Impact" included a set of questions designed to help readers uncover the purpose behind leadership.[6] Your purpose in business and in life should be one and the same—a holistic, all-encompassing identity that captures the essence of who you are as a person and who you aspire to be. To discover your purpose or internal "why," Craig and Snook recommend that you explore life stories and patterns that reveal unifying threads and themes. Review your life story to find the connective threads and recurring themes that authentically connect you with your inner purpose statement. Is this self-help? Not according to the authors. They argue instead that a leadership purpose statement is an important and meaningful developmental exercise for everyone.

These three questions can help you identify your core, lifelong strengths, values, and passions—in short, those pursuits that energize you and bring you joy. Writing down your answers to these questions will likely produce a stronger, clearer, and more thoughtful response.

- What did you especially love doing when you were a child, before the world told you what you should or shouldn't like or do? Describe a moment when you experienced this love and how it made you feel.

- Tell us about two of your most challenging life experiences. How have they shaped you?

- What do you enjoy doing in your life now that makes you feel the happiest?

I would venture to add a fourth question to this list, which complements the first and third questions: *What is it that you do naturally better than almost anyone? What is your superpower?* I constantly ask or at least think about this question when looking for good people. At first, this may seem to contradict my earlier argument that goodness should focus more on character and value traits and less on competencies. After all, isn't talk about superpowers biased toward competencies? But we should remember that strong skills and talents aren't a bad thing; they just can't be the *only* thing. This question asks people to closely reflect on their strengths on a relative basis. Though most people immediately focus on a particular skill or competency, I'm always delighted when this question prompts a person to engage in a deeper conversation about a value or set of values they practice. In and of itself, this discussion can help us select people who are inclined toward goodness.

While this type of self-reflection may seem relevant only to people starting a new endeavor or experiencing a transition point in their careers, I would argue internal walkabouts are useful for all of us to do regularly. We should expect our purpose statements to evolve over time, especially as we grow and add more depth, nuance, and meaning to our work. Deeper reflection helps us appreciate how our values respond to pressure and conflict. My firm's annual off-site meeting, for example, is an invaluable period for such reflection. In business, we tend to spend so much time "in it" that we forget to spend time working "on it." The same can be said of our own personal lives. If we just continue living "in it" without stepping back to consider the bigger purpose to which we aspire, our quest to become the fullest versions of ourselves can stall. In the end, it all comes back to self-awareness; pause, meditate, and ask, "What purpose am I trying to achieve?"

Whether you use the three questions posed by Craig and Snook or focus on my "superpower" question, once you've reflected, generate a purpose statement and run it by people you trust to make sure it's relatable. Again, your dream must be relatable—don't lead too far ahead of the parade—but make sure your purpose statement doesn't read like hundreds of other flat corporate mission statements filled with business jargon.

Consider the differences between these two purpose statements:

- Continually lead and consistently develop while mentoring the growth of others in order to be able to lead innovation in markets and gain new market share.

- With tenacious commitment to others, eliminate chaos and create brilliance.

It probably goes without saying that most people would respond to the concision and aspiration of the second purpose statement. A purpose statement needs to be an energizing dream statement, one that expresses your authentic and truthful inner self, but it should also be grounded in pragmatic idealism.

Values Anchor the Dream

Whether you work at a new or established company, setting relatable values is key to anchoring the dream. Again, avoid just using a list of the "right" words; tailor and define what these values mean in a language consistent with your company's culture. One of my favorite recent examples of a set of company values came from an early-stage start-up we evaluated called Jumpcut, which creates online educational video courses that feel like movies. During Jumpcut's presentation, and afterward, I was struck by the company's five core values[7]:

- **Help People Grow**—Help others get a little better, every single day.

- **Run into the Wall**—Aim for the difficult first, instead of avoiding it.

- **Bad Ideas Welcome**—You have got to wade through the shit to find the golden nugget.

- **Be a Barrel**—Don't complain, solve.

- **Sign Your Name on It**—Your work should be like a work of art, so masterful that you would sign your name on it.

I love the authenticity of these values, and I bet if I were to survey Jumpcut's founders and employees, they would know them pretty close to word for word. This start-up's spirited commitment to using the right language to capture its values reminded me of the powerful, values-driven culture of Zappos. I have spent considerable time at Zappos talking to employees about the company's values, and all have had something to say about their first core value, especially: "Deliver the WOW through service." The same goes for WD-40, where the number one core value is "Do the right thing." These values are memorable to and relevant for the people and cultures they serve. And even more important than being memorable, they are amplified and lived by members of their organizations.

Pick the five to seven values that matter the most to your organization. Reflect on your overarching purpose and be informed by your past experiences and relationships. In reflecting on those experiences, what people and things have had the greatest significance in your life—and in the business's history? These will help you identify the recurring values that should serve as your uncompromising truths. In the end, your values should be the things that truly matter the most to you and your organization, because these are the things you are committing to live by.

Ultimately, values are only enforced through actions. When we are trying to balance tensions, our daily habits, shared experiences, and gatherings serve as vessels of these values. In times of doubt or imbalance, a company's values serve as filters and priorities.

Just like your personal leadership statement might change over time, your company's values might become more refined over the long life of a business. That said, the core meaning behind your values needs to stay stable in order for them to be a useful guide for decision making and the shaping of culture. For entrepreneurs, the tension between pragmatism and idealism—and the need to return to foundational values—occurs most often when they are trying to scale their vision. Launching a vision is generally easier than scaling an idea or creating a culture to support that idea. Purposeful trade-offs require leaders to maximize value-creating impact while minimizing negative cultural influences. This requires self-awareness and an innate understanding of one's values. To help provide objectivity and new skills, entrepreneurs must sometimes look outside for a new CEO who both embraces the values that got the business to where it is and also understands how to make necessary trade-offs elsewhere to take the business to the next level. In these situations, your pragmatism should ideally remain consistent with your original core values, even if this means replacing yourself as CEO.

Harvard Business School professor Noam Wasserman has researched the trade-off between wealth and control, what he calls the "rich versus king" dilemma.[8] Of the 460 start-ups in his study, Wasserman found that the equity stakes of founders who continued to serve as CEO and maintain control of the board were only about half as valuable as those belonging to founders who ceded their role as CEO position and control of the board. In this dilemma, what one intellectually knows is the right thing to do is at odds with how one feels about relinquishing position and power. A pragmatic idealist in this situation would look for balance points, perhaps moving from the CEO role to that of the board chairman, with less direct day-to-day oversight of the business. Or perhaps a pragmatic idealist founder would initiate a two-step transition, hiring a highly seasoned president to work alongside him before allowing the president to assume the CEO role.

PRAGMATIC IDEALISTS—THE TANDEM DANCE
BETWEEN VISION AND REALITY

What matters most in business and life are the deep values underpinning our dreams. In order to create long-term happiness and success, we need to focus on what we know *must* endure over the long run. The right purpose with the right values gets us most of the way toward realizing our dreams.

But in all business-building journeys, there is also a tandem dance— yes, another dance metaphor—between strategy and execution. "How can we put in place resources to help the company get to its next level of growth while also facing the reality of what we need to execute right now?" is probably the most common question CEOs face. Leaders need to continually push the company to the next level while also dealing with the urgent day-to-day tasks required to execute the business's operating plan.

"Tony, I understand that we want and need to rethink the brand work and urgently put in some of its new elements, but what do you want me to do with the seven stores we currently have being built midstream?" To answer questions like this, we must come back to our values, seek counsel from those we trust, and use a logical decision-making approach. Inevitably, there will be times when the values of the business seem to have been compromised. At these times, self-aware leaders need to ask themselves two questions: Did we genuinely make every best effort to live up to our values? And did we give ourselves sufficient time to realize our vision while upholding our values?

There is also nothing wrong with drawing a line in the sand, provided time frames have been honored. As we will discuss in the upcoming chapter on the tension between short-termism and long-termism, there is often a mismatch between the idealism of our dreams and the practical time frames people are willing to wait for these dreams to bear fruit. Even though most things take longer than we want them to, this doesn't mean they won't happen. Nothing can happen without execution, just as nothing can progress unless entrepreneurs dream and believe they can shatter convention.

In this context, let's briefly consider how the pragmatic idealist Lee

Kuan Yew might have used the R.I.S.E. framework to implement his vision and business plan for Singapore.

Recognize: After Singapore won its independence from Malaysia in 1965, Lee faced the looming decision of what to do with the spit of land he now governed. But there was one thing Lee knew for sure: Singapore is strategically situated as a natural hub at the mouth of the Strait of Malacca, where up to 40 percent of maritime trade passes.[9] Lee *recognized* that adding infrastructure to the port was critical, and to bolster this natural advantage, one of Lee's first key strategic decisions was to transform Singapore into a welcoming economic region for foreign nationals. Today, Singapore is a haven for expats, but at the time it was not obvious how best to convince about two million Singaporeans of this necessity. Lee's dilemma then was how to attract the foreigners he needed while winning the confidence and loyalty of his people.

Internalize: How could Lee attract foreigners with capital and skills to his island nation without losing the support of local Singaporeans? On the one hand, he had to create open and pro-business economic policies, but on the other, he had to be tough on crime, corruption, drugs, gangs, and poverty. Lee's policies were informed by a strong, *internalized* set of values, like competition, meritocracy, and civility.[10] Most important, however, was the value of respectful citizenship—and Lee's concomitant belief in the Confucian ideal that individual rights should be fully embraced and celebrated, but not at the expense of society.

Share: Lee built a nimble government that could act quickly to put in place economic policies conducive to foreign investment and jobs. Lee was brilliant, but he still sought counsel from a handful of trusted advisors. One of the best known of Lee's advisors was Dr. Albert Winsemius, a Dutch economist who ended up serving for more than twenty years as Singapore's chief economic advisor. Dr. Winsemius designed large portions of Singapore's economic development policy and helped attract key multinational corporations, like Shell, to the region. Moreover, Dr. Winsemius's work in Singapore was inspired by his desire to do good in the world. When once asked what his legacy would be, Dr. Winsemius replied, "There is quite a lot of satisfaction, perhaps not like that of, say, an architect who can look at something and say, 'I made it.' But there is that satisfaction in knowing that you have contributed to the well-being of people you don't know."[11]

Execute: Lee followed through on his model. He was tough-minded in his quest to clean up crime to the point that, by the time he retired, Singapore had one of the lowest crime rates in the world and was practically free of corruption. And Lee was adamant about creating a level of financial security for Singaporeans through the Central Provident Fund, a statewide pension plan and corporation that helped citizens feel a sense of ownership in the new Singapore. Lee Kuan Yew firmly believed his paternalistic style was critical for transforming Singapore into a first-world economy. And the historical record seems to suggest he was right; from 1976 to 2014, Singapore grew an astonishing 6.81 percent year over year.[12]

• • • •

One final note on how to be a pragmatic idealist: you don't need to do it alone. One of the most straightforward ways to balance pragmatism with idealism is finding the right complement of people around you. This takes the "S" in R.I.S.E.—"sharing"—to the next level, and asks you to consider doing something similar to what Lee did with Dr. Albert Winsemius, and formally recruit the right mix of capabilities to your team. I like to create a diversity of excellence but commonality in character and values to ensure high-performance teams.

From the examples of historic leaders as well as executives in modern organizations, we learn the undeniable lesson that pragmatism and idealism can find a natural equilibrium through diverse but complementary team relationships. Consider the well-known case of Lincoln that historian Doris Kearns Goodwin chronicles in *Team of Rivals*. There is no question that Lincoln presided over one of the most historically significant presidencies, and that his presidency's successes, including emancipation and the end of the Civil War, were shaped by the diversity of the cabinet he formed between 1861 and 1865. To the surprise of many, when Lincoln was elected in 1860 as president, he chose to appoint Salmon

Chase, William H. Seward, and Edward Bates—all of whom had run against him in the election.

Or look at some of the strongest partnerships in the modern business era. Prior to joining Facebook, Sheryl Sandberg already had one of the biggest jobs in the valley as vice president of Global Online Sales and Operations for Google. But in 2008, Facebook's founder, Mark Zuckerberg, made the decision to hire Sandberg into the role of chief operating officer for Facebook without conducting a formal search for the role. It turned out to be one of the most important and prescient decisions he has made while leading the company. Sandberg instantly lent legitimacy to the young, pre-IPO company. Over the past eight years, Sandberg has been a key driving force in increasing Facebook's user base from seventy million to 1.65 billion users, and most important, developing a scalable business model to monetize that user base.[13] None of Facebook's successes—from establishing the largest social media advertising platform to shifting to mobile and video social ads to staying relevant and powerful in the rapidly changing digital advertising space—were likely to have happened without a Zuckerberg-Sandberg partnership. Still, it would be incorrect to think of Sandberg as only a pragmatist or Zuckerberg as only an idealist. All leaders who are as successful as they have been have struck a balance between the two. But their complementary strengths have evolved into a "pragmatic-idealist" approach to strategy and execution. As Zuckerberg said of Sandberg, "Without her we would just be incomplete."[14]

When we are idealistic, we live by our values, morals, and ideals even when they inconvenience us or cause us suffering. Pragmatism, on the other hand, looks for answers and prioritizes action. Idealism and pragmatism aren't combatants incapable of coexistence. Rather, they are two halves of an exquisite tension that is a reality of business and even life. This tension is often palpable, high-pressured, and challenging, but it also forces us to create things that are better and more beautiful. Business builders who can both lead with values and patiently execute on their vision will win high levels of respect and admiration. These men and women are textbook examples of pragmatic idealists—dreamers who are equally doers.

SUMMARY OF KEY POINTS FROM CHAPTER 6

• • • • • • •

• **Pragmatism and idealism are collaborators rather than enemies at war.** While this tension challenges the cornerstone goodness values of truth, in some ways it is a false dichotomy. Pragmatism and idealism should be thought of as a productive tension in search of the right balance point.

• **Dreams and idealism lead the way, but it is execution that creates the new reality.** Idealism cannot be considered without pragmatism; in business, a grand vision is nothing without eventual execution. The best leaders are able to set goals and realize their dreams.

• **Purpose and vision should be grounded in a set of enduring and relatable values, or immutable truths, that can guide us through dilemmas and difficulties.** Articulating our values as truths can help us discern those who want to be on this journey with us from those who are looking to jump ship. The question to ask here is: To what degree do I subscribe to these values?

• **Ultimately, business building is a tandem dance between vision and reality, between strategy and execution.** The task of leadership is to dream big, but not *so* big that no one else can follow our dreams. A leader's imperative is to be a pragmatic idealist who can understand and integrate this balance.

7

———

SHORT-TERMISM VERSUS LONG-TERMISM

We often mistake the journey of entrepreneurship as a sprint or dash. We crave results but aren't willing to wait for them. It's only natural to want to fix things that aren't working as quickly as possible. This facet of human nature holds true with respect to our business goals, relationships, diets, and even our largest global and economic problems. We desire light-switch solutions.

In this chapter on the tension between short-termism and long-termism, I suggest we should reconsider our bias for the short term. Why are short-term beliefs and behaviors so intoxicating? One reason is the aggressive expectations we set for companies and their leaders. Many public company CEOs face an unforgiving, quarter-to-quarter burden to produce an unbroken series of short-term wins. Even privately backed companies confront this bias against the long term when they are pressured to set their businesses up for sale or resale just a few short years after they're begun. Few might frame it this way out loud, but in my view the world is often more focused on value capture than value creation.

I structured my own investment firm, Cue Ball, with permanent and flexible capital for this very reason. Our firm is deliberately oriented toward the very long term. We have an evergreen structure and flexible investment mandate, with no fixed end date to the fund and therefore no artificial pressure to sell any of our assets or investments. We see this as an advantage, one that differentiates us from the majority of venture and private equity funds with limited life spans (i.e., they must liquidate or distribute the fund proceeds or assets within eight to ten years). Those firms are in the business of investing in companies in order to sell them. By contrast, we feel we're in the business of investing in companies in order to build the people and vision *behind* those companies. This allows us to sell if and when we want to, even if that's in the long-run future. We've taken many pages from Warren Buffett's playbook, including his mandate to "only buy something that you are perfectly happy to hold if the market shut down for 10 years."[1] The basis for my long-term philosophy at Cue Ball is simple: it is incredibly hard to find that rare company with the potential to endure and sustain, so if you ever do, you should be able to hold on to it! Despite all the recent talk of unicorns and now decacorn companies and valuations, I've always been more interested in looking for sea turtles—slow-moving but deliberate, long-lived, and majestic creatures that have graced our oceans for millennia.

The challenge with long-term perspective is that we now expect leaders to deliver short-term returns using short-term strategies. We've been conditioned to think this way—we eagerly await the next quarterly results, the next fund-raising round or big project we land, the next game to play, the next election. While the short term is a reality in and of itself, it presents particular dangers. "We are living in a world in need of long-term solutions, but we are surrounded by short-term thinking," Mats Lederhausen, my partner at Cue Ball, once remarked. Together, we could address and potentially solve the world's biggest, most urgent issues—inequality, health care, climate change, and many others—if only our political and economic systems operated on longer-term time frames. But unfortunately, this just isn't the case today. Imagine a politician or a CEO of a public company who does the right thing in the long run but is unable to offer constituents or shareholders tangible proof of results in the short run. In both cases, these people are barely in office long enough to accomplish anything of value— especially given the scale of the issues they face—before they have to worry about being reelected or replaced. Long-term thinking is increasingly rare, and so the tension between short-term and long-term thinking is one of the most critical trade-offs contemporary leaders must face.

Consider another example of our short-term bias. All of us witnessed and were personally affected in some way or another by the two last major economic downturns: the dot-com bubble that peaked in the year 2000 and the financial crisis of 2008. On a universal time scale, each lasted less than a nano-instant, but at the time, both were perceived to have done significant and perhaps even permanent damage to our economy. These market downturns are perfect examples of Amara's law, which states that we tend to overestimate short-term effects and underestimate long-term effects.[2] Although Stanford researcher and futurist Roy Amara was speaking about our perceptions of the impacts of new technology, short-termism is also a deeply embedded psychological bias, one that is particularly acute in times of risk and uncertainty.[3] For example, overestimating the shorter-term negative impacts of economic downturns might cause us to rush out of the market altogether. During these times, someone with a long-term view might double down on her investments, which have suddenly become significantly undervalued. Evidently, patience has long-term value.

Li Lu, a highly regarded value investor and friend, told me once that—from an intellectual point of view—investing is easy. It's our psychology that makes it difficult. He explained that it's difficult for most people to follow the most basic rule of investing: to buy low and sell high. The undisputed champion of value investing, Warren Buffett, describes this strategy as buying into fear and selling into greed. Straightforward, but much easier said than done. Amara's law predicts many investors will do precisely the opposite and follow a lemming-like strategy instead of one based on common sense, independent research, and long-term thinking. There are precious few investors who have stuck to their principles in the long term, and not coincidentally, they have performed the best.

In 1999, many criticized Buffett's investment game plan to acquire businesses with certain fundamental, intrinsic qualities, like cash flow and defensibility born of durable competitive advantage. Critics said Buffett was too old-school, that he'd become naïve about new investment opportunities. What good were Buffett's horse-and-buggy business models in a world where everything—including business models—had been revolutionized by the Internet? In late 1999, *Barron's* ran a cover story on Buffett titled "What's Wrong, Warren?"[4] The story did suggest that Buffett was down, not out, but the authors of the piece couldn't resist sticking it to the old Oracle of Omaha. "To be blunt, Buffett, who turns 70 in 2000, is viewed by an increasing number of investors as too conservative, even passé," the writer stated. Online readers of the *Barron's* article were just as harsh: "Middlebrow insurance company studded with a bizarre mélange of assets, including candy stores, hamburger stands, jewelry shops, a shoemaker, and a third-rate encyclopedia company."[5]

Yet Warren stuck to his belief that all things, technology based or not, ultimately become valuable in the long run based on durable competitive advantage and superior cash flow. In 1999, a year when companies were going public at the rate of almost one a day, Buffett's big acquisition was Jordan's Furniture, in New England.[6] That same year, the Internet economy reached its irrational peak. More than a dozen dot-coms bought their first—and last—Super Bowl ads. The value of Yahoo! reached $100 billion, more than Berkshire Hathaway's entire portfolio.

One of my mentors once told me that history has the benefit of being factual. Fast-forward to today: as of October 2016, Berkshire Hathaway is worth at least $300 billion *more* than Yahoo! Who would have imagined in the heyday of the dot-com bubble that fifteen years later Verizon would offer to buy Yahoo!'s core business for less than $5 billion? The lesson for us is that the best investors patiently wait things out, stick to what they know, and refuse to be swayed by fads or trends. Buffett's patience over the long term puts him in a class of his own.

Above all, both Buffett and his partner, Charlie Munger, recognize that the short-term reward for being a "market timer" is more ephemeral and random than a sound long-term strategy. Buffett and Munger recognize the "what" and the "why" of good value and wait patiently for the "when." Buffett even uses this approach for his retirement plan and the trust he'll leave behind for his wife; 90 percent of the fund is in a low-cost S&P 500 index fund like Vanguard, and the remaining 10 percent is in short-term government bonds. With time and patience, that money will go to work for his family.[7] It's profoundly simple, but also profoundly true—for investing in good companies and in good people, too.

We can also think of people as long-term investments. When we value character and goodness just as much as competency, we end up rewarding those people who create and receive the most value. The system is more or less equitable. It rewards not just those people who are the most admired, but also those who create and receive the most value. Just look at some of Buffett and Munger's "people bets." One of their best-known investments was in Rose Blumkin, or "Mrs. B," who founded Nebraska Furniture Mart with $500 in 1937 and built it into one of the nation's largest home furnishings stores. Rose, who passed away at the age of 104 in 1998, was known as a pistol of a personality. Her motto was "Sell cheap, tell the truth, and don't cheat nobody." Buffett bought a majority of her business in 1984 on a handshake with no audit of her books or inventory.[8] Buffett had gotten to know Rose and her family over the years as a customer. He simply believed in her as a person and was impressed by the business she had built over sixty years. He bet on her truth, work ethic, and commonsense wisdom.[9] After the business was acquired, he commented, "Put her up against the top graduates of the top business schools or chief executives of the Fortune 500 and, assuming an even start with the same resources, she'd run rings around them."[10] Today, Mrs. B's store is worth about $1 billion.[11]

The pursuit of goodness and good people is a long-term game. Consistency in values and purpose ultimately drives real results.

GOING AGAINST OUR SHORT-TERM BIAS

The Road goes ever on and on
Down from the door where it began.
Now far ahead the Road has gone,
And I must follow, if I can,
Pursuing it with eager feet,
Until it joins some larger way
Where many paths and errands meet.
And whither then? I cannot say.

J. R. R. TOLKIEN[12]

There are countless other areas in which we exhibit a short-term bias. Consider eating, health, and rehabilitation. America has some of the world's worst eating habits; we consume fast food, supersized portions, processed junk foods, and on-the-go energy shots, all because we're seek-ing the quickest possible fix. The pharmaceutical and medical industries don't fare much better, with their never-ending stream of prescription and over-the-counter drugs that target symptoms rather than causes. Media and marketing suggest that there is always an instant solution for any-thing we're told is wrong with our bodies, which is part of the reason America leads the world in total number of plastic surgery procedures. But our short-term bias hurts us most by cutting short the development of our goodness and our quest for wholeness.

Goodness isn't something you can turn on and off with an on-demand app or remote. The values of truth, compassion, and wholeness come from an internal place, and their realization requires stoicism, commitment, and a belief in the value of long-term results. Along the way, not surprisingly, come distractions and temptations. Living with conflict, ambiguity, and adversity isn't pleasant, which is why many people like to apply temporary Band-Aids. We forget that good things take time to ripen and mature, and that great things take even longer. What things worth doing can really be done quickly and easily?

True, business building sometimes requires quick decisions with near-term impact. But these decisions are the relatively easy ones! For example, we might see a gap in a product feature and allocate budget to fill it—done. An employee might be a clear misfit and cultural disaster—so fire fast. Even some larger decisions, like choosing to acquire a longtime part-ner who comes to you first after being approached by a competitor, can be made with lightning speed.

The problem is that we want every decision to be as quick and simple as these previous examples. But developing character and goodness, building purpose, and transforming a company take time and patience. Unfortu-nately, we tend not to fully realize or appreciate those defining values of goodness until many years later, when we are able to see them expressed longitudinally over long timescales. When I started working to transform the Thomson organization with Dick Harrington, we could not have imag-ined we'd be able to change as much as we did, let alone acquire Reuters. I remember Dick telling me that, given the sheer number of people involved and how long it would take for this shift in cultural mind-set to set in, we would have to be patient, honest, and empathetic with those people who had worked at the company for years during a very different period in its history.

No shortcuts exist to goodness and character, just as there are no shortcuts for deep skill sets and competencies. It's neither quick nor easy to develop humility, self-awareness, and integrity. Character- and truth-based leadership can only flower when it is rooted in a bigger, deeper purpose or initiative. The tension between our short-term bias and long-term value ultimately comes back to the cornerstone qualities of truth and wholeness. Our values are tested every day, and in the long run the consistency of our actions will define us. The problem is, while most people want to do good and build character, patience is increasingly rare because we want more, faster, with less effort and more pleasure. Unfortunately, this get-rich-quick approach almost never works. It doesn't produce the quality and enduring value that most of us claim we want. And this type of thinking can prevent us from working on the bigger things that truly matter.

When Marvin Minsky—the celebrated MIT faculty member who coined the term "suitcase words"—passed away on January 24, 2016, the world lost one of its greatest minds. Minsky tackled some of the most complex issues in computer science and co-founded the MIT Artificial Intelligence Lab. During his memorial service, one speaker remarked on how rare it is for people today to actively confront the world's biggest and most pressing and intractable problems. The speaker remarked, "Instead of putting in the time, the contemporary flavor of strategy is a preference for people to 'fail fast' and iterate in rapid cycles toward success." Failing fast allows us to creatively iterate toward new innovations, but the question remains, What is the cost of this mind-set? Do we avoid tackling complex problems that can't be solved in quick, iterative development cycles? The speaker at Marvin's memorial service closed with the following: "Marvin took on the biggest issues and opportunities related to artificial intelligence and computing, knowing the direction that was needed, but succeeding slowly, stoically, and patiently over his lifetime."

Speed and convenience all too often trump quality and long-term potential. When making a decision, we should constantly ask and test whether we are biased toward quantity and speed, and whether pursuing these near-term benefits sacrifices the quality that can be achieved through patience. To be clear, speed and convenience should neither fall by the wayside nor come at the expense of quality and sustainability. We need to understand the consequences of our short-term bias—the opportunities we might miss, the problems we might cause. The long-term big picture should never be an afterthought.

The businesses that really matter are those that last. It's no coincidence that these businesses also are often purpose driven and focused on creating true long-term value, without regard to what markets or critics think. Over the years, many CEOs of public companies have told me they wished their public companies were private so they could bypass the dull cadence of the quarter-to-quarter drumbeat. Playing the long game allows for higher-quality, sustained performance, whether in investing, research, sports, or other endeavors. How does this pertain to good people? Goodness is a long game because it takes time to become good and reach wholeness while helping other people become fuller versions of themselves along the way.

Big changes and elite performances demand a bigger-picture perspective, relentless focus, and an inexorable drive to achieve a higher purpose. This requires extraordinary discipline and patience, and acceptance of the fact that you may not get credit for your hard work and discipline until many years later. Short-term results matter relatively less than long-term sustained performance and truth to one's purpose. This is just as true for leaders as it is for one of the most recognizable and accomplished sport legends in New England.

DISCIPLINING OURSELVES FOR THE LONG TERM

On a Sunday in late 2001, the NFL held its first game since the September 11 attacks. This game—in which the New York Jets faced off against the New England Patriots—was more than just a contest between two teams. It symbolized a return to normalcy after a time of terror. Coincidentally, this game also thrust one of the greatest leaders in National Football League history into the national spotlight.

With only five minutes left in the fourth quarter, Patriots quarterback Drew Bledsoe was forced out of the pocket and Jets linebacker Mo Lewis tackled him out of bounds. The hit, which injured Bledsoe's chest and forced him to leave the game, altered the course of Patriots history. An unknown twenty-three-year-old sixth-round draft pick from the University of Michigan trotted onto the field to take Bledsoe's place and play backup quarterback. His name was Tom Brady.

Five Super Bowl championships, four Super Bowl MVP awards, two regular season MVPs, twelve Pro Bowls. Tom Brady is now one of the world's most accomplished athletes, whose confidence is best understood in the context of his passion for excellence, which dwarfs that of his competitors'. Brady is proudest of the discipline he has exercised to sustain his superstar performance over seventeen seasons. Over the years, Brady has done everything in his power to eschew short-term thinking and commit to a long-term perspective. His holistic training program is geared to a single purpose: achieving *sustained peak performance.* Brady has not been afraid to go against the grain of traditional strength and conditioning training and rehab programs. For the past decade, Brady and his body coach, Alex Guerrero, have complemented traditional strength and conditioning training with a focused nutritional and functional supplements program, cognitive exercises, and other "prehab" methods designed to help the body better defend against injury.

Brady has been remarkably healthy since he began practicing what he and Guerrero call his TB12 prehab method. The TB12 method enhances muscle pliability through performance training that incorporates intense, hands-on tissue and muscle manipulation, which is much more focused and intense than regular massage, other pliability exercises to complement traditional strength and conditioning training, and a carefully considered diet with an intensive hydration and supplementation regimen. Brady is a textbook case study in discipline, evidenced by his clockwork-like training schedule and strict eating habits—e.g., no caffeine, no white sugar, no white flour, heavily plant-based seasonal foods but no nightshade vegetables such as tomatoes (as they are not anti-inflammatory), healthy nuts, and water, water, water. That said, this discipline has become the by-product of practiced positive daily behaviors such that it does not feel regimented and constraining, but rather has become just a way of being. Taking this back to what makes for goodness from a values perspective, it is a similar philosophy and approach to life and work. With the right values and practiced behaviors, things become increasingly innate and natural.

The TB12 method makes good common sense—keep your muscles soft and supple, eat and hydrate right—but it only works when paired with focus, discipline, and a long-term perspective. For nearly two decades, Brady has sustained an extraordinary level of performance in the National Football League. When I spoke to Tom recently about his pre-hab defensive system, he pointed out that the real benefits of his discipline matter most now, more than a decade after he began the program. He explained, "I never felt so good throwing the football. Early in my playing, I used to think that pain and injury were just part of the way it was in sports, but I've committed myself to a different path and truly feel that I've never thrown the ball as well as I'm doing so now."[13]

Peak performance over the long term. This is what motivates Brady and what he'd like most to share with the world. In the interest of disclosure, not only am I a longtime New England Patriots fan, I also sit on the board of the TB12 organization, which Brady founded in order to help as many athletes as possible attain and maintain peak performance by building up their own prehab defense systems.

Brady's commitment to long-term, high-quality athletic performance is rooted in a deeply personal purpose and calling. Over many years of playing, he has witnessed countless athletes reluctantly accept rehab as a regular part of their training regimen. From Brady's perspective, this is akin to accepting that the rate of injury in athletics will never change. Without a more holistic approach, elite athletes become trapped in a vicious cycle: play, rehab, play, and repeat. Nearly two million high school athletes get injured each year, with about five hundred thousand requiring doctor visits.[14] College athletes are equally susceptible to injury, and nearly 70 percent of them confess to playing through injuries at least once. Says Brady, "The current athletic training system is done in such a way that it is short-term oriented, trying to get people back out playing as quickly as possible, and more prone to injury. It doesn't have to be this way.

"At age eighteen, I did not know I'd be here more than twenty years later," Brady said. "With the fortune of having the success I have had, and an opportunity to play a role—not just in the NFL, but beyond—to advocate for the thing that has allowed me to play as long as I have, and at that level." As in the case of Warren Buffett, Brady's long-term value creation isn't difficult to understand. What is difficult is finding people capable of maintaining such consistent discipline over the long term.

R.I.S.E. IN START-UP STRATEGY: TRADING OFF BETWEEN THE SHORT AND LONG TERM

Developing purpose and goodness in people is also a long-term practice. Arguably, it's a lifelong journey. As with the strategies of Buffett and Brady, it is more easily learned, or intuited, than it is expressed. Becoming good ourselves and cultivating goodness in others requires a rare brand of a stick-to-it-ness that yields disproportionate dividends over time. It certainly did for one of my favorite entrepreneurs, Dr. Rajiv Kumar, cofounder of ShapeUp and current president at Virgin Pulse.

In 2005, Rajiv was a first-year medical school student at Brown University. He and a classmate, Brad Weinberg, were frustrated and dismayed by how many patients struggled to stay healthy because they lacked the resources necessary to eat well and exercise right. Rajiv and Brad believed that peopled needed a social support system in order to make positive and successful behavioral changes. So they created an online social wellness platform called ShapeUp that encouraged people to become healthier *together*. Early clinical research showed that people lost seven pounds on average after using the platform for twelve weeks. It worked! Soon, Rajiv and Brad realized corporations were in dire need of better wellness programs, and before they realized it, they were running a rapidly growing online enterprise platform that helped people stay healthier at work. At the base of the business was the central premise that the best way for people to become healthier is for employees to support one another's goals and hold one another accountable.

Cue Ball was fortunate enough to lead ShapeUp's first round of institutional financing in 2010. But as the company grew and won new clients, we as a board had to discuss a new dilemma: a wide range of customers wanted ShapeUp's solution, but who would actually be the best core target customer for ShapeUp to focus on and grow for the future? Demand was high among small- and medium-size businesses; winning smaller clients would be faster and easier, and it would lead to more near-term growth. But the accounts of large Fortune 500 companies were also growing—and that was a different animal. We had to choose whether to trade these smaller clients for the opportunity to land larger ones. Ultimately, we chose to focus on larger customers but were confronted by how best to transition to this new model while still finding ways to do right by our existing mix of clients. How could we manage the present and plan for the future at the same time?

Rajiv's approach during this period inspired the R.I.S.E. framework I introduced at the beginning of part two. Rajiv is one of the most self-aware founders I've ever worked with, so it's not surprising he was the first to *recognize* the situation at hand—namely, how to plan, strategize, and fully serve more large clients while still being loyal and helpful to smaller ones who helped them get there. Rajiv took his time and sought other perspectives, approaches, strategies, and insights that he could *internalize* before making a decision. He also spent considerable time on the road speaking with customers to allow his thinking to marinate. After soliciting this input, Rajiv *shared* what he had learned with the board, and we spent considerable time discussing the pros and cons of the different approaches. Rajiv took these inputs, filtered them through the values of the company and the strategic objectives he wanted to accomplish, and then came up with a plan on how to get there that we all resoundingly supported. Rajiv stood steadfast and worked alongside his field team to make sure it was *executed*. He explained to his team why this was important and inspired them to land and serve larger clients. During this period, he met with every single key client and partner.

In the end, the choice to allocate more resources to secure and serve large clients paid off: ShapeUp had a blue-chip roster of clients that was the envy of all the early-stage companies competing in this space. In February 2016, we decided to join forces through a merger with Virgin Pulse to create the world's largest online wellness platform. Rajiv's discipline and attitude were no different in this situation. First, he considered whether it would be the right thing for the company in the long term. Once the decision was made, he doggedly focused on closing the deal, all while thinking very carefully about the implications for his people. It was a terrific outcome for Rajiv and his team and for Cue Ball as well. We decided to maintain shareholdings in the new Virgin Pulse company, where we continue the journey of promoting healthy behaviors and positive employee engagement in the workplace.

. . . .

By now I trust you've got the point that it takes time—sometimes a long time—to realize our dreams, desires, and visions, but if you truly commit, the rewards make the whole journey worthwhile. To be long-term focused, we need to stay true and disciplined to our values and principles, day in and day out. Typical business training tells us we must measure what we want to manage, but far too often this measuring occurs on the wrong timescale. Every parent struggles at times to believe his or her child will get bigger or taller. After all, from day to day we all look pretty much the same. If you took a photo of your child every day, or every week, you wouldn't notice all that much. But if you compare your child year after year, or every five or ten years, these changes become dramatic. Parenting is a long-haul game. So, too, is developing goodness and character.

One last reason we should choose the long view is that people who are willing to take the long road tend to have fewer long-term regrets. You can't get back time. Our actions and decisions have consequences both on the present day *and* on the long term. Again, Amara's law states we tend to overestimate short-term benefits while underestimating long-term effects. But the back-end values of life cannot be bought or quickly acquired.

The artist, designer, and entrepreneur John Maeda once described a thought experiment he learned from one of his mentors. Imagine your life will last one hundred years, with four equal twenty-five-year-long quarters. Many won't make it to the last quarter with their bodies and minds intact. This leaves most of us with three quarters, each twenty-five years in length, to accomplish what we want in life. What quarter are you in? To paraphrase what the retired woman from North York who inspired me to begin a lifelong exploration of what goodness and good people means once asked me: Are you really doing what you love? The earlier on you dedicate your life to goodness, the more these efforts will compound, and the fewer the regrets you'll suffer. So commit to goodness now. Start today.

Millennials are driving and leading a palpable movement for companies to transform themselves into purpose-driven organizations. (Note that I'm not talking about social-enterprise initiatives, but rather businesses that believe that by living their values and pursuing a higher purpose, they can generate greater impact and greater profits.) Still, there is more work that can be done. Back in 2001, I sat on a World Economic Forum panel where we were asked, "Is youth truly wasted on the young?" My response, I remember, was hedged. Today, I've come to believe that impatience makes many young people miss important opportunities for growth toward goodness. Impatience is hard to temper, even in the later stages of one's life and career. I've had many conversations with people in the later stages of their lives and careers, and I've found most express some regret that they did not give their dreams the time and resources they merited.

Swiss-born Jean Piaget, one of the most renowned psychologists of the twentieth century, put forward many of our most important theories on cognitive child development. Interestingly, when Piaget toured the United States giving lectures on the positive education of children, he became accustomed to waiting for what he called "the American question." Piaget—only half joking—reported that this question was always something along the lines of, "Can parents do something to speed up the normal developmental process in children?" Despite how regularly it was asked, the question continued to surprise Piaget because he could not imagine why anyone would want to speed up normal child development.

If we are willing to patiently wait out the normal development process for our life and business goals to mature, what time frame should we regard as appropriate? The answer is: longer than we would like. Good things take time to develop and, like a child's cognitive development, have to be allowed a natural and patient cadence in order to be realized. As we have shown, this dynamic holds for most things. From renovating my own home, I've learned a good general rule of thumb: set your expectation to two times the intended project budget and two times the intended project length. For life's bigger goals—like changing the trajectory of a business or deepening a set of relationships—the right rule of thumb might be to think in terms of *decades*, not years, and sometimes longer.

Indeed, some things might even take more than a lifetime. Large-scale political, environmental, or cultural changes will transcend individual life spans. This shouldn't discourage us; it should remind us of the scale of our work and the impact it will have long after we are gone. Think of Eva Duarte de Perón, the First Lady of Argentina from 1946 to 1952. Eva's life was cut short by cancer, but her tireless work for laborers' and women's rights is still remembered not only by Argentines but also by people around the globe, as evidenced by the enduring popularity of the musical *Evita*. And then there is Anne Frank, perhaps the greatest example of what ordinary people can do to shed light on our understanding of history. Her posthumously published diary provides a first-person, and touchingly human, narrative of what it was like to live under Nazi occupation. Frank's diary has become one of the world's most treasured documents and a critical teaching tool of history, read every year by millions of students around the globe.

Without question, the people I respect most are ordinary people who have left behind extraordinary legacies precisely because their long-term view allowed them to overcome their short-term bias. As with all the tensions, we must find the right moderation and balance. I have learned this from the strong, good leaders who have mentored me over the years. When I ask these mentors to name people they respect and look up to, they often identify leaders with visions and values, and a willingness to patiently work toward realizing those visions and values. Slow and steady wins the race; in the modern world, it still pays in the end to be the turtle instead of the hare.

SUMMARY OF KEY POINTS FROM CHAPTER 7

• • • • • • • •

- **We tend to be biased toward the short term.** We must understand and develop self-awareness of this bias. Not all quick wins are bad, but very frequently, our bias for short-term returns comes at the expense of long-term objectives and opportunities.

- **We need to be more realistic with our time frames.** It takes time to realize any truly worthwhile goals. We need to give our strategies sufficient time to take root, germinate, and flower. It's not the "what" that's hard to see and select as we strategize; it's the "when."

- **Goodness and good people take time to be realized.** Invest in goodness and good people—yourself and others—intentionally and with the knowledge that this will be a long-term pursuit. You can enjoy significant upside just by investing in those who adhere to their values with diligence and patience.

- **The long term is almost always more important.** Some things require rapid iteration and quick wins, but in general, the long view matters most. You will rarely, if ever, regret patiently giving things the time and resources they deserve.

8

VULNERABILITY VERSUS CONVICTION

Photograph by Nicole Bengiveno/*The New York Times*/Redux.

It all started in the mid-1970s when famous actress and Hitchcock muse Tippi Hedren traveled to postwar Vietnam and began working with an organization to bring relief to Vietnamese refugees. Returning to the United States to visit the refugee camp Hope Village in Sacramento, Hedren flew in her personal manicurist, Dusty Coots Butera, and asked her to teach a group of twenty Vietnamese women, mostly the wives of high-ranking military officers, the art of manicures. Hedren then helped sponsor more Vietnamese refugee women to come to the United States to learn from Butera and to enroll in a local beauty school, after which she helped them find work across Southern California.[1] Thus began the growth of a service once limited to the elite and the start of an immigrant-dominated nail care services industry that today includes over sixty thousand locations across the United States.[2]

But, as is the case with almost any new innovation, the rapid growth of this industry has brought with it some of the good, some of the bad, and some of the ugly. On the good side, there are tens of thousands of immigrants who have brought home honest pay and provided support to many family members while allowing their customers to obtain a small piece of luxury at an affordable price. On the bad side, standards have been uneven—to put it in the most polite terms—and while there are independent shops that do things right and provide good service, the vast majority do not meet reasonable occupational health standards. You only need to walk into a shop and see technicians wearing masks to know something is not quite right, as there is rampant use of toxic products. And then there is the ugly side of the industry, where stories of labor exploitation, stolen wages, trafficking, and infection rates (due to improper cleaning of instruments or poor process protocols) make an impartial observer wonder how things could still be this bad in this day and age.

In the fall of 2006, my partners and I were still working through what our first new business creation and investment project would be for our newly formed Cue Ball Group. We had no idea at the time that our own history would be forever linked to the pioneering work of Tippi Hedren. We had imagined Cue Ball as a type of holding company of growth businesses; but all we had was a name, and in fact, the structure of the fund hadn't even been settled. The fact that now we are an investment firm that started as a nail salon (today branded as MiniLuxe) deserves a bit more context and background.

At the time we were only certain that we wanted to get behind projects with long-term potential, where we could take an active role in their growth and ensure they had a strong purpose behind them, simpatico with a people-first philosophy. That's pretty nonspecific. So the range of ideas we saw at first included everything from new pricing search engines (not quite Priceline, unfortunately), an online social image board (not quite Pinterest or Instagram, unfortunately), a people database (not quite LinkedIn, unfortunately), a database of real estate listings (not quite

Zillow, unfortunately), to an Asian-inspired hot pot restaurant concept. Quite simply, we were all over the place. My partner John Hamel and I were actually pretty certain that Asian hot pot, based on Japanese shabu-shabu, would be the winner. So much so that we spent ten days overseas trying as many hot pot restaurants as we could throughout Asia. We returned from that trip with stomachs sated but unfortunately no closer to a winning idea.

We knew there was something else that we still weren't quite hitting on. Following Charlie Munger's investment maxim to "invert, always invert," I asked my colleagues to try to look for investment inspiration not in the dazzling world of the Internet, but in the daily landscape of the prosaic. What had other entrepreneurs or investors ignored in their search for sexy new business concepts? Could we find something that we'd want to hold on to for a long time by using "boring" as an operative search term? We figured if you start with the decidedly unsexy, that might lead to greater opportunity to reimagine the experience, change people's lives, and create real value along the way. So we asked ourselves: What could we consider doing that would be true to our values and principles, offer new models of empowerment for employees and customers, and equally benefit from a little added excitement in the experience?

After we decided, or perhaps our potential operating partner decided for us, that we were not going to be setting the world on fire with hot pot restaurants, I suggested the following as a thought experiment: What businesses do we encounter in our daily lives that are still "Starbucks-able"? With that question in mind, my partner John spent the following weekend driving around the streets of his North Shore hometown when the idea suddenly hit him. On nearly every corner he saw independently owned nail salons.

For the next several months, we decided to dig deep into the space. Some four hundred thousand technicians were employed in an $8 to $10 billion market (a good part of the industry is part of the informal cash economy, so exact estimates are difficult). But the numbers part was easy. Really understanding the nail care industry meant spending time in salons, visiting and speaking with owners and technicians, and making more trips across the country to see what various nail salons had in common and what they didn't. It was important to see both the typical corner salon and the luxury salons. I made trips to Florida, Miami, New York, San Francisco, and Los Angeles and perhaps set a record for the number of pedicures and manicures a middle-aged businessman can receive in a given month.

What we saw simultaneously frightened and excited us. On the one hand we were faced with a newly found set of vulnerabilities and atrocities, and on the other we had the conviction and determination to do something about it. We all immediately saw how wildly inconsistent health and hygiene standards were across the board (and in a good number of cases, frankly nothing short of deplorable)—because nail care service is simultaneously the most-used and least-regulated beauty service in the world. John has long-standing experience in real estate development, and he brought up the fear that landlords had of getting "another nail salon" in their building. When I asked why, the answer was that landlords generally shared a negative stereotyped image of this particular business, stemming from an aversion to the toxic fumes and odor associated with nail services and products.

If we were going to launch MiniLuxe, before we focused on the experiences and services we wanted to offer, we would first need to tackle the issue of health and hygiene. We also wanted to ensure fair labor practices and growth opportunities for the people who worked there. Our purpose was defined as creating a people-first business that happened to do beauty, not a beauty-first business that happened to employ people. Belying this strong sense of purpose was a sense of trepidation as we considered the challenges ahead.

Some of our sense of vulnerability was simply due to our unfamiliarity with the industry as both customers and operators. We were obviously completely unknown to the community of nail technicians, and for John and me the sum total of our prior visits to nail salons was negligible. We were also feeling vulnerable because we did not want, out of principle, to offer certain traditional nail services associated with health concerns such as acrylics. Would that hurt us? And then there was the human factor. We were sensitive to the stories of hardship some technicians shared with us, like not being able to make ends meet, feeling shorted on their cash tips, and being overworked, but we also wanted to run a profitable business. There was an absolute need to establish trust as an outsider. In addition to these human capital challenges, the conversations with technicians who told us how hard it was to make money, especially during down periods, and how manual the work was made us quietly wonder if the economics could ever work for this business.

But, on the other hand, a number of observations helped strengthen our conviction. First, no one had ever made a bold investment in this space to reimagine what a nail studio experience could be—we didn't know what we didn't know. What would clients think if we were able to change everything from the way colors are selected to a clean lab to sterilized tools? What would happen if we celebrated the technician as our hero and provided a clear career path? What if we put in place technology and data analysis to better match service supply with client demand? And we felt it was also reasonable to think that clients might be willing to pay a little more for an enhanced experience and high-quality services with a clear purpose behind the brand (and a no-chip guarantee!). When we looked again at everything through our analytical lens, we felt confident that there was a case for an affordable luxury that would sit in the space between mom-and-pop corner nail salons and full-service spas—in short, we had high conviction that we had hit on our "Starbucks of X." Most important, we were bolstered by the opportunity to create significant change and try to transform an industry—from both the employee side and client side. So despite this push and pull between our vulnerabilities and our convictions, this bigger purpose fueled our passion and our ultimate belief in the MiniLuxe concept—and tipped us to the side of conviction.

So we decided to cofound and form our first venture for Cue Ball, a nail salon brand that would deliver a mini moment of "me time," a small reprieve, and hence "MiniLuxe." We put forth self-care as its central purpose, meaning the belief that you cannot fully take care of others unless you first tend to yourself. We started in 2007 with our first nail salon in Newton Centre, Massachusetts. One of the first things we put in place was a surgical-grade autoclaving system in an exhibition clean lab. We established competitive wages, flexible hours, and benefits from health care to paid time off. We also put a lot of time into the design, creating an architecturally award-winning space. But we would start with only one location and be careful about growth, adhering to a principle that our partner Mats Lederhausen has practiced throughout his career: think big, start small, and scale appropriately.

MiniLuxe reminds me each day that what drives me, my colleagues, and our firm across all our ventures is one simple thing: to ensure that human capital remains the guiding principle behind everything we do. Candidly, of all the businesses I've either backed or participated in, with MiniLuxe I experienced the push and pull between vulnerability and conviction most intensely. I was unfamiliar with the industry but saw the obvious need for change; and perhaps the cultural side of it also influenced me, as I came from an immigrant background with several family members in the service retail industry. The business idea felt consistent with principles that I hold closely, along with my partners: to create positive change through good people. MiniLuxe in some ways informed and inspired Cue Ball's overall human-capital-centric philosophy, and also a number of the goodness themes in this book.

MiniLuxe is now almost ten years old and still early in its journey. But now with studios in four different states across the United States, it's gratifying to see the budding fruits of our labor, though we still have a long way to go before claiming victory. Still, every time my partners and I reach a milestone—opening a new store, increasing the loyalty of our employees or customers, or launching in a new state—and we celebrate and toast the evolution of our central purpose of self-care, I can't help but feel my heart skip a beat.

RECONCILING VULNERABILITY AND CONVICTION

What we do when we feel the tension between vulnerability and conviction is as relevant in our personal lives as it is in business. Isn't that the paradox of the entrepreneur, who gingerly balances on a tightrope of vulnerability while also finding the courage, conviction, and intuition to pursue what might be possible on the other side? The truth is that any business builder—whether starting something new or facing a critical decision—feels vulnerable.

In the case of MiniLuxe, the founding team had been building our track record over the years, but this concept was really quite different—so what would happen if this time around we failed? I'm happy to say that my partners didn't share this mind-set. It wasn't that we did not think there were risks, but we focused on mitigating those vulnerabilities and risks, reminding ourselves that our overriding purpose and conviction was so great, it was impossible *not* to try.

Without knowing it, we took on a collective process to consider the things that we could positively influence and thus gain better comfort around some of the vulnerabilities that we felt. Here is our MiniLuxe journey quickly recapped through the lens of R.I.S.E.:

Recognize: We recognized the opportunity to look for a concept with great longevity that could amplify our Good People Mantra principles. While we hadn't yet articulated the R.I.S.E. framework or the mantra, we were discussing the same principles without knowing it. In particular, we knew we wanted to be people-first and to take on something that had the opportunity to help others become fuller versions of themselves. We knew our strengths in experience design, data, and technology as well as our weakness of inexperience in the nail care services industry. We tried to be self-aware and go into the venture with an outline of the most important steps we would need to take and the roadblocks that might slow us down or prevent us from succeeding. Our question to reconcile: Could we make the leap from vulnerability to conviction?

Internalize: Even after we recognized that MiniLuxe fit with our values and we validated that there was a reasonable business model to support what we wanted to do, we spent many months letting the concept marinate, iterate, and evolve. We did the equivalent of an actor going "method" to learn everything we could about manicures, pedicures, and waxing services, until we understood enough to give us the conviction to push forward.

Share: One of the best things I did early in the concept evolution was to share it with Mats Lederhausen, who is now my partner but was at the time managing director of McDonald's Ventures and the lead director of Chipotle. I told him that we had been waiting for something to work on, and it was either hot pot restaurants or nail salons! But he and other people who became extended members of the founding team were instrumental in helping us shape the concept. As part of the internalization process, we did quite a bit of customer research and discussed the findings with people who could help. For example, we went to medical professionals and hospitals to learn how best to develop our clean lab for the sterilization of instruments.

Execute: Once we took the leap of faith to start the concept, we were all in. We executed across the board, including building the first MiniLuxe over Christmas week, and spent sleepless nights worrying about how pedi stations or dry bars should be redesigned, and securing relationships with landlords and even some nail salon owners as consultants and employees to make sure we could confidently deliver high-quality services, commit to our hygiene differentiation, and have a more fulfilling career model for technicians. We put our dollars, our time, and our souls into getting that first location up and running. Whatever skepticism we may have had we pushed to the side. We put our heads down to work knowing that "retail is detail," and that it was all in the execution now.

POWER IN VULNERABILITY

Embracing our vulnerabilities is risky but not nearly as dangerous as giving up on love and belonging and joy— the experiences that make us the most vulnerable.

BRENÉ BROWN[3]

In contrast to the mostly positive associations we have with the words "confidence" and "conviction," the word "vulnerability" sounds faintly shaming or weak. But I am defining vulnerability in this context as a conscious choice, as amenability to novelty and experimentation that allows for the possibility of stumbling upon even bigger ideas. Vulnerability is the awareness and willing acceptance of taking risks toward the purpose of a bigger goal. It requires us to be open about our set of assumptions and revisit how we think about things while maintaining conviction in our most core values. You cannot reach your larger goals without making yourself vulnerable at times. The easier word in the business vernacular to use would be "risk taking" instead of "vulnerability"—but what we're really talking about is a self-aware vulnerability and the ability to proactively confront it rather than adopt a passive naïveté. If you choose to have vulnerabilities and risks (for the sake of potential rewards), you can figure out the ways to manage the attendant risks. This is what great leaders and entrepreneurs do; they do not just accept risks, they manage them. Framed this way, vulnerability not only becomes more nuanced, it becomes a trait that buttresses our strength to try new things.

If we perceive risk takers as bold, driven, persuasive, and extroverted, we may look at "vulnerable people" as weak, helpless, introverted, and undefended. But business building and vulnerability are inextricably linked—if you don't allow yourself to have active vulnerability toward risk, there is little chance of reward or change. Some of the people I respect the most are active seekers and managers of their vulnerability. They are at ease with who they are. They know that by revealing themselves, they engender authenticity in themselves and in others. Just as we can actively pursue goodness, we can also consciously practice vulnerability or, if you'd like, measured conviction, knowing the parts we can control and those riskier ones we can't.

Since writing my first post on vulnerability in 2009 for *Harvard Business Review*, I've been inspired by Brené Brown's TED Talk on the topic and her book *Daring Greatly*, and more recently by the work of Sarah Lewis, whose 2014 book *The Rise* explores the missteps of great artists who ultimately achieved success. Both express why so many greater callings and admired successes have required embracing both vulnerability and failure. "From a certain height we can see it," Lewis writes in *The Rise*. "Many of our most iconic endeavors—from recent Nobel Prize–winning discoveries to entrepreneurial invention, classical works of literature, dance, and visual arts—were in fact not achievements, but conversions, corrections after an arrow's past flight."[4]

Without allowing for some vulnerability, for the acceptance of failed paths or unexpected speed bumps, the world would be flatter, shallower, duller. That said, understand that there are two main types of vulnerability: one is passive, docile, and unlikely to lead to much that is good; the second is self-selected, proactive, and productive risk taking that can create new thinking and new things. Let's be clear: there is a vital difference between what I call *passive* and *active* vulnerability. Passive vulnerability refers to the condition of being vulnerable without choosing to be. Active vulnerability stems from a contemplated risk that considers the intrinsic (e.g., personal fulfillment) and extrinsic payoffs (e.g., financial reward) for that risk.[5] Further, active vulnerability considers ways for those risks to be managed. Active vulnerability is in essence proactive and informed risk taking. Passive vulnerability is reactive and submissive exposure. If passive vulnerability leads to failure, we shouldn't be surprised. But even when active vulnerability ends up in what the world calls failure, it is still among our most humanizing traits, across any field we may be in, whether it's in the arts, the sciences, or business.

Consider this example of active vulnerability: the story of how entrepreneur and inventor James Dyson went through 5,127 prototypes and 5,126 failures over fifteen years before he eventually invented his massively successful vacuum cleaner is the stuff of entrepreneurial legend. Dyson liked saying that the inventor and entrepreneur's life is one of failure.

> *I've always thought that school children should be marked by the number of failures they've had. The child who tries strange things and experiences lots of failures to get there is probably more creative. . . . We're taught to do things the right way. But if you want to discover something that other people haven't, you need to do things the wrong way.[6]*

Failure and vulnerability can serve as an almost spiritual source, an inner inspiration, a mysterious energy that leads us down creative paths we could never have imagined. Accepting the premise that we all have flaws of competency and character should give leaders the courage to share these flaws, confront them, and find strength in them. This is the basis of both trust and authenticity.

Through failure we can sometimes find our inner confidence. WD-40 came about after thirty-nine prior attempts failed, but that history left an indelible mark on CEO Garry Ridge. He is emphatic that there are no failures at WD-40, just "learning moments" that encourage employees and give them confidence going forward. In addition, every one of Dyson's 5,126 failed attempts at his vacuum prototype allowed him to learn something new. With that new knowledge, he gained greater conviction that he was going to get to the final, correct prototype.

THE LEAP FROM CONFIDENCE TO CONVICTION

Confidence and conviction are close cousins—but they also differ in important ways. In Buddhism, for example, a clear separation exists between confidence, which is self-directed, self-empowering, and therefore mostly internal, and conviction, which connotes a belief in something larger than one's own self, whether it's a principle, a set of values, or even a higher power. Confidence often leads to conviction, but by itself confidence is fraught with risks (as Icarus can attest), especially when it curdles into arrogance or self-righteousness. That danger point? When a person succumbs to pride and loses self-awareness and is short on his compassion, he becomes more selfish than selfless. Between our confidence and conviction lies a white space in which we have the option to surrender and make the leap toward true conviction.

Another difference between confidence and conviction: if you're confident, you can support a given decision. If you have conviction, you get that much closer to true accountability. So while vulnerability and conviction may be at war with each other, ultimately you need enough conviction to feel fully accountable for your actions. Leaders and decision makers have to recognize that they are the ones directly responsible for the consequences of their decisions. They also need to realize they are accountable across all levels of their organizations. Leaders also have to know when to apply conviction judiciously and when it can give them the most leverage. Every leader (and every person) knows that there are times when the troops require someone to tell them what to do and lay out a course of action. This is when confidence and conviction are both able to deliver on the goods—inspiring and elevating an organization toward greater focus, alignment, and intensity. The key is figuring out what situation calls for conviction and knowing how to comport yourself between those conviction points. Which, inevitably, brings the conversation back full circle to vulnerability.

COMING TO TERMS WITH DIFFICULT DECISION MAKING

The best part of putting this book together was having the opportunity to speak to many leaders, ranging from serial entrepreneurs and artists to Fortune 500 CEOs and military generals. What has been fascinating is hearing them describe how they've motivated their teams, and how their teams have motivated them, especially in difficult decision-making situations. Many told me that they simultaneously worked hard to manage and restrain their quiet inner vulnerabilities while choosing the right times to project the confidence and conviction necessary to get things done— often what leaders need to just stay the course. Staying on course doesn't mean that leaders have banished their vulnerability, it simply means that they've managed to maintain their team at a calm equilibrium and that they have a process and temperament that serves them and their team members well in such situations.

Even the strongest, most confident, most experienced, and most eloquent leaders recognize that they won't be right every time. Generally, great decisions and outcomes involve making the right call in the face of embedded risk. "No risk, no reward," as the mantra goes, touching on the balance between conviction and vulnerability. Once leaders make a decision, their goal shouldn't be to protect others from vulnerabilities that may arise as a result, but to be transparent about the risks that need to be mitigated. Leaders should give their people the opportunity to stretch and excel in the challenge while always reminding them they have the strongest possible conviction and faith that the team will do what they set out to do. Ultimately, this is how leaders can inspire their teams into action.

> *A "no" uttered from the deepest conviction is better than a*
> *"yes" merely uttered to please, or worse, to avoid trouble.*
>
> MAHATMA GANDHI

You need to be persistent, and even relentless, in communicating your beliefs—but only up to a certain point; or to put it another way, "stubbornness is great when you're right, but hell when you are wrong."[7] The best leaders exhibit an intense conviction that derives from a deeply held belief in the rightness of their decisions, one that can be misinterpreted as arrogance. Only a few leaders are adept enough to reconcile this balance, and fewer still can simultaneously maintain sufficient self-awareness and humility to adjust their plans in response to changing conditions.

• • • •

Vulnerability and conviction are dueling forces that challenge us in our pursuit of goodness and across its three cornerstone values. The foundation of goodness that underlies our truth characteristics and values needs to rise to the challenge of embracing vulnerability but never to the point that our conviction weakens or vanishes. If the basis for good decision making begins by recognizing and internalizing a given situation, then being aware that this tension will always exist should lead to better decision making. So facing vulnerability head-on, *and* as a potential source of strength, can even help energize our convictions.

Of the five tensions I've explored in this book, the one between vulnerability and conviction is the most frequently encountered. It's the one entrepreneurs and leaders face almost daily. I couldn't help notice a pattern common to each person who faced this tension and faced it with courage: the usual stages of *recognize, internalize, share,* and *execute* had become unconscious, automatic functions. Such leaders gave themselves permission to be uncertain and were comfortable navigating their seas of ambiguity in the belief that any vulnerability that seeped in was the natural consequence of their search for a bigger purpose. The clarity of a purpose in a business can serve as its own faith during moments of vulnerability and uncertainty. What balance point in the tug-of-war between vulnerability and conviction best serves your purpose?

As Dominic Barton of McKinsey & Company once said, "Whenever we as a partnership have had to come to a difficult decision, I have used as a filter the firm's mission and asked how is this decision or action going to help the two principles we care most about: furthering client impact or furthering our own firm's talent development."[8] Barton's filter for purpose is driven by a profound commitment to the values of his firm. The same goes for anyone in business. We need to reflect deeply on the human-centric values that guide us, and decide whether or not they complement our company's overall values and purpose. Is there consistency, integrity, and resonance between our personal and professional values? What makes someone a truly good, and even great, person in his or her personal life is no different from what makes a good or great business leader. With our human-centric values of goodness in truth, compassion, and wholeness guiding our purpose, we can find balance in this and other tensions, allowing us to stare down uncertainty with courage, authenticity, and, yes, conviction.

In 2015, the *New York Times* released a front-page two-part investigation into some of the shocking conditions in many New York City nail salons, including how poorly the employees were treated.[9] Reporter Sarah Maslin Nir highlighted many of the issues we confronted in the industry before founding MiniLuxe eight years earlier, when we were balancing our vulnerability and conviction for the concept. While we were surprised it took this many years for a major investigative story to break about nail salons and the range of issues found in many of them, the story was an important marker of validation for our concept. It was also key for a newspaper of such repute to shine a light on the issue after all this time. As for

MiniLuxe's place in the industry—we had been privileged to be included in a (positive!) story by the *New York Times* just a few months prior to Ms. Nir's article publication. That said, the company hardly rests on its laurels and continues growing as ever—starting now to extend its national footprint by going into Los Angeles, right back to where Tippi started it all. It's going to be heads down as it ever has been, but our excitement could not be greater.

SUMMARY OF KEY POINTS FROM CHAPTER 8

· · · · · · · ·

• **Leaders, business builders, and entrepreneurs face a paradox:** Taking risks involves vulnerability, but once they make decisions, leaders need to show unwavering conviction in their purpose and calling.

• **Purpose can serve as our guide toward balance.** What's the best way to handle the struggle between vulnerability and conviction in times of difficult decision making? Use purpose as a North Star to see how the values of any decision either serve or detract from the overall purpose at hand.

• **There is power in sharing our vulnerability.** We should directly confront our own vulnerabilities, accept them as risks, and then proactively work to mitigate those risks. If we are strong enough to take on our vulnerability, it can fuel the conviction of our purpose.

• **Confidence and conviction are different.** Confidence is an internally directed trait that helps us back up our decisions, whereas conviction is more an internally directed trait that allows us to take on full accountability for the consequences of our decisions and actions.

• **There is a clear difference between passive and active vulnerability.** Passive vulnerability carries with it the conventional connotations of weakness and submissiveness. Active vulnerability is something that we initiate; we expose ourselves to risks and challenges as a means toward becoming or doing better.

9

———

IDIOSYNCRASY VERSUS CONNECTEDNESS

Everybody has their idiosyncrasies.

QUINCY JONES[1]

"Do you know what a phatic question is?"

I was sitting in the living room of a West Village apartment in New York across from Margo Feiden, or as many of her friends insist on calling her, "Ms. Feiden." I began my conversation that afternoon the way most people do, with a polite "How are you doing?" Ms. Feiden replied with a question of her own: Did I *really* want to know how she was doing? Moreover, did I know the meaning of the word "phatic" or even "phatic communication"? If I didn't, no worries, she said; even her most literate, educated friends had no idea what it meant.

Phatic communication, she told me, refers to the act of relying on convenient, conventional—and not always meaningful—words, phrases, or even topics. Added Ms. Feiden, "You see, if you *really* wanted to know how I am, we would have scheduled a much longer meeting—several hours or even a day. This meeting isn't really about how I am, but about what is on your agenda, something having to do with your book project? And by the way, that's okay."[2] Little did she and I know that, ironically, just by introducing me to the term "phatic," she had already helped me with this book. It was Margo who inspired me to explore this topic earlier in our chapter on compassion and how we can ask more non-phatic questions.

More than almost anyone I've ever met, Ms. Feiden is completely and utterly true to herself, and at ease in her own skin. And why not? Her eclectic, passion-filled life began at sixteen years old, when she produced her first Broadway play. She later became an avid aviator. For the past fifty years, she's been the gallery representative for Al Hirschfeld, the late renowned caricaturist.

"Margo Feiden is a real, old-fashioned New York bohemian character," *Interview* magazine wrote once.[3] It's hard to argue with that. If Ms. Feiden ever invites you to tea, my best advice is to fasten your seat belt and prepare to let your tea grow cold. During our meeting, I heard one story after another about encounters and friendships with people ranging from Charlie Chaplin to Luciano Pavarotti, interspersed with a wide range of other topics, including countless stories about Mr. Hirschfeld, who died in 2003. The stories Ms. Feiden tells are infused with a human spirit. At times, I felt like I was listening to a piece of music whose honesty and quirkiness left me feeling strangely moved and more humanized in the moment. After only two hours in her company, I knew she possessed one of the world's most enviable traits: a self-congruence defined by a belief in the truth and integrity of who she was. There was a seamless consistency between every one of her words, thoughts, and actions. Despite or maybe because of her idiosyncrasies, you seemed to know exactly who she was. She didn't shun what made her unconventional, nor did she flaunt it. She was who she was.

The tension pair between idiosyncrasy and connectedness brings us back to all the layers of the Goodness Pyramid. In the truth layer, our idiosyncrasies are about the congruence of what we say, do, think, and feel. This tension also activates the compassion layer of our framework; it calls us to have openness and empathy for the diversity of our personalities and the capacity to appreciate these differences while remaining connected. And with respect to wholeness, it's about being satisfied with our waypoint in life.

The discussion of this tension pair reminds me, too, that there are people in business or leadership who seem absolutely clear about who they are and what they stand for, including the likes of business leaders such as Alan Hassenfeld of Hasbro to rising stars like MIT Media Lab's Neri Oxman to creative giants like dance choreographer Bill T. Jones. Hassenfeld, Oxman, and Jones are near fearless about trying things differently and celebrating the unique traits and habits of their leadership styles, all while remaining humble and receptive to new information and ideas. After various conversations with them, I'm left with the feeling that if asked, they would all without hesitation list off their salient quirks and personality traits. And they would garner significant respect because they know who they are and don't back down from it.

· · · ·

The late Oscar Levant—American pianist, composer, actor, hypochondriac, and world-class neurotic—once remarked, "There is a thin line between genius and insanity. I have erased that line."[*] Levant believed this blur drove his creativity. Musicians, entrepreneurs, artists, and writers often need to be a little, well, out there. Fearless creativity, maverick thinking, and risk taking seldom appear in the midpoint of a bell curve. It is these quirks of endearment in our friends' personalities that make them more well-rounded human beings. Like Ms. Feiden, the world's most iconic personalities often look to remove that thin line. At the same time, too many quirks and too much eccentricity can be disconcerting and make these people challenging to respect or love. How can we begin to connect with those people?

Artists are often stereotyped as being difficult, idealistic, and even self-absorbed in their own worlds, often at the expense of practicality or even reality. Businesspeople are similarly stereotyped as being difficult, idealistic, and even self-absorbed in *their* own worlds, at the expense of appreciating the cultural and human impacts of their work. I think much could be gained and advanced by starting a school where the arts and business meet. We need to remove some of the silos of our thinking to innovate and find new white spaces. It goes back to the belief that multiple perspectives and multidimensional thinking almost always lead to a better and more beautiful answer. We need more humility and compassion with respect to one another's ways of thinking.

It starts by celebrating what is different about an individual. Think of how some idiosyncratic approaches have made people famous in the art and literary worlds. Emily Dickinson's unusual syntax and punctuation in many of her poems—especially her use of the dash—and e. e. cummings's use of lowercase letters are recognized now as defining elements of their work. What might have been once seen as out there or overly avant-garde is often later seen as groundbreaking, singular, and distinctive. At a bare minimum, it's fair to say that our idiosyncrasies bring out the texture, depth, and hue of our personalities.

People in business seem to feel that if we bring in too much humanity, poetry, or emotion, we are being soft or getting distracted from performance, which is what really matters. Yet these two worlds needn't be as separate as most people believe. We've already discussed the power of the concept of lovemarks in chapter 5; brands need to establish emotional connectivity as well as functional trust through their performance and the passion of their personalities. Business can learn from the expansiveness and inclusiveness of arts and culture, where difference and singularity is accepted and often celebrated. I am biased because I cofounded my first venture with the late Kaming Ng, who was my creative counterpart. We had just enough of the other's strengths to make for a productive and innovative firm—my appreciation for the arts and design coupled with his appreciation for strategy and analytics. The premise we had when we started that company twenty years ago is one that I still believe in today: left- and right-side thinking across business, design, and technology will always lead to more innovative, integrated, and holistic solutions and products.

MiniLuxe was no different. If we had launched the business focusing only on the market and unit economics, and created a clean and functional store that was neither on brand nor tech enabled, I have no doubt that the client experience would have suffered. When disciplines coexist, you eliminate the broken telephone syndrome. You don't ask the businessperson to write the business case, then pass that to the engineer for the technical specifications, and then pass this to a designer instructed to "make it look pretty." Instead of making things sequentially, you should work in parallel, with greater appreciation of the trade-offs one might need to make to achieve the goal of a better whole. For example, if you are designing a product and you can drastically simplify the user experience by tweaking the underlying code, it's better to do this early and collaboratively. What a businessperson may see as a creative person's idiosyncrasy works the other way as well. In the very best products, all disciplines are synchronized and working toward the same goal.

If we believe in goodness, and in the truth and compassion that accompany it, we should also believe in the strength of people's diversity. As ever, the challenge is to find a balance between being so out there that you're disconnected from your organization's core center and striving so hard to be a part of something that you erase whatever elements make you distinctive and human, not just in your personality but also in the uniqueness of your potential contributions.

IDIOSYNCRASY DRIVES BETTER IDEAS AND INDIVIDUALITY

Recently, the MIT Media Lab and its director, Joi Ito, have been exploring what it would mean to reward researchers for disobedience. Ito himself is a renaissance man with deep curiosity in all things related to human capital. The MIT Media Lab often derives progress from idiosyncratic research or thinking that many people have no interest in backing. At its inaugural Forbidden Research symposium in July 2016, the MIT Media Lab announced a $250,000 award, supported by Reid Hoffman of LinkedIn and Greylock, for any work by an individual or group that pursues disobedience for the express purpose of improving society. Said Ito, "How can we most effectively harness responsible, ethical disobedience aimed at challenging the norms, rules, or laws that sustain society's injustices?"[5] As a member of the Advisory Council for the MIT Media Lab, I was proud they were pushing for such a forward-thinking and idiosyncratic award that might lead to breakthroughs in areas including but not limited to nonviolence, human rights, freedom of speech, and freedom of innovation. The prize is meant to inspire individuals committed to righting society's wrongs.

I had heard the rewarding and celebrating of disobedience described as a guiding principle for progress before. Consider one of McKinsey's core guiding principles and values for its employees, which is to encourage a willingness to dissent—to proudly and frankly say what you truly believe. When I was at McKinsey, I used to joke that I may have too often exceeded expectations on professional reviews for my willingness to dissent. But valuing dissention provides permission for our differences and idiosyncrasies to come out in an open and safe way. Today, it's now generally accepted that diversity in critical thinking is absolutely key to better performance. Leaders should seek people who think differently and also come from the widest possible variety of backgrounds—again, so long as they can balance this idiosyncrasy with the right level of connectedness.

Idiosyncrasy and connectivity have a love/hate relationship with each other. Alone, idiosyncrasy can produce a disarming and alienating level of weirdness, unconventionality, or even craziness. But frequently, they converge to fill out different sides of the same personality. When appropriately balanced, the two express the thing we love about good people, namely, their strong sense of self and the uniqueness of their personalities.

Some of the world's most iconic figures' idiosyncrasies come to mind—Tom Wolfe's white suit, Lady Gaga's meat dress, Glenn Gould's insistence on wearing gloves when playing the piano, the German poet and novelist Friedrich Schiller's practice of keeping rotten apples on his desk in the hope their stench would inspire his writing. I once knew a Fortune 500 CEO who placed pennies in his shoes before every speech. The most famous CEO of the last decade, Steve Jobs, wore a daily uniform of black mock turtlenecks and blue jeans. The idea came to Jobs after a trip in the early 1980s to visit Sony in Japan, where he learned that Sony provided uniforms to employees after World War II. Jobs loved the idea and took it back with him to Cupertino, but it did not take among his employees. However, Jobs's mind was made up; he had fashion designer Issey Miyake create a signature black turtleneck. The Levi's he paired daily with it were his own doing.[6] These idiosyncrasies and rituals are a way of bringing order and control into our chaotic lives and are a form of self-expression for those who are most at ease with the truth and wholeness of their character.

Idiosyncrasy in Business

But beyond the white suits, rotten fruit, and designer black turtlenecks, are there any idiosyncratic strategies that have actually led to superior results? Consider Zappos's Tony Hsieh's now-regular practice of paying new employees $3,000 to quit after their first month if they don't feel the job is right for them. As a result, the most culturally simpatico employees self-select into Zappos, a core value of which is to "create fun and a little weirdness." Is this vision quixotic or brilliantly shrewd and forward thinking? As ever, the secret is balance. "On a scale of one to ten, how weird are you?" Hsieh typically asks prospective employees.[7] No, Zappos isn't necessarily seeking candidates who respond with a nine or ten, but the company isn't looking for employees who reply with a one or two, either. If Zappos's core purpose is delivering happiness to customers, its staffers need to accept that some small peccadillos come with the territory. If you're at ease with who you are, chances are you'll mesh well with Zappos's service and values-driven culture. Hsieh likes to emphasize his preference for an appropriate modicum of idiosyncrasy in new hires, but moderate enough that they can connect with Zappos's other employees.

Most of us like to believe we are individuals, but few of us have the courage to let the world know who we *really* are. When interviewing candidates, I like to ask whether the person is willing to confess one of his or her idiosyncrasies. Are they comfortable telling me about one or more of their quirks, or are they fearful they might break everyday decorum? Idiosyncrasies aren't necessarily negatives; they're the individual ways we express the human traits we have in common. We tend to remember the idiosyncrasies of good people or great leaders because their unusual behaviors, tics, or stories not only make them who they are, they also make them human.

Southwest has been long known to audition new prospective employees in addition to conducting a more formal interview, one that emphasizes behavioral questions like "Describe a time you helped a colleague succeed." Like Zappos, Southwest seeks to live its cultural values as a way of being. Southwest prides itself on developing interview systems that help ensure they are hiring for the right attitude and cultural fit, because they believe that skills can be learned. Prospective candidates might be asked to share a joke or share their personal statement for "why Southwest" on the spot.[8] In 2015, Southwest received about 371,202 résumés and hired less than 2 percent of that group, and over the past twenty years, Southwest has consistently been rated a top place to work by *Fortune* and *Forbes.*[9] It's not surprising, then, that when you are on a Southwest flight, you feel their culture—their endearing and light-spirited wonkiness makes it fun to fly on the economical airline.

The point is that idiosyncrasy can connect to a culture so long as it adds a distinctive soul and personality to a business or brand. Organizations or new start-ups shouldn't take this as license to fill their offices and boardrooms with men and women adrift in their own cult of weirdness. This, then, is the balance businesses seek: to be forward in their thinking but still grounded enough to achieve performance. Both Zappos and Southwest have come to understand where their balance points of weirdness or idiosyncrasy lie. Hsieh wants employees just weird enough— probably a six or seven on a one-to-ten gradient. The ultimate test of any culture or innovative approach is just that: In the end, does it produce a consistent way of being that consistently attracts the type of people who truly reflect the essence of the company?

Idiosyncrasies don't only define people and organizations; they also function as a source of value by spurring innovation through multidimensional thinking. There is much inspiration to be found in idiosyncratic approaches as long as they are balanced with a level of connectedness to one's coworkers and organizational purpose, and are matched with steady, high-level company performance. Idiosyncrasy reminds us that each one of us can express who we are in odd, beautiful, imperfect ways that ultimately connect us with the rest of humanity. We all have things about us that are unusual, even strange. We shouldn't be afraid to express these things consistently in our daily lives and at work. Ironically, we become more human and more connected when we feel free to reveal the quirks that make us who we are.

We will occasionally push too far in the direction of idiosyncrasy. This occurs when we're so centered on our individual selves that we expect everyone else to follow suit. This type of idiosyncratic behavior can become inappropriate or even dangerous. Idiosyncratic behavior is *not* a blueprint for everyone else to follow; by definition, idiosyncrasy is highly individual. But idiosyncrasy should never be pushed to the point where it serves as an excuse for outcast behavior that comes at the expense or even the offense of others. Skills and competency can be replaced, trained, or mastered. Positional power is almost always a short-lived source of strength, and sometimes it commands only bogus respect. Leadership requires a rarer, less tangible capacity to maintain and construct human connectivity, which derives from revealing our vulnerabilities and idiosyncrasies.

CONNECTIVITY AND CONNECTEDNESS

On Partnership and Presence

> *The quieter you become, the more you are able to hear.*
>
> RŪMĪ[10]

Business aside, think of someone you like and respect. Do their quirks and foibles drive you away, or make you love them even more? If idiosyncrasy is angular and alienating, connectedness is collective and inclusive. Connectedness means coming together as a community. It means allowing certain idiosyncrasies to dissipate, though never to the point that they disappear. As we have said, we need to balance our shared connectedness and shared humanity with the imperfections and quirks that make us human. To be connected in this sense starts with two core principles: being present and being in partnership with another person.

With partnership, it goes back to the filters we use to find the colleagues with whom we will work the best. Great partners share common values and common standards, which helps to generate respect, affiliation, and mutual pride. With respect to being present, this is much harder than it sounds. Presence requires carefully and authentically listening to what someone else is trying to say and what they want to do, whereas being in partnership has more to do with recognizing that, titles and positions aside, we are all equal and deserve trust and respect. With presence and partnership as the ground rules for connectedness, what remains is how we express ourselves, through stories and storytelling.

On Communication and Storytelling

"I do not claim that I can *tell* a story as it ought to be told," Mark Twain once wrote. "I only claim to *know* how a story ought to be told."[11]

Good people and great leaders are superior communicators who can make the complex clear. They have *internalized* their ideas. They know who they are, why they do what they do, and where they're going. Having internalized their purpose, they are able to speak in simple, relatable terms. But this isn't easy to do! My own efforts to write about and frame subjects like good people and goodness have shown me so. I think, too, of the hundreds of researchers, authors, and leaders who have spent years studying and internalizing complex subjects before they were able to understand and communicate their findings to the world. In the end, we all want to produce something simple and relatable, but I can personally attest that translating any topic or problem into straightforward and simple words is anything but straightforward and simple.

For starters, making things clear, understandable, and inspirational isn't about dumbing things down. It's about incorporating anecdotes, metaphors, and analogies in ways that bring both logic and emotion to any message. Most entrepreneurs and leaders have a vision; the hard part is getting others to understand it. The best communication is clear and authentic. When listeners intuit that a leader is present and open to partnership, they will eagerly engage with his or her message. Leaders would be well advised to sculpt their words so that the audience doesn't just understand them but also *feels* them. In the meetings I run with my team, I increasingly push them to internalize their own messages so that they, too, can help others feel that the main points of the meeting have not just been remembered, but truly *internalized.*

Like it or not, interconnectivity—once implicit—is now explicit, thanks to the Internet. More than ever, we rely on others to help advance our ambitions. Technology and the convergence of multidisciplinary thinking have yielded a huge number of creative expressions, innovations, and advancements, but the core of human connectivity remains the same. In a conversation I once had with then CEO of NPR, Gary Knell, about how technology would change the future of radio, Knell told me instead what *wouldn't* change—namely, the power and passion of storytelling. Every new disruption or change reminds us who we really are as humans. The connectedness of our core story comes up time and again; we simply need to unlock the story inside ourselves, while helping others find theirs.

> *What I am committed to is being witness to my own life*
> *and to the lives around me, and telling stories that ask*
> *the listener to consider nuance, particularly in the context*
> *of African identity construction, and how we see ourselves in*
> *the world, and how the world sees us.*
>
> SOMI, SINGER AND SONGWRITER[12]

At my venture capital firm, we're always looking for the human story behind the entrepreneur. How did the person seated across from me grow up? What were her past successes and struggles? Why does she *really* want to pursue her big idea? What's her underlying purpose? More than the answers themselves, how a candidate shares the *story* of her vision—the narrative, tone, its overall packaging—often determines whether or not we will offer to back. After all, it's not easy to "smart" your way to a great idea. In the early stages of company creation, we're looking for fire in the belly, heart, and a capacity to *connect.* Without this connectivity, leadership and partnership won't last very long. Connectivity is what gives good people the ability to excite *others.* We ask the questions we do in order to get a sense of whether an individual is able to lead with goodness and be true to themselves while still having sufficient compassion and respect for a larger group.

There was a period at ZEFER when I asked anyone we interviewed to take fifteen minutes to build anything that they wanted with a set of LEGO blocks, and then tell a story around what they had built. The goal wasn't to put anyone on the spot or make them uncomfortable, but to see how they might respond to an unconventional and idiosyncratic question and then connect the results to a story we might not have heard otherwise.

Goodness always happens best in the company of others. This is why you should put your weight behind people over ideas. Jim Goodnight at SAS is one shining example of this strategy, though other companies—like Google, Bloomberg, and the Container Store—have a long-standing history of being employee-centric in ways that foster collaboration and community, whether through training and development programs or other benefits.

THINKING NEW, THINKING OLD

How, then, do we find a balance between clarity, simplicity, and the need for authentic, sometimes quirky expression? I believe the answer begins by understanding what the *core* of something is. John Maeda, the former president of the Rhode Island School of Design who eventually became a design partner at Kleiner Perkins, is the author of numerous books on topics ranging from hybrid thinking to the laws of simplicity. When I asked Maeda the best way to cultivate crossover and multidisciplinary thinking, he didn't hesitate. "The starting point of good thinking is actually not to be multidisciplinary but to be pure. We need to go to that isotopic level. Gain deep and full understanding of an area before cross-pollinating."[14] In other words, we must go deep inside a specific discipline before we can discover what lies outside its confines.

By understanding what is fundamental and what is peripheral, we can recognize how two ideas can work together. Consider the structure and frame of a building versus its costuming, like the color or accent hues of its walls. In architecture, design, and even fashion, it is possible to balance and combine the two forces of idiosyncrasy and connectedness, but only after you've grasped each at its core, or as Maeda calls it, "its isotopic level." Once you've done that, the varieties are infinite.

Often, the most interesting, insightful interplay between idiosyncrasy and connectedness comes from good people who are also multidisciplinary—people who can easily transcend the boundaries we erect between separate fields of thought, practice, inquiry, or creativity. Underneath all the fact-based knowledge we gather are mysteries that go deeper than we'll ever understand. As biologist E. O. Wilson has suggested, as we gain more facts our curiosity only increases.

We will be able to clarify the core qualities of human goodness and character by combining patterns, thoughts, dreams, and anecdotes borrowed from business, art, design, literature, poetry, science, and history. This multidimensional perspective may call upon us to be unconventional or even idiosyncratic, but it will ultimately help us better appreciate the commonalities cut across different fields and disciplines. In the end, these same qualities form the essence of what it means to be human. In my mind, the most novel, intriguing ideas converge in white space; beauty is often found in these same in-between spaces.

When we default to traditional words, types of people, or categories of expertise, our perspectives narrow. For example, consider former street performer turned accidental entrepreneur, Guy Laliberté, the billionaire founder and CEO of Cirque du Soleil. What began with street performers walking on stilts and breathing fire is today one of the biggest live entertainment companies in the world. What if you had seen Guy back in the day when he was a street performer? Would you have been able to look beyond his current role as a street artist to see the genius behind his act?

Multidisciplinary people also tend to be better problem solvers and thinkers with distinctly human-centric perspectives. The smartest people I know are deeply curious. But they are not just mile-wide/inch-deep people. Charlie Munger is a lifelong student of history, cultural civilizations, and science. Is this one of the reasons for Berkshire Hathaway's performance, results, and overall success? "I went through life constantly practicing this model of the multidisciplinary approach," Munger told me. "You can't really know anything if you remember only isolated facts. You've got to have models in your head and array your experiences—both vicarious and direct—on this latticework of models."[15] This latticework-like thinking helps us to think differently.

Having an assortment of mental frames that describe how the world works across different disciplines helps lead to the kind of smarts I've long believed is essential to success: pattern recognition. As Munger suggests, a wide variety of mental models allow us to overlay patterns and distill learnings from them when we are problem solving. These mental models can help us to test how several different disciplines would resolve a problem and to observe how their answers either converge or differ. Being more multidisciplinary in our thinking also allows us to be more compassionate to other perspectives and viewpoints and more open-minded about how an idiosyncratic approach might connect to something that is closer and more grounded to being human.

If all this sounds too far-fetched or impractical for business, consider Katherine Collins, the CEO and founder of Honeybee Capital and the former head of research at Fidelity Investments. With nearly a quarter century of investing behind her—and a track record that includes successful early investments in companies like Lululemon—Collins argues that long-term themes and insights are best discovered not by just relying on the traditional, mechanized, analytical models favored by the industry, but by also using the scientific framework of biomimicry.[16]

Before we make any decision, we should ask ourselves, "What would nature do?" Collins connects the core principles of biomimicry to finance investing by asking, for example, if nature were designing this product or company, would she strive for optimization or maximization? Would nature seek to make this product intricate and complex or simple and direct? Would nature be holistic and systemic or insulated and closed?

Collins believes that the most crucial question in the investment world is risk versus uncertainty, and she argues that a broader, multidisciplinary perspective would retrain us to invest in regenerative, sustainable ways that—not coincidentally—bring together the worlds of nature and finance. To achieve balance we must be open-minded to an unusual or even idiosyncratic approach, while remaining connected to our investment objective: to invest in purposeful companies that can do well (e.g., generate shareholder returns) while doing good.

CELEBRATING THE IMPERFECTIONS WITHIN OUR PERFECTION

I want to stand as close to the edge as I can without going over. Out on the edge you see all kinds of things you can't see from the center.

KURT VONNEGUT[17]

We should strive to achieve a balance between idiosyncrasy and connectedness; their coexistence is productive and artful. This is the very rationale behind the MIT Media Lab's Award for Disobedience, discussed earlier. Sometimes we need to reward those who go against the grain. Joi Ito, the director of the MIT Media Lab, is himself a balanced persona and leader who toes the line between idiosyncrasy and connectedness. Ito was an unconventional choice for MIT: he's not an alumnus, and in fact, he doesn't even have a college degree. His eclectic background includes everything from working as a disc jockey at New York's Limelight nightclub, to working as an activist, to becoming an Internet entrepreneur, to acting as the former chairman of Creative Commons, a nonprofit seeking to expand the legal availability of creative works for people around the world. All too often, we feel compelled to choose between our eccentricities and the pressure to conform. But again, the quirks and oddities that make us complex are just as beautiful—and as good—as our traits that are more simple and straightforward.

We should champion the nonlinear, the quirky and the idiosyncratic. They should push our thinking and boundaries, just not *too* far. The best leaders are just quirky and idiosyncratic enough to effectuate groundbreaking change, but grounded enough to actually make that change happen. Innovation rarely sparks without idiosyncratic risk taking. Guy Laliberté, Richard Branson, and Warren Buffett have succeeded because they are true to who they are; they are different but connected to a purpose to which other people respond. Consider, too, some of the entrepreneurs of our modern era. Sara Blakely tried being a stand-up comedian, among other things, before inventing a body-slimming product, the now-famous Spanx. She managed to get a meeting at Neiman Marcus, where she made her first sale in the women's bathroom! Perry Chen of Kickstarter built a company and model that challenged the traditional way capital and funds could be raised for the arts and creative projects. Stewart Butterfield of first Flickr and now Slack built and sold a wildly popular enterprise software without a sales force, relying solely on the virality of its user base. All these people and the others profiled in this chapter straddle that line between idiosyncrasy and connectedness. If we make it our work to manage and master this tension pair, I strongly believe we will all be that much closer to changing the world and, like Levant, erasing the line that holds back truly creative thinking.

If entrepreneurship is the relentless commitment to and pursuit of potential without regard to limitations, how different is a venture-backed entrepreneur from a street performer walking on stilts from a single parent looking to make ends meet or an immigrant who's just arrived in a new land? Every day, everyone makes choices and trade-offs between their desires and aspirations and their resources, whether they involve time, money, or other people. In our own way, each of us is an entrepreneur on a similar journey.

SUMMARY OF KEY POINTS FROM CHAPTER 9

• • • • • • •

• **Idiosyncrasies are positive attributes that should be celebrated.** Our endearing quirks are an essential part of who we are. They tie back to the truth and wholeness layer of our Goodness Pyramid because they demand that we be self-aware and true to who we are and what we stand for. We want to truly express who we are and be comfortable with ourselves.

• **Connectedness is not mutually exclusive with eccentricity, provided we maintain a sense of presence, partnership, and clarity in our overall purpose and communication.** Our connectedness ties back to the compassion layer of our Goodness Pyramid; we should ensure our thinking and actions do not veer so far outside the realm of reality that they isolate or offend others.

• **Finding a balance between idiosyncrasy and connectedness is a challenge embraced by those people who bring a multidisciplinary mind-set and approach to their problem solving.** Multidisciplinary thinking makes us more empathetic to new ways of being and helps us to distinguish the old roots of an idea from the new, boundary-pushing branches.

• **Leaders who balance idiosyncrasy and connectedness have a real chance to create forward progress.** We should celebrate the idiosyncratic and unconventional leader who is rooted in a larger purpose that furthers our connectedness and our ability to be good for ourselves and for others.

10

GRIT VERSUS ACCEPTANCE

In late December 1999, in the central Massachusetts city of Worcester, a homeless pair stood huddled inside a large abandoned building that straddled an entire city block. Once a meat-storage unit, the building had been abandoned nearly a decade earlier, and many of the city's homeless population used it for shelter, lighting fires inside to keep warm.[1]

That night, the weather was chilly and overcast, but clear enough for an observant off-duty police officer to notice a thread of gray-white smoke seeping out from a corner roofline. It was around 6 p.m., and evidently, an hour or so earlier, two homeless men squatting in the empty building had accidentally knocked over a candle, reported it, and then left.

Built in 1906, the Worcester Cold Storage and Warehouse Company did not meet fire code. Above the ground floor, the building had no windows, and a single staircase led from the basement to the top floor. It was impregnable, too, with three-feet-thick walls. Inside was a dizzying labyrinth of one meat-storage locker after another, each sprayed with highly combustible insulation, and none connected to fire doors or exits. In short, ideal conditions for a nightmarish inferno.

By 6:30 p.m., when the first two fire trucks were dispatched, an initial search had revealed that the building was empty, but no one was certain whether the two homeless people remained trapped inside. No one knew that they had already left, nor did anyone suspect how large and destructive the fire would become. Burning across nearly one hundred thousand square feet and six floors, the fire chewed through the building, devouring the flammable insulation as fuel. It was a vicious cycle. The fire burned the insulation. The insulation released fuel-feeding by-products that the fire lapped up as it grew wildly and quickly in size.

Presiding over this inferno was incident commander District Fire Chief Mike McNamee. Nearly two hours after the blaze had started, six men were already lost and disoriented in the building. A veteran lieutenant who had fought his way out told McNamee he hadn't even been able to reach the third floor.

Glancing around him, McNamee saw a dozen firefighters, all primed to enter the building in groups of three. He imagined their family members, their spouses, their children, their parents. With half a dozen of his men still lost inside the building, and the blaze refusing to back down, McNamee stood thinking for what he remembers to be about one full minute and then heard the words coming out of his mouth: *Look, it's over. No more.* As some of his own men objected loudly, McNamee braced himself in the doorway. He faced the men, spread his arms, placed one foot against the jamb, and replied, "We've already lost six, we're not going to lose any more."

The aftermath of the Worcester fire was laden with shock and grief. It took more than a week to recover the bodies of the six brave firefighters. There was an outpouring of national support; President Bill Clinton, Vice President Al Gore, and Senators Ted Kennedy and John Kerry all attended the memorial service, which was broadcast live on national television. In its scope and complexity, and the number of lives lost, the Worcester fire was one of the most significant fires in United States history; it's remembered for the scale of the disaster as well as the courage of the six firefighters who were lost.

Less discussed is that single moment of leadership and decision making when McNamee told his men that it was already over. To me, it's a profound illustration of the tension that exists between grit and acceptance. In the following years, even the firefighters who didn't understand his decision at the time have thanked him for the courage it took to accept that the firefighters already inside the building had little chance of survival, and that sending in any more firefighters would have led to their deaths. McNamee himself was later quoted as saying, "We failed that night. . . . The building kicked our butts big-time. The building won."

The fire may have claimed six lives, and prevented a dozen more fire-fighters from doing what they were trained to do—but McNamee's decision was about as far from failure as a person can get.

. . . .

Do most people move forward against adversity but also recognize when to surrender? Where is the tipping point? This is a difficult and challenging question. In this chapter, the last of the five tension pairs—grit and acceptance—will be discussed. Grit versus acceptance is a pair that fights primarily against our wholeness.

While the stakes are almost never as high as losing lives to a fire, all of us try every day to reconcile and balance the tension between grit and acceptance. Give up too early and you are thought to lack guts and perseverance. Give in to a failed situation too late and you are thought to be stubborn or even reckless. Some of the most respected people in history often died trying, but as everyone knows, there are also times when surrendering is the best possible course of action. How can we develop our ability to discern whether we should lean one way or the other? This is one of the most challenging balance points we must face—we need to allow our rationality to weigh in (and not let emotion override us), to look back at our values, to get external perspective to keep us objective. But first let's look to some of the characteristics of grit and how we can best sense and respond to different situations.

SOME CHARACTERISTICS OF GRIT

While we always look for a balance point between grit and acceptance, I often find grit most admirable. Grit is that no-nonsense work ethic, determination, and "grind it out" quality that gets things done. When interviewing job candidates, I'm always trying to get a sense of whether someone has this quality of grit. In chapter 12, we discuss some of the questions that you can ask to make you a better judge of people, but here are a couple of those questions and a few others that help tease out whether someone has grit:

- *Does the person act or react to a situation?*
- *Has this person gone through any struggles or setbacks, and how have they responded in the past?*
- *Overall, has the person's performance been driven by smarts or heart and guts?*
- *What's the person's best example of a time he or she showed stamina?*
- *Is the candidate impatiently patient?*
- *Is this person adaptive?*

The ability to find the balance between persevering and giving up is actually enhanced by one's grittiness. Knowing, as Wooden has suggested in his definition of success, that we have given a situation our fullest effort is the most important driver of wholeness. Grit allows us to give our full efforts before assessing whether acceptance or a course change is appropriate. Recognizing that you have put in effort, stayed true to your values, and were able to sense and respond in critical moments, you'll be in a better position to gauge whether to call it a day or correct your course.

TRUE PURPOSE, CORE VALUES, AND THE ABILITY TO SENSE AND RESPOND

What best practices do we have for dealing with change and uncertainty and fulfilling one's ultimate purpose? In addition to staying rooted in core values, I have found it helpful to employ a "sense and respond" strategy. "Sense and respond" refers to a strategic management theory coined in 1992 by Stephan Haeckel, the former director of Strategic Studies at IBM's Advanced Business Institute. Haeckel's theory begins with the premise that we live and work in a complex adaptive system, and that leading, doing business, and living successfully is about knowing how to sense and respond to changes within this system.[2] Arguably, this more adaptive form of strategy has its roots in work carried out by strategic gurus including Henry Mintzberg, who during the 1970s proposed a new approach to the more analytical strategies. Today, all these theories have been repopularized in a new language filled with words like "lean," "agile," and, of course, "pivot."

Adaptive systems and organizations consistently absorb information from the environment and its surrounding context before adapting accordingly. This doesn't mean they lack a plan, only that they may adjust; or as the boxer Mike Tyson once said, "Every plan makes sense until you get in the ring and get punched in the face."[3] Similarly, the tension between grit and acceptance begins with understanding and accepting whatever situation is at hand, and figuring out how it can be adapted to optimize the outcome. In the case of the Worcester fire, McNamee and the engine and ladder companies on the scene had a plan that night. They would fight the fire. Their decisions were based not only on their training and experience, but also carefully derived assumptions, including the belief that two homeless people were still inside the building. As information became available, and it was clear that the six firefighters inside the building were disoriented and potentially trapped, McNamee accepted the situation. He would fail at saving anyone inside the building, and he would fail the firefighters who wanted to keep fighting the fire.

Obviously, it wasn't that simple and, in fact, was far more painful, tragic, and complex. Yet sometimes the tension between grit and acceptance is no clearer than the situation McNamee confronted in 1999. There are challenges, information is murky, and no one may step in to help. Such was the case for another incredible individual who fought the battle between grit and acceptance alone, against all odds—a man named Steven Callahan.

I first learned about Callahan when I read his memoir *Adrift* many years ago.[4] The book, originally published in 1986, chronicles Callahan's experience alone and lost at sea for seventy-six days, clinging to a survival raft, and remains among the most amazing stories of grit, resilience, acceptance, and ultimately, triumph that I've ever read. Since I first read it, I have had the opportunity to have several discussions and interviews with Callahan, and I now appreciate even more the challenges he faced over those nearly eleven weeks out at sea in solitude. The magnitude of the decisions that he had to make on each of those days and the stress and enormity of the consequences of those decisions remain unfathomable.

So what happened? In 1982, Callahan, a naval architect and lifelong seaman, was sailing alone toward Antigua when his boat, a 6.5-meter sloop that he had hand built, collided during the night of a storm with what he later determined was a whale, forcing him to find shelter in his emergency life raft. Over the next few days and weeks, Callahan was forced to create his own ecosystem, spearing for fish, using a pair of solar stills to distill water drops for survival, fighting bouts of sickness, and wondering daily how much fight he had left in him and whether he should simply accept that his death was imminent. Along the way, he was forced to respond to ever-changing conditions, ranging from shark attacks to unpredictable weather conditions. He told me later that he maintained his natural disposition—a stoic, resilient attitude, coupled with comfort with ambiguity—and that he believed this helped him survive as his raft floated 1,800 miles across an especially desolate stretch of the Atlantic Ocean. Finally, on his seventy-sixth day, a group of fishermen spotted his raft.

Years later, as Callahan successfully battled cancer, his attitude remained the same: you have to focus on the things within your control while maintaining faith that things will turn out the way they are supposed to. To many, this approach may sound either fatalistic or obscurely spiritual, but in common with most of the good people we spoke to for this book, Callahan humbly believes that some things in life are bigger than we are.

Whether you're crossing the Atlantic Ocean in a raft or leading a business, the balance, or resolution, of grit and acceptance exhibits a few common themes worth noting. There is not one clear line in the sand to serve as your signal for which side to lean toward. As with many tensions, that bright line, and the clarity that comes with it, is more often a deeply personal decision. The following eight considerations are the ones I have found most useful in finding balance between grit and acceptance:

1. *Purpose, values, and people should always lead.* Purpose can sound abstract, but make it more concrete by sitting down at your desk to write a purpose statement for you and your organization. We all need a North Star that helps guide us through stormier decisions and environments, and if we lack clarity, it just becomes that much "grayer" of a decision. I asked some of the experienced doctors we interviewed for this book how they make the call whether to fight to save a patient's life or give in and allow him to die peacefully. Many answered with the Hippocratic oath—first, do no harm. This simple purpose provides a clear, ethical guide to challenging situations.

2. *Think about how the issue will impact others.* Carefully consider how your decision will affect others. I ask myself: Which members of my team will help me make this decision and also embrace its consequences? Who will be affected the most? Will this decision advance our purpose of putting people first—and if not, how can I ensure it does? Compassion goes a long way toward imagining how others will receive, and perceive, a given decision.

3. *Recognize, internalize, share, and execute (R.I.S.E.) on the situation.* As discussed, R.I.S.E. is one of the most useful approaches for achieving balance. But first pause whenever you can. Take time to think about what is really going on and to help internalize and gather many perspectives from trusted people's points of view or through different multidisciplinary lenses. Then just go out and execute with conviction!

4. *Be open to new information.* A sense-and-respond strategy can be helpful when you find yourself in the heat of the moment trying

to decide between leading with grit or accepting the situation and moving on. When Callahan was lost at sea, new situational factors emerged every day and sometimes every minute. We cannot be stubbornly relentless in our quest to achieve a goal if the landscape changes, at least not if we don't respond to, or adjust for, these new inputs.

5. *Be self-aware enough to know your bias.* The ultimate test of self-awareness is understanding your own biases. Just knowing whether you tend to be relentlessly determined or to cut your losses short will help you make better decisions.

6. *Read broadly, read deeply.* I keep coming back to the importance of reading. In the fight between grit and acceptance, history is a valuable teacher, so read broad and deep. The more you read, the better your thinking. Steven Callahan talks often of how different his outcome and willingness to persevere might have been had he not been well-read in survival techniques and the knowledge that there were others who survived even longer periods at sea. Get as deep as you can in your calling's subject.

7. *Know your council of advisors.* Surround yourself with good people who can inform and provide input on big decisions. Having a set of folks who have your back and whom you trust is important. People on the outside can be objective, less emotional, and fully in your corner. I recently found myself in this position for a friend and former colleague who had been wronged by a business partner, which caused instability in his business. While the situation was highly emotional for him, it was immediately obvious to myself and others advising him that the right answer was to quickly wind down the business and start fresh. He elected to do so but needed reassurance and clarifying logic from a set of people on the outside.

8. *Making a decision is necessary and empowering.* The decision to push forward and the decision to give in are both active ones.

Even when you decide that it is best to accept a situation, there is greater power in *deciding* that path than passively waiting for that path to be decided for you. I remember the difficult time this past spring when my cofounder from my first venture, Kaming Ng, was diagnosed with terminal late-stage pancreatic cancer. There was little he could do but choose how he wanted to leave this world. At a certain point, he made the decision not to delay the inevitable through more procedures or medicines given the pain he was in and would feel over the ensuing days. Even as he became less conscious, there was a peace that I could hear in his words. All of us who were close to him knew that he had elected the path and way that he wanted.

Few of us will have to confront dilemmas of the magnitude and weight McNamee faced or fight for survival like Callahan, but we can look to what has made these decisions stand out. In the case of McNamee, in the moment he had to do the quick math of the lives at stake. It was a grueling decision to make, but he's sure of his choice, he says, because he's certain more lives would have been lost. Going in at all costs may sound like the heroic course of action, but the chances of rescue had already diminished to nearly zero. Heroism is finding the balance between grit and acceptance and doing what many would not do or be able to do. Each time we learn to balance that tension, we get a better sense of what is within our control and what is outside of it, echoing Niebuhr's serenity prayer.

People like McNamee and Callahan strive beyond their training and knowledge and, despite their different roles in life, are alike in that they hold strong values and are at their core good human beings. This brings us to the next and last section of the book, in which we look at how the essence of what makes us good or even great, like McNamee and Callahan, is actually something we can cultivate for ourselves. We can all put more goodness into practice than we may think.

SUMMARY OF KEY POINTS FROM CHAPTER 10

• • • • • • •

• **Grit and acceptance.** This last tension pair is about balancing the tension between grit and acceptance—that desire to fight toward a desired outcome versus knowing when to call it quits.

• **Acceptance and surrender aren't necessarily bad.** As in our discussion on vulnerability, power and control often come from either surrendering or accepting a situation for what it is.

• **Resolving the tension between grit and acceptance** requires a strong and clear sense of purpose, and a strategic philosophy that embraces a willingness to sense and respond to new information.

• **Other principles to help balance between grit and acceptance include the R.I.S.E.** framework, especially being self-aware enough to *recognize* the situation and see what biases we may have; pausing to fully *internalize* the situation; reading up on a topic; leaning on the good people you have around you; and ultimately knowing that making a decision is always better than not making a decision.

PART THREE

. . . .

THE IMPERATIVE TO PUT GOODNESS INTO PRACTICE

But 'tis a common proof
That lowliness is young ambition's ladder,
Whereto the climber upward turns his face.
But when he once attains the upmost round,
He then unto the ladder turns his back,
Looks in the clouds, scorning the base degrees
By which he did ascend.

WILLIAM SHAKESPEARE[1]

The ultimate test of our goodness isn't whether we do the right thing when our character is in question; it's whether we do good whenever we have an opportunity to do so. Do you have the courage to embody truth, compassion, and wholeness even when no one is watching? Remember that goodness is a *proactive* commitment to making yourself and others the fullest versions of who you can be.

You couldn't have arrived where you are today without the support and graciousness of those people who helped you along the way. As Shakespeare's Julius Caesar reminds us, do not turn your back on the goodness and generosity that's helped get you where you are today. Even if you genuinely believe that you've received little help from anyone, you have an obligation to take your own success and pay it forward.

When we talk about goodness, and what it means to be good—a good parent, a good mentor, a good friend, a good business leader—core commonalities emerge that speak to a deeper, shared definition of goodness.

In the end, to be good is to help ourselves and others become our fullest selves, in a manner that is true to who we are and compassionate to others, and in the service of a quest toward wholeness.

This is the core of our Good People Mantra and Goodness Pyramid. You may want to keep your personal and business personas separate, but as Zappos's Tony Hsieh once told me, it's best to eliminate the boundary between our private selves and public roles. "It is way too hard and confusing to try to be two different people," he explained.[2]

Ultimately, typecasting ourselves can seriously prevent us from becoming the fullest possible versions of ourselves. When my ZEFER cofounder Kaming was ill and in the hospital, a good friend of ours told me, "Hey, let's be careful not to define him by his disease—he's still the same stubborn, witty, and ruthlessly smart Kaming we've known all these years." Whether we're the parent or the child, the boss or the employee, the mentor or the mentee, we should remember that rigid roles are usually neither useful nor practical. Like Zimbardo's Stanford prison example so clearly illustrated, we'll revert to "prisoner" or "guard" roles and become disconnected from who we really are. As Kurt Vonnegut once said: "We are what we pretend to be, so we must be careful about what we pretend to be."[3]

What binds us together is the simple fact that we are all human. There can be no pretending here. At the most elemental level, there are things like our capacity for humility, self-awareness, integrity, empathy, openness, generosity, love, respect, and wisdom. While we strive for these things, to some extent we already possess them. We can access these values when we break from rigid roles and return to what is most foundational in life. So much of good leadership is seeing our position as an opportunity to serve. For servant leaders, the title is unimportant; what matters is the good we do for the people around us. If leadership truly is about how we interact with other people and imprinting our goodness upon them, then all of us are capable of becoming good leaders.

When we can forget our titles and lower our guards, we can more easily see the common truths that bind us together. While words like "goodness" and "good people" seem at first to lack precision, in truth they precisely capture the most quintessential decision of leadership: whether to treat others as equals deserving of our respect, and in doing so enable them to achieve their goals and move closer to who they want to become.

In this final section, we will discuss what's possible if we choose this goodness for ourselves and others. What might this change mean for us collectively? What change can we ignite together? We explore practical and tailored ways to increase our goodness in our daily lives, like asking questions that help us become better judges of character. If we devote more time and energy to choosing to surround ourselves with good people, we will multiply the number of opportunities to drive positive change.

This change starts with a commitment to changing ourselves and each other. Perhaps over each of our lifetimes, we'll be able to help ten people—maybe even more—to realize their potential and the power of goodness. It is this human factor, which resides in each and every one of us, that empowers us to share and collectively grow our goodness. Inside a business, the human factor is manifested in a set of lived values and an enduring culture. If we extend our reach even further and imprint this goodness on the many people in our lives, we will begin to glimpse and feel how truly human leadership can catalyze real and amazing change.

11

———

BEYOND ORDINARY MENTORSHIP

The cameras were rolling in August 2011 when the phone call came in for Justin Kauflin, who was seated in his doctor's waiting room. His mom was sitting on one side, and his ever-present guide dog, Candy, was lying on the other. Kauflin was born with a hereditary eye disorder and had lost his sight completely by age eleven. Many children in his position would have been bitter and given up their dreams. But Kauflin, a classically trained musician, grew even more committed to becoming a jazz pianist.

That day in his doctor's waiting room, it was as if the planets aligned to let Kauflin know that he'd made the right decision. The moment wasn't planned, even though it took place during the filming of a documentary, *Keep On Keepin' On*, which since 2009 had chronicled the relationship between Kauflin and legendary jazz trumpeter Clark Terry (known by his friends as CT).[1] On the other end of the call was the Thelonious Monk Institute calling to notify Kauflin that he'd been selected as one of a dozen finalists for its renowned annual jazz competition. The call wasn't only pivotal for Kauflin—it also reshaped the arc of the documentary. The filmmakers shifted their focus over the next few months as Kauflin prepared for the final competition and CT's health worsened from advanced diabetes.

The story of how Kauflin and CT met, became friends, and developed their extraordinary relationship began shortly after Kauflin graduated from high school in 2004. A top-ranked student, Kauflin was awarded a Presidential scholarship to attend New Jersey's William Paterson University, where Clark Terry was a faculty member. By then, diabetes was causing CT's own eyesight to falter. A mutual friend asked Kauflin if he'd be willing to share his experience with blindness with the older musician; perhaps it might help CT prepare better for the loss of his own sight.

The bond between the two men—one barely twenty, the other in his eighties—was instantaneous. It didn't take long for CT to recognize Kauflin's talent and sound and choose to mentor this musical prodigy, just as CT had mentored many students over the course of his long, distinguished career. As Kauflin later told the *New York Times*, Clark "was an expert in making the band feel good and about making the whole audience just so happy to be there."[2]

CT's only hope was that Kauflin could attain the pinnacle of his dreams and his potential.

Theirs was much more than just a teacher-student relationship. Both a friend and a mentor, CT offered Kauflin one of the greatest opportunities any young artist or person can hope to receive—the opportunity to learn a few choice lessons about music and life from a true master. The scenes in the film where CT is riffing off tunes with Kauflin ("We've got a million of them!" he says) are beautiful and moving. But it was far from a one-way friendship. In return, Kauflin reciprocated and mirrored CT's own values back to his mentor—serving as a model, a support system, and a close friend for both CT and his wife as he underwent one medical procedure after the next. CT anchored and mentored Kauflin, and Kauflin anchored and mentored CT in return. By breaking from character, each was able to serve the other in the most human of ways. Released in 2014, *Keep On Keepin' On* begins with a letter CT once wrote to Kauflin that simply and movingly captures the depth of their relationship:

> *Dear Justin, challenges are a part of life. As you know, your mind is a powerful asset. Use it for positive thoughts and you'll learn what I learned. I believe in your talents and I believe in you.*

Most memorably, *Keep On Keepin' On* illustrates the respect, compassion, and love between two human beings. Beyond shared mentorship, it's a story about what is possible when people have authentic relationships that help carry each other forward. In one later scene (small spoiler alert),

Quincy Jones, one of Clark Terry's former students, pays a visit to CT when Kauflin happens to be at the house. With Terry's prodding, Kauflin plays the piano for "Q." Some days after, Kauflin receives another monumental phone call: Quincy Jones Music wants to represent him. As Quincy himself put it to Clark: "We need to introduce this kid to the world."

MENTORSHIP BEGINS WITH A RELATIONSHIP

Think back: When, and in what context, have you encountered goodness? Who was responsible for it? For me—and for many other people I interviewed for this book—parents are at the top of the list. After parents, the people I interviewed usually named a close relationship, like a spouse, relative, or—in the case of Kauflin and CT—a close friend. Several people mentioned the name of an influential teacher, and some referred to various professional mentors or community members outside of work, such as a nun or rabbi, who offered guidance whenever needed.

When I followed up with the question "Who has most fundamentally shaped who you are in life or work?" parents again invariably topped the list. But this time around, this answer surprised me slightly. Where were all the career mentors, those who had helped shape a person's *work*? It came as no surprise that parents, partners, relatives, or close friends were at or close to the top, but I wondered why so few people mentioned a professional mentor, a boss, or a superior who helped them improve at their work.

In its purest and fullest form, mentoring takes work and deep commitment. The results of a 2015 Gallup Poll of 2.5 million Americans showed that a large majority of employees remain disengaged at work.[3] This is a dispiriting fact. Gallup defined "engagement" as employees who are "involved in, enthusiastic about, and committed to their work and workplace." Using this definition, only 31.5 percent of Americans are engaged at work. Even more worrisome, the engagement level among millennials comes in at only around 29 percent.

During one interview, when a respondent told me that his father was his best mentor ever in life *and* work, it finally struck me. What did this response really mean? What might the business world learn from people who play natural mentoring roles but are not immediately associated with the word "mentor" because they lack official titles and positions? Only then did I begin to acknowledge and appreciate the people outside work who have affected and shaped my career just as much as those at work. And I realized that many of my workplace mentors over the years were individuals who made me feel like an extension of their family.

How we define business leaders and entrepreneurs comes back to my longtime belief that the world's most important start-up is a family. It takes extraordinary work, sacrifice, commitment, and support to raise a family "right." But millions of people around the world may not realize that parents are *already* entrepreneurs. Like most business leaders, they try to make the most out of limited resources while offering support and growth to a small team. We don't necessarily think of our families as teams, but maybe we should. And it might even make sense to consider our business colleagues as a parallel family.

More than one of my interviewees remarked that we look to our families for inspiration, for mentorship, for support. Our families are our teams and they can provide the most loving and supportive environments possible for growth and development. We can't compare businesses to actual families, but businesses *can* learn how real, caring relationships encourage the growth of both the family's individual members and the overall family organism. Judy, a supermom I interviewed for this book, told me that she has gone so far as to codify her family's mission and values to remind her family members every day of their commitment to one another. And isn't this just another way to describe mentorship?

In fact, this mother of four's core family mission statement went along these lines: "A family is a team that needs a core mission or purpose just like a business. For us it is a place where we can encourage good values in one another, celebrate our individual peculiarities, and always be that refuge of committed support." Is it any surprise that Judy has a wonderful and successful family and is an equally great mentor in her business? A few other families I'm close with have chalkboards in their kitchens where they've written down a set of values to greet them every morning. I admired this practice so much, I adopted it myself (our list begins with "Love one another" and ends with "No whining!"). This all sounds a little hokey, but you would be surprised by how often we refer to that board.

Businesses that consider their peers and colleagues as part of a family, or who have a deeper commitment to the employer-employee social contract and bond seldom think about competency and profit first. Instead, they consider the values of support and commitment, which link back to our Goodness Pyramid.

This is why I think it's a good idea for leaders to consider the relationship equity—or lack thereof—they have with each one of their employees. Relationship equity requires a shift in attitude. Can leaders and bosses think more like the parents who topped most respondents' mentor lists, and put in place values, support, and care that will make employees happiest and most fulfilled? As my literary agent, James Levine, has said to me, "The trick in making this attitudinal shift successful with colleagues and employees is to be paternal without being paternalistic."[4] It is about saying "I care" and offering advice, not because you are wiser or have authority, but simply because you hope it might be helpful.

When we think about good people in the context of business, we see our informal and formal mentors often exhibiting and living by the principles of the Good People Mantra:

1. Be people-first.

2. Help others become the fullest version of themselves.

3. Commit beyond competency to the values of goodness.

4. Find balance against the realities and tensions of goodness.

5. Practice goodness whenever possible, not just when tested.

Businesses need to start from a place of goodness and develop true relationships with their employees, and the principles of the Good People Mantra can help leaders and employers do just that. Good people make good mentors, but a mentor (one defined as such by their title) doesn't necessarily make for a good person.

In many organizations, mentoring has become a must-do but not a must-believe-in activity. Without substance and belief behind it, mentoring comes across as flat and empty. On the other hand, when mission and mentoring are more than just empty morale boosters, they can be an organization's North Star and a cultural advantage. Research beginning in the 1980s and 1990s shows that while many companies have formal mentoring programs in place, their efficacy is often marginal. In cases where neither the mentee nor the mentor finds mentoring to be useful, inspiring, or significant, the practice can be downright negative.

Professor Belle Rose Ragins of University of Wisconsin–Milwaukee has extensively studied mentorship, specifically the relationship between career workplace attitudes and the presence, quality, and design of workplace mentor programs. At the conclusion of one of her seminal studies—conducted in 2000 and involving more than 1,100 employee subjects in varying work environments—she and her fellow researchers found that even the best-designed formal mentoring programs are no substitute for the quality of the mentor, and that satisfaction in the mentor relationship varies significantly.[5] They also concluded that mentees who don't form satisfactory relationships with their mentors fail to derive any discernible benefit from mentoring relative to peers who were not mentored. The researchers described these situations as "marginal mentoring." It comes back to our first principle of the Good People Mantra: it's all about the people. When mentorship feels forced or procedural and people participate without authentic connection, rapport, and commitment, the relationship is unlikely to ever bear fruit. Mentorship cannot and should never be a "check the box" activity.

The quality of mentorship is directly correlated to the quality of the relationship between a mentor and mentee. The two must authentically connect in order to establish trust. That is more likely to happen when the Goodness Pyramid is in place—truth and compassion are the bedrock on which to build a real relationship where there is a shared sense of humility, self-awareness, integrity, openness, empathy, and generosity. A relationship of integrity is a trusted connection, one that balances the best interests of *both* the mentor and mentee and allows people to honestly speak what they think and feel.

When relationships are built on this foundation, mentors and mentees are champions of each other. Neither necessarily seeks nor needs the depth of the relationship we find between parents and children, between partners or spouses, or perhaps even between CT and Kauflin, but the baseline for effective mentoring is a minimal level of authentic connection and rapport. This is a critical point—when you are choosing a mentor, do an internal gut check: Can you develop a rapport with the person? As with any relationship, you need chemistry. If there is no basis for the connection except the formal act of mentoring, my advice is to find a different mentor or mentee.

MENTORING AS GOODNESS VERSUS MENTORING AS TRAINING

Professional mentoring today mostly happens formally in the workplace, but as I just noted, this experience relies on the quality of the relationship between the mentor and mentee. Even when there is a good relationship, we also must identify and understand the type of mentoring we seek and the type of mentoring we are receiving.

We should first focus on establishing common values and deepening the workplace mentoring relationship before improving competencies. Both steps are critical, but the order matters. We need common values before common competencies and standards. Sometimes we can find "Master Mentors" who can help us on both the values side *and* the competencies side, but more often we will need to draw on the experiences of different types of mentors. More on that soon, but let's look first at the typical experience of a mentor.

Mentoring is usually biased toward competency and career-based advancement. While nothing is wrong with this approach, it can dominate mentoring programs or be mistakenly leaned on at the starting point of a mentoring relationship. Professor Ragins posits this widely accepted definition of mentorship: "A mentor is a higher-ranking, influential individual in your work environment who has advanced experience and knowledge and is committed to providing upward mobility and support to your career. Your mentor may or may not be in your organization and s/he may or may not be your immediate supervisor."[6] There is no mention here about establishing a rapport between mentor and mentee or a common ground of values or goodness beyond competency. It emphasizes workplace advancement, rather than addressing whether your workplace is right for you and whether you find your work engaging and fulfilling. A great first or last question every career mentor should ask is: *Does this place make you happy?*

If we can deduce a leadership lesson for mentoring, it is that we need to go beyond ordinary, conventional definitions of mentorship. Mentorship as training is vital and integral for building the skills needed for organizations and individuals to succeed and produce results. But to optimize the results of mentorship, start at and aim for a higher level of engagement. Whether you carry out your mentoring formally in a program or informally ad hoc, ask yourself whether your mentoring looks more like training or more like goodness (along the lines of our Good People Mantra and Goodness Pyramid). What are the gaps you might need to fill on either side?

THE ROLE OF A MENTOR: HELP YOU FLY WHILE KEEPING YOUR FEET ON THE GROUND

What is it that we want most out of a mentor? Throughout history, different terms have been used to describe the various roles that mentors play. In ancient Greece, a muse was a source of knowledge and inspiration for songwriters and storytellers. Other mentors are more like coaches who guide and provide psychological support to players who may actually be more skilled than the coaches themselves. Sometimes, mentors are highly respected practitioners, like artisanal masters of a craft to aspiring apprentices. Or think of the ultimate mentor of mentors, a Jedi Master like Yoda from whom younger hopefuls seek inspiration and wisdom. These and others are master mentors—the men and women who teach us to fly toward a dream while keeping us grounded to everyday realities.

Imagine a world in which you work with the following people. The first is a brilliant, iconic superstar in your industry, someone who is a true master in your field of work and with whom you can apprentice as much as you need. The second is a constant champion for your goals. The third is a go-to copilot, a comrade in arms with whom you can work side by side in the trenches. And what about when things take a wrong turn or hit a speed bump? You would be fortunate to have an anchor—someone to re-mind you of the values that matter, prevent failures from turning into long-term scars, and transform these obstacles into moments of growth. Then, when you do succeed—because who wouldn't with a team like that?—you might be inspired to pass on the mentorship you received and the skills and values you learned to younger associates. At the same time, you would build on your own wisdom and reach new levels of collegiality and collaboration. Perhaps you would even "reverse mentor" the original mentors who helped you along the way.

Sound too magical and unrealistic? Perhaps it would be to get all this in one place or in one person, but it isn't overly optimistic to believe that this type of mentoring is possible as long as we commit to working with the right set of good people. While it is up to each of us to be good, I discovered early in my career that having just a handful of people committed to your fulfillment and success can determine whether or not you are able to realize your aspirations. We all ultimately choose how and with whom we spend our time; whether or not we are surrounded by good people is up to us.

So let's consider the different roles that mentors can play and what they can contribute to our lives. The following roles described here are not mutually exclusive but they are often embodied by different people.

Masters of craft

Master mentors who are at the highest level of their craft are usually among the most iconic figures of their respective fields. They tend to be members of the old guard, all of whom attained their superstar station and accumulated wisdom only after years of practice and experience. Master mentors inspire us by executing day-to-day tasks and duties that resemble our own in their highest form. Masamune was Japan's greatest swordsmith, but of his many apprentices, only ten became known as the "disciples of Masamune." Who is the Masamune of your field? Masters of craft can give you insight into the history, values, and current state of your industry and help you better see why other respected leaders in your area are so good at what they do. Master mentors share their wisdom with us and teach us the values and the skills we need to become the best in our professions. He or she should help you identify, realize, and hone your natural strengths toward the closest state of perfection as possible.

Champions of our cause

As the relationship networking expert Keith Ferrazzi says, you need to have someone "who's got your back."[7] In any organization, you should make sure there is someone who will champion your cause. There will be times when the thing you need most from your mentor is emotional support and the knowledge that there is someone there who cares about you. But champions are not just advocates; they should also be able to help connect you to others. Your champion is usually a superior in your workplace who is looking out for you and supporting your career path.

Copiloting colleagues

Not all mentors need to or should be superiors. It can be immensely useful to have a copilot, buddy, or mentor. This type of relationship can develop when you are on-boarding someone new, helping him figure out where to go for lunch, showing him how the office tech works, and introducing him to others. A copilot is a peer mentor and your go-to colleague for working through major projects or tasks. This type of mentor is valuable because the relationship is reciprocal—you are peers committed to supporting each other, collaborating with each other, and holding each other accountable. When you have a copilot, both the quality of your work and your engagement level improves. The reason is simple—who really wants to work alone?

Anchors

Who can you go to when you need a confidant or a psychological boost to help get you through a difficult situation? Anchors are trustworthy mentors who always show up when you need them. They may play less of a day-to-day role in helping you hone your skills, but they are there for objective advice and compassionate support as needed. We need people who can counsel us while keeping our best interests in mind and help us see how we can grow and improve, even in uncertain times. Often, anchors are close friends, parents, or community leaders. Whoever they are, they support us in our professional and personal lives—from task prioritization, to work-life balance, to remembering our values.

"Reverse" mentors

I asked one of my mentors to identify the one thing mentors should expect in the mentoring journey. His response: "Be prepared to be mentored." By 2020, the millennial generation—those born between 1980 and 2000—will represent 50 percent or more of the workforce.[8] Because I frequently invest in new technology, I'm constantly meeting and learning from folks younger and more technologically skilled than I am. But reverse mentorship is about much more than just "the young" up-mentoring "the old" on technology. For leaders, reverse mentoring is an opportunity to collect candid upward feedback on engagement and leadership style. Moreover, when millennials feel that their perspectives matter too, they become more open to learning. Organizations need to equally embrace younger workers' fresh perspectives and older workers' wisdom and experience to create more flexible, meaningful, and collaborative workplaces.

LEARNING FROM OUR MENTORS: KNOWING THE RIGHT QUESTIONS AND PRINCIPLES

In retrospect, I won the lottery with my mentors. I've been lucky—while some of my mentors are unquestionably among the best in their field, they are also some of the best people in terms of sheer goodness. My mentors taught me to put values first, and then helped me develop requisite competencies and useful relationships. However, it's taken time for me to recognize that I've actually had many different types of mentors, many of whom spanned the categories I've described above. I needed a team of complementary mentors in my corner to succeed. In reality, mentors frequently crisscross categories and play two or more "positions," but some end up specializing in one particular role. Below, I profile just a few of my mentors to illustrate their roles.

Masters of craft in practice

Tsun-yan Hsieh, Mats Lederhausen, and Henry McCance are all influential mentors of mine who are masters of their craft. In strategic leadership advisory, retail services, and venture capital, respectively, these people have reached the highest echelons of their fields, and I have been fortunate to learn from their experience. Their insight and advice have been critical as my work at Cue Ball has pulled me across these three seemingly disparate, yet still inter-related, fields: I need to advise entrepreneurs (strategy consulting) whom we back with early stage capital (venture capital), and some of our most significant investments have been in branded consumer businesses, such as MiniLuxe (retail services). Each of these three master mentors sees their work as much more than a career; rather, they view their work as a craft, the nuances of which must be learned in an apprenticeship form.

These mentors have inspired me to reframe how I think today about each "craft" at its highest level of practice. Tsun-yan, for example, has taught me that consulting needs to go well beyond mere analysis, and instead be seen by clients as true and trusted counsel. Mats explained to me that we cannot think of our shops just as stores. "When you walk into a store, you are walking into a brand story," he told me; everything in that story must begin with the purpose and the people, starting from the inside out.[9] Henry reminds all of us at Cue Ball that we are really aspiring to be true partners with our founders. He teaches us that if we, as venture capitalists, were to seek an award, we should aspire to receive the best supporting actor award—not best director, not best lead actor, but best *supporting* actor. Upon reflection and writing, it's quite remarkable—but not coincidental—that all three mentors express the highest form of their craft in terms of being in the service of others.

Champions of our cause in practice

I had my first experience with champion mentors at McKinsey, where people like Tsun-yan and Dominic Barton were champions of my career path there. Their example of paying it forward has stayed with me through the years. At Cue Ball, the partners work with each member of our staff to develop personal goal sheets that we discuss at length twice a year. But the first time I felt a real need for a champion was at my first venture, ZEFER, and I happened to find a mentor in the first venture capitalist who invested in our company. Vernon Lobo, the managing director of an investment firm located in Toronto called Mosaic Capital Partners, became much more than an investor and lead director; he was a true champion, and at times he served as an anchor as well. By lending me commonsense advice on business models and helping me think about how to better build our team and develop client relationships, Vernon guided my thinking. He also supported my decisions to colleagues and other board members.

During one of the most critical points in ZEFER's trajectory, we had to decide whether to accept a major infusion of capital from a large private equity firm. The negotiations were tense at times, and for me, selling a large part of the firm was not without emotion. All of this was compounded by the fact that I was still young and relatively inexperienced, yet I was the CEO and I had to make key decisions. I vividly remember when the time came to decide on the final deal economics. It was a lonely time for me as a leader. So when I had to travel to Miami to negotiate the final terms with people who were clearly more experienced and above my pay grade, I called Vernon and asked if he would join me on the trip. Instead of sitting in my hotel room alone contemplating what was truly most important to us in the deal, my champion mentor and thought partner was by my side. As ZEFER grew and went through all its ups and downs over the years, Vernon was a constant resource. Even when my ideas were unconventional—like doing a LEGO test for potential candidate interviews—he championed my vision.

Copiloting colleagues

I learned the importance of having supportive copilots during my first year away from home at boarding school. I was fifteen and intimidated by the advanced workload, and I know I could not have managed without the people with whom I did my homework day in and day out. Since then, I have always believed that I perform better with a copilot by my side. Today, I have colleagues and partners with whom I collaborate every day to solve issues and prioritize projects. These activities range from exploring an investment opportunity to preparing for board and investor meetings, to setting agendas for key internal meetings such as our largest external annual gathering, On Cue, which brings together three hundred of the best and brightest from around the world for a day of connectivity.

For those early on in their careers, it is worth noting that while copilots mostly tend to emerge at the peer level, one of the best ways to work closely with a senior team member is to find a project that is of importance to them and offer to be a supporting collaborator. Finding ways to be a "junior copilot" can be a way to stretch your role with someone you normally would not work with day to day. As I shared earlier, this was in fact the way that I came to know Tsun-yan. I asked if he might be interested in having me work with him on a piece of intellectual capital about overseas Chinese family conglomerates—a topic that I knew was of interest to both him and to me.

Anchors in practice

I was speaking at a large technology conference in 2000, and a man named Kosmo Kalliarekos approached me after my talk. He explained he was a founding team member of The Parthenon Group, a boutique strategic consulting firm, and asked if we could meet some time later that day. Kosmo and I immediately hit it off. He was a big-picture thinker and had an infectious optimism. At the end of the meeting, he said he was not sure how, but he was quite certain that we'd find a way to work together. Little did I know at the time that I would later spend close to seven years as a senior partner at Parthenon and fifteen years as its vice chairman. Kosmo became an anchor and trusted confidant for any project I took on at work. Most important, he helped me during challenging times, like when my brother and Kaming were ill. Today, Kosmo is the godparent to our twin daughters.

"Reverse" mentors in practice

At Cue Ball, I've tried to install an open and transparent work environment that allows colleagues to give upward feedback, which in turn helps me become better at my job. At each feedback or mentoring session, I try to remind myself to ask, "Is there anything that I could be doing better?" Serving on the boards of businesses run by millennials has also allowed me to learn from my younger colleagues. One example of this is when Fabian Pfortmüller and his colleagues asked if I would serve as chairman of their startup, Sandbox (now Thousand), a global community of young leaders under the age of thirty years old. My interactions with the Sandbox community—especially with Fabian—have inspired my thinking on how to stay relevant to a younger generation of leaders.

•   •   •   •

All of these mentors have influenced my mind-set and approach over the years. Together they have helped teach me an overarching set of "learning questions" for every mentoring interaction. These learning questions provide a consistent means of understanding how to best support your mentee. Knowing the right questions is the first step toward establishing a productive mentoring relationship.

Specifically, every time I lead a mentoring session, I have the same critical questions in my mind that I know I must ask in order to better understand my mentee and be a more effective mentor. I always begin the same way, first by trying to discuss values and principles, and then by listening very carefully to where it is they want to go. As a mentor, this is without a doubt the most important question to ask and understand, because it centers on what your mentee values and what they are trying to achieve. We often think we are on the same page, but more often than not there is discordance between where we want someone to be and where they themselves want to go. If the core of goodness is the desire to help others become the fullest versions of themselves, then carefully listening to where they want to go is absolutely the critical first step.

THE FIVE CRITICAL QUESTIONS OF MENTORSHIP

When you are formally or informally mentoring, your first question should be: "What are you truly trying to achieve?" You always want to begin by checking in and affirming the big goal. There are four other logical questions that follow from this that you should ask your mentee:

What are you doing well that is getting you there? What is slowing you down? What will you change tomorrow? How can I help? These questions pave the way for enhanced understanding and create a space of shared consciousness to guide mentoring discussions. It may sound obvious to adopt a more structured approach to mentoring, but from my own experience, mentoring is usually done on a more ad hoc basis. The sequence of five mentoring questions I have proposed has been developed through years of being mentored and serving as a mentor to many others. Together these five critical questions of mentorship create more mindful conversation, spark greater inspiration, and generate more practical ways to be supportive and effective in your mentoring relationships. Try to find a way to ask these questions—in your own words—but always in the following order:

1. *What are you truly trying to achieve?* This question hits all levels of our Goodness Pyramid. What is the thing that will make this person feel true to themselves? Are you listening with empathy and compassion? If this person realizes this set of goals, will they feel they have moved a step closer to being whole? Are their foundational values aligned with what they want to do? Find ways to encourage them, even if their dream is unconventional or difficult to reach. In this mentoring situation, you are likely playing the roles of a master, champion, and anchor.

2. *What are you doing well that is helping you get there?* This question tries to look beyond where someone is on their journey to discern what their natural superpower is. By asking this question, you can get a better sense of how their capabilities align with their passion.

3. *What is slowing you down?* This question can begin a conversation about whether a mentee's values are misaligned with what they want to do or whether a particular skill or key relationship is missing.

4. What will you change tomorrow to help get you there faster? This question helps mentees develop self-awareness and act with wisdom. Wisdom is the self-awareness to know the difference between what you can change and cannot change. As a champion and cheerleader of your mentee's cause, you can provide them with encouragement and psychological support. A boost from someone trusted and respected in a time of need can go a long way. Help mentees do everything possible to do more, faster, toward their goals.

5. How can I be of help? Mentors can exhibit great generosity not just by listening with openness and empathy but also by looking for ways to act in their mentee's best interest. Is there someone whom they should meet for another perspective? Perhaps you have a "copilot" colleague who could help in the day-to-day execution of a task. Alternatively, this question may provide an opening for you to receive feedback or mentoring from your mentee on how your relationship can be enhanced. Often, this question sets the stage for what might be discussed or better fleshed out at the next meeting.

These questions are critical to internalize in order to mentor effectively. The next time you lead a mentoring session, reflect afterward on whether you found a way to ask each of the five critical mentoring questions, and if you did so in an effective sequence. Although it's not difficult to practice asking these questions, it does require practice to *internalize* them. Try holding a mentoring discussion over lunch or dinner and look for a natural way over the course of the meal to go through the five critical mentoring questions. You can open up with what they are really trying to achieve, and hopefully, by the time coffee is served, you'll be more prepared to share how you can best help them achieve their goals.

While these questions are a good beginning for any formal or informal mentoring session, they should not be asked in a forced manner. This brings us to the guiding principles that will help you go beyond ordinary mentorship.

PRINCIPLES FOR GOING BEYOND
ORDINARY MENTORSHIP

When preparing for mentor-mentee sessions, you should consider not only what questions to ask and in what order to ask them, but also how these are asked and how to listen to your mentee's responses. Mentors need to be genuine and avoid sounding paternalistic. Be in the right mind-set to thoughtfully ask and listen to answers to the five critical mentoring questions. Use the right tone and come with the right preparation to appreciate the common patterns of your mentee's responses.

To ask to be a *mentee* is a highly personal and vulnerable thing. Don't forget the humanity! These types of questions are not, as Margo Feiden would remind us, phatic questions. If you take on a mentee, take that duty seriously. You should listen carefully to your mentee's responses to your questions, give thoughtful feedback and answers, and approach the task with a mind-set of openness and kindness. What's the best way to do this? Keep the Goodness Pyramid, our meta guide on truth, compassion, and wholeness, in the back of your mind to help with how to ask and what to listen for. Think of the five mentoring questions as an instructional guide and "checklist" for mentoring. But the questions in and of themselves do not work if they are delivered in a phatic or merely procedural way. Mentoring must begin with a real relationship. So while the questions go a long way toward helping us ask the right things, equally important is asking them with the right tenor and the right mind-set, knowing that there are some common patterns that can help you give practical responses and advice. The following points build on the Good People Mantra and the Goodness Pyramid to present ten specific, applied mentoring principles you ought to be mindful of when asking and listening to your mentee's responses to the five critical questions of mentorship:

1. Choose to be of service and listen, really listen. Mentoring is a proactive choice, and you need to go into each mentoring session with the mind-set that you are there to be of service to your mentee. The most important thing you can do in this regard is to not only ask the right questions, but to listen—really listen—deeply and carefully, to your mentee's responses. Great questions are futile without great listening. Great listening, in turn, requires time, a strong sense of your own values, and an earnest attempt to understand another person's values. Make sure to give mentoring discussions sufficient time. Remember the compassion layer of the Goodness Pyramid and approach the meeting with openness, empathy, and generosity. Remember that you are trying to listen to—and be—*where the other person is*. Be careful not to be biased by where you are or where you want them to be.

2. *Help uncover and celebrate their superpowers.* The mentoring question "What are you doing well that will help you get there?" can help us discover another person's superpowers. When you are listening to their response, be on the lookout for the person's real natural strengths versus those that come from a great work ethic. Both are important, but if you uncover their superpower, help them see it, too! Inspire confidence in these superpowers and celebrate what is effectively their natural comparative advantage. Incidentally, this is also a great interview question: "What comes to you most *naturally*? What is it that you do better than most people?"

3. *Shout loudly with your optimism, and keep quiet with your cynicism.* Mentoring sessions should always be honest and direct, but your overall tone can still be upbeat and positive. When a mentee shares an idea, for example, always remember to begin by thinking about why it might work before you consider why it might not. Use the 24 x 3 rule; try going 24 seconds, 24 minutes, or even 24 hours considering all the ways the idea might work before criticizing any aspect of it. Be a giver of energy, not a taker of it.

4. *Encourage unconventional success.* Closely related to being optimistic is being helpful to those who wish to take that path less

traveled. If you sense the possibility that your mentee wants to do something unconventional, but that they're not fully expressing it, help him or her express it! Too frequently, people don't share what is in their heart because they think their goal is unreachable. It's been said that the world prefers conventional failure to unconventional success. As mentors, we should encourage exploration of the latter.

5. Find meaning. Whether it is a traditional career path or something unconventional and completely out of the box, after you've hit on what is truly meaningful in a role—the intrinsic "why"—the rest is easy. While balancing pragmatism and idealism, find ways to infuse what your mentee is doing today with a little more of what they'd ideally like to be doing. People might not see how their current work relates to their future goals, but you can help to frame the connection for them. Give people a sense of true ownership over something and explain why their contribution is valuable.

6. Meaningful roles are what make us engaged in our work. Help them find other good people. One of the most practical ways to support your mentees is to connect them to people who are willing and able to help them. Share with them the taxonomy of different types of mentors, and encourage them to find others who can help fill the gaps you cannot fill or who complement the areas in which you best serve them. Help your mentees themselves become better judges of people, and provide them with a framework they can use to evaluate how other good people will support them and their goals. This will be discussed in greater depth in the next chapter, where I share questions and approaches that can help us become better judges of people.

7. Share wisdom but choose kindness over rightness. Pride is the natural enemy of humility and openness. Being kind is always more important than being "right." Instead of trying to be right all of the time, do as Wayne Dyer once instructed: "Choose kindness over rightness."[10] Next time you are in a debate with someone, observe how much you follow Dyer's advice.

8. *Let them come to the answer themselves.* My partner, Dick Harrington, has often said that working with colleagues and entrepreneurs has taught him to allow others to arrive at the answer themselves. The mentor-mentee relationship isn't hierarchical. Good mentors allow their mentees to come to the answers on their own. Your ultimate goal should be to have your mentees internalize what is in their best interests.

9. *Let them control the volume dial.* As active investors, one of the questions we frequently receive is, What exactly does it mean to be "active"? While entrepreneurs ask this question because they are sincerely interested in knowing how we would add value, I know they also ask it because they fear we will become intrusive. It is immensely gratifying to be a mentor, but one needs to exercise some caution to avoid crossing the line. I encourage our entrepreneurs and mentees to be in control of the volume dial. Sometimes it's useful to nudge them to engage in a discussion, but in general, mentees should be able to turn up or down the level of mentoring that they feel they need.

10. *Always show up, whether for yourself or for others.* Respecting commitments made is a core barometer of a person's character. Mentorship requires reciprocal respect. When Adam Bryant of the *New York Times* speaks about leadership, he likes to ask the audience how they feel about their bosses: "Do you trust and respect them at a gut level to advocate for you, treat you fairly, and not throw you under the bus when things get tough?" On average, only about half the hands go up. Be on the right side of this question—respect your mentee. Building trust requires following through and showing up.

MENTORS ARE MENSCHES

A simple, common bond connects the five critical questions of mentorship and the ten principles for how to ask and listen to those questions. Simply remember to ask and answer with the attitude and style of a mensch—a "warm human being" in Yiddish. Being a good human being is a big part of being a great mentor. Being a mensch means living out all the aspects of the Goodness Pyramid, but especially the compassion layer. Practice your "bedside manner" by keeping the ten mentoring principles described above top of mind. Think of what a good person would do—ask the five critical mentoring questions and thoughtfully react to the mentee's responses. If you do the same, you'll be well on your way to being a good mentor.

While all good people are mentors, not all mentors are good people. It's possible to say the right things but without warmth, compassion, and care. When we mentor, we must remember to step outside the boss-employee relationship. Remember that when we act as mentors, another person has entrusted us with a huge responsibility. Just as there are highly competent doctors who suffer from a poor bedside manner and there are technically perfect musicians who lack emotional connectivity, there are mentors who do and say all the "right" things but not in the right way—they mentor without feeling, without being mensch.

In 2013, Mike Myers released the documentary film *Supermensch: The Legend of Shep Gordon.*[11] His subject, Shep Gordon, is one of Hollywood's best-known talent managers and agents. He has helped sculpt the careers of celebrities ranging from Alice Cooper to Michael Douglas, and he is in part responsible for creating the modern celebrity chef and the subsequent foodie movement. Shep is an atypical Hollywood agent, antithetical in nearly every way to the archetype embodied by Ari Good, Jerry Maguire, and other superagent caricatures. He sets a pretty high standard—not just for Hollywood, but for all of us.

Spending a few days together with Shep reminded me once again just how much goodness drives success. Whether you are a CEO of a Fortune 500 company, a senior partner at a consulting firm, a venture capitalist working with entrepreneurs, or a superagent, goodness for others should be a priority. The core purpose of our jobs should be to make others great. This just happens to be Shep's actual job, and when you are in his presence, you quickly experience the goodness that has enabled his success.

In an ideal world, agents and business managers are more than just transactional brokers of deals; they are their clients' champions, confidants, and counselors—in this way, they, too, are mentors. Shep's clients think of him as a good person and a mentor before they consider his managerial role or his list of accomplishments. It works so well that Shep doesn't need to sign contracts with his clients. People don't "sign" with Shep—they commit to a trusted relationship. When I recently reconnected with Shep, I asked him what drives him and how he avoids getting caught up in fame and money. He replied:

> *Human nature—and good human nature—is pretty easy to override. Life is a difficult journey in the best of times, and the way you deal with that journey and the choices—even the little tiny choices—really add up to whether you are fulfilling a purpose on this planet or not. Try to see the miracle in everything. When you meet a person, try and see to find their miracle. It is hard not to be nice to a miracle. Another trick I learned to help stay grounded is to say "thank you" as often as you can. It is amazing when you just remember to say thank you and have gratitude for what is given to you.*[12]

Our innate goodness and humanity, the mensch inside us all, is under constant pressure from the tensions of money, fame, fear, and greed. We may even experience negative peer pressure if we're around the wrong people. Mentoring is something that can and should bring joy to the work we do to give it a higher purpose: to help others succeed in a world that so often pressures us to be people we don't want to be and to do things we don't want to do. We want to mentor with the attitude, style, and grace of a mensch. We should be cautious not to fall into the de facto role of boss or employer, and instead relate to others primarily as fellow human beings. This mind-set is what makes a great mentor.

Mentoring as Your Lasting Legacy

> *Generativity is a concept originally developed by Erik
> Erikson and defined as the desire and the act to leave behind
> at the end of one's tenure better people, places, and things than
> at the beginning. The phenomenon is the basic human desire
> that becomes prominent starting at around the age of forty,
> when we become conscious of our full self. It's the idea of
> "agented immortality." We all die, we all mourn the end of
> our tenure, but we live on through better people, places, and
> things—through the things we leave behind. The problem
> with the word "legacy" is that it's used so often. People
> focus on material things, not motivation. You can have a
> legacy—but no generativity.*

TSUN-YAN HSIEH[13]

Earlier during our discussion on wholeness, we discussed Erik Erikson, the psychologist who described adult development as a quest for fulfillment through what he calls "ego-integrity." The concept of generativity, espoused by Erikson and encouraged by Hsieh above, explains why mentoring is the only noble way to leave behind a legacy that is worth leaving. In the end, all we can do is pass on the good we know to others. We must be hopeful that this "agented immortality" will go forward to do more good. We have a duty to mentor and be good if we want more overall good in the world.

The greatest mentors I've known have been selfless and honest in their ongoing quest for self-awareness. They've devoted themselves to helping others develop into the best, fullest versions of themselves. This is the core lesson that has guided me over the decades as I've tried to mentor colleagues. Like parents, the best mentors sometimes believe in you more than you believe in yourself and find ways to communicate this confidence. But being a mentor and keeping another person's best interests at heart requires deep commitment. Do you have the desire and will to commit to someone else's education, skills, and future? Are you willing to stay the course for a year, a decade, or even longer? Mentoring doesn't simply entail checking in with a person routinely. It is a partnership that requires committing to your mentee's overall education, skills, character, and goodness for the long haul. Organizations that are able to cultivate a culture that prizes helping others succeed are poised for greater success because they encourage greater engagement, loyalty, and performance from their employees.

Mentoring and being good allow us to see what we share in common: our humanity, virtuosity, and character. This expression of our inner humanity connects us all. But this is only possible if we recognize that the highest level of achievement is to serve a higher purpose: to seek ways to be a master, champion, anchor, copilot, or reverse mentor and to do so in a relatable, connectable, and amazingly human way. This challenge is yours to take: to encourage goodness in yourself and in others, and to go beyond ordinary mentorship.

SUMMARY OF KEY POINTS FROM CHAPTER 11

· · · · · · ·

• **Effective mentoring requires a baseline relationship.** There needs to be authenticity, chemistry, and mutual commitment for a mentoring relationship to bear fruit.

• **Mentoring for goodness is different from mentoring for training.** Like our bias for goodness of competency over goodness of character, mentoring is sometimes biased toward training and acquiring skills. Mentoring for goodness is equally if not more important than mentoring for competency. It requires that we really think about what the mentee's larger goals might be, even if they don't benefit the mentor (like when their goals require that they leave your organization).

• **Different types and roles of mentoring exist.** Mentors can be masters of your craft, champions of your goals, copilots in your work, anchors in times of need, and reverse mentors who help you develop greater self-awareness. We need all these different types of mentors at different times. While there are mentors who can occupy many of the different supporting roles, most times it makes sense to cultivate relationships with a set of complementary mentors.

• **Know the right questions to ask.** Effective mentorship requires knowing what questions to ask and in what order to ask them. Five key questions to pose to a mentee are: What's your goal? What are you doing that is getting you there? What's slowing you down? How will you change that? How can I help?

• **Mentoring as a mind-set and as a mensch.** As a mentor, you not only need to know the right questions to ask, you must also respond with the right mind-set, tone, and patience. Mentoring is a choice, and it requires careful listening. To convey the right attitude and tone to a mentee, uncover their superpowers; express optimism and meaningfulness; encourage success, even if it's unconventional; choose kindness over rightness;

help them find other good people; and let them guide the discussion at their pace, so that they can discover and internalize the answers for themselves. In the end, remember good mentorship requires the right "bedside manner." Show up when you say you will and put the mensch in mentorship.

12

———

BECOMING A BETTER JUDGE OF PEOPLE

Good judgment of others is a skill we all could probably stand to improve. The choices we make about our colleagues and associates are the foundation of our personal fulfillment because, in the end, we are just the sum of the interactions and experiences we have with others. Everything we do and everything we are is influenced by the people with whom we choose to surround ourselves. It's taken me many years of taking the right steps—and several missteps—to see how the success I've had in my business career and personal life ultimately reflects the quality of the decisions I've made about people. American writer and activist Rita Mae Brown once said, "Good judgment comes from experience, and experience comes from bad judgment."[1] The truth is, I've found that a lot of bad judgment revolves around people.

Leadership is only respected and organizational cultures only endure in the long run if you decide that choosing the right people is your top priority. Recall our general definition for good people: *those committed to continuously cultivating the values that help them and others become the fullest possible versions of who they are.* But therein lies the conundrum—goodness is about positively influencing others, but our own ability to do so is significantly shaped by those who influence us. How we treat others is a function of our memories and experiences—good and bad—of how people have treated us.

If you want to become a better judge of good people, you have to look beyond competency or status. Famous names and important titles are the easiest to assess—and perhaps the least useful measures of goodness. What we need to do more of is get a sense of a person's character and values, in particular, whether they espouse the values I've identified across the categories of truth, compassion, and wholeness. But just as most of us struggle to define and explain what exactly we mean by goodness and its concomitant values, so, too, do we wrestle with choices when asked to judge other people. If we are in the business of choosing goodness in others while practicing it ourselves, there's one question that looms above the rest: How can we become a better judge of good people, not just for the sake of business, but in our everyday lives?

You make judgments about people all the time, whether or not you realize it. You constantly hire new employees, meet new people, interact with prospective partners, and court potential investors of your business. Each and every day you develop and deepen your relationships and in so doing make more judgments of people. Over time, most leaders and people can develop a pretty keen understanding of a person, their character and their goodness, but that's just the thing—it takes a long time.

Is there another way to learn how to judge people and get better, quicker? Throughout my career, I have used an almost embarrassingly large array of tools, diagnostics, and frameworks to analyze companies, but *none* of them specifically addressed how best to judge and develop good people. We clearly need to remedy this.

BECOMING A BETTER JUDGE OF PEOPLE

The first step is to become aware of the biases we harbor. Two biases are particularly problematic. The first is judging goodness by familiarity— by what we already perceive as good. While I was working on a definition for "goodness" and "good people," my friend John Maeda cautioned me against falling prey to one of humanity's natural blind spots—the tendency to look for and reward that which is most familiar to us. We want to think of ourselves as good, so we seek and affirm others who look and act like us.

The second bias we should avoid is what I call the "competency bias." We are biased toward competency because we have been conditioned to focus on what David Brooks calls "résumé virtues." We tend to use status or other extrinsic markers like social media following, wealth, titles, and accolades as the key yardsticks for determining how people measure up. These metrics and signals are all helpful, but they do not allow us to dive into a person's intrinsic values or how they express those values in their character and goodness, including their willingness (or not) to help bring others along the way.

It Goes Back to Having a Language and Framework

Just knowing about and acknowledging these two biases can make us more thoughtful about what makes for good people. But if we want to sharpen our people senses even more, it is helpful to use an objective framework or mental model as a filter for good people. This is where I hope the language and Goodness Pyramid from part one of this book can reduce our biases. To remind you of those values that define goodness and good people, I have reproduced the Goodness Pyramid here.

GOODNESS PYRAMID

WHOLENESS
Gratitude for the people around
you and for your waypoint in life

WISDOM
RESPECT
LOVE

COMPASSION
Selflessness made possible by
understanding others' experiences

GENEROSITY
EMPATHY
OPENNESS

TRUTH
Honesty and congruency
across your actions,
thoughts, and feelings

INTEGRITY
SELF-AWARENESS
HUMILITY

	MIND-SET ⟶	PRACTICE ⟶	ACTION
WHOLENESS	LOVE — A mind-set of caring for and nurturing your spiritual growth and that of others	RESPECT — The practice of having appropriate regard for and fulfilling obligations to yourself and others	WISDOM — Acting with an understanding of what is truly important and knowing what you can and cannot change
COMPASSION	OPENNESS — A mind-set of being without bias and seeking to understand the actions, thoughts, and feelings of others	EMPATHY — The practice of understanding and sharing in the experiences and emotions of others	GENEROSITY — Acting on an understanding of others by being kind and giving them what they truly need
TRUTH	HUMILITY — A mind-set of modesty and accepting that there is much that you do not know	SELF-AWARENESS — The practice of reflecting on your actions, thoughts, and feelings to fully understand yourself	INTEGRITY — Acting in accordance with the insights that arise from self-awareness to achieve self-congruence

Are We Asking the Right Questions?

Armed with a definition and framework for goodness, the logical next step is to formulate the right questions to ask to help us better see and judge whether others embody and practice the values of goodness. A few years ago, I wrote a blog post for the *Harvard Business Review* on how to become a better judge of people by asking yourself ten simple questions.[2] The post touched a nerve both inside and outside of the business community. The questions help us get past brand-name credentials—that irresistible shorthand for how to judge people—and help us focus on a person's authentic character and values.

Twelve Questions to Screen for and Develop Goodness

Leaders constantly make decisions and judgments, but judging others and ourselves is one of the hardest things in the world to do consistently well. Below are a dozen questions that apply the Goodness Pyramid to real life. I hope they will help you better understand the concepts of goodness and good people. While these questions will surely prove useful in the context of professional job interviewing, I believe they're also helpful when thinking about any relationship or person and the frequent interactions we have that require us to become a judge of people.

1. *Do You Believe This Person Is Self-Aware?* (*a question of truth*)

I place an enormous premium on self-awareness because I believe it is the nucleus of success and happiness. Is the person intellectually honest about who she is, about her strengths and weaknesses? Is she actively curious about learning new things? Is she humble? Are her thoughts, words, and actions consistent?

There are many ways to become more self-aware, but the core of self-awareness is honesty and consistency in what someone says, believes, and does. My advice is to look for people who are willing to put down on paper what they say they'll do and actually follow through on it. There is enormous power in writing down intentions and then later going back to assess the progress made on those promises. In addition to seeing if someone is willing to codify their intentions, consider soliciting formal feedback from peers and having them take a psychometric test to better understand their biases. It is also worth just asking them directly how they carve out adequate time for self-reflection.

2. Does This Person Feel Authentic or Obsequious?
(a question of truth)

There are few things worse than phony praise. We've all been in a restaurant or other situation where the service or presentation feels over-the-top, obsequious, and even staged. Good people do not feel compelled to tie themselves into knots in order to impress you. When good people offer praise or criticism, it comes across as authentic, genuine, and in the service of objective truth. Ask yourself, does this person seem modest, down-to-earth, and even unafraid of showing vulnerability? All people get nervous in new situations and in front of superiors, but good people find a way to still be who they are. Be on the lookout for those who alter their core behaviors among different sets of people. Authenticity is simple; it just means being yourself honestly and consistently.

3. What Is the Talk-to-Listen Ratio?
(a question of compassion)

Self-confidence is intoxicating, but if a person talks more than he or she listens, it's worth diving deeper into this behavior. Is the other person drunk with self-importance? Is he indifferent to what others have to say? Does he believe he has nothing to learn from others?

In my experience, listening and caring go hand in hand. Listening is—or can be—among our most important learned skills. One good litmus test for assessing whether a person is a good listener is to follow the example of Dominic Barton, managing partner of McKinsey, and mark the number of times in conversation that person uses the pronoun "I" versus "we." Another is to watch out for the "topper"—that person who always has to "one-up" the last person who spoke in a conversation.

4. Is This Person an Energy Giver or Taker? (a question of compassion and wholeness)

Some people exude negativity. Others are positive, passionate, optimistic, open, empathetic, and generous. There is a Chinese proverb that says the best way to get energy is to give it. The next time you're at a cocktail or dinner party, ask yourself whether the person sitting across the table from you is an energy giver or an energy taker. You'll soon separate the good people from the emotional vampires. Look for people who smile more—smiles are contagious—and for people who tend to speak with optimism. Does this person chip away at skepticism and enhance positivity, or does he increase cynicism and negativity?

One way to test and even develop positive energy in another person is to employ our 24 x 3 rule. If someone follows an approximated 24 x 3 rule in their thinking, they're more likely to be an energy giver than an energy taker. Energy givers are more likely to listen compassionately to other people's ideas because they approach the world with an open mind. Finally, a fun question to ask yourself is this: If this person were a song, what song would they be? Would they be an uplifting and energizing "fight song," or do they remind you of the most depressing tune you know?

5. Is This Person Likely to Act or React to a Task? (a question of compassion)

When asked to do something, some people become critical and defensive. Others jump in at once, push forward, and try to solve the problem. It is the latter you should keep in your circle. I've never forgotten a phrase an old business school classmate of mine liked to say: "Action, not reaction, please."

Many people are quick to say "no" if asked to do something outside of their job description or everyday responsibilities. They fail to see the bigger picture of collaboration and shared goodness. This is a fundamental difference between team leaders and individual contributors. We should be wary of those who have reflexive negative responses. Think hard about what jobs the person you are evaluating would be willing to take on, large or small, and how collaborative you think they'd be.

6. *How Does This Person Treat Someone He Doesn't Know?* *(a question of compassion)*

Many of the good people we interviewed for this book follow a basic mantra: we are all equal. Closely watch how someone interacts with a stranger, a cab driver, a waiter, or a colleague. Is she polite or brusque? Does she engage with that person or treat him as a social and professional inferior? Can you picture that person coming to a stranger's aid? Is she compassionate enough to treat a stranger as she would want to be treated in return?

Condescension, brusqueness, rudeness, and snobbery often derive from a tacit fear that, in the end, we are all pretty much the same—that in different circumstances, given different breaks, we could find ourselves in worse roles or positions. If someone treats his inferiors dismissively, think hard about why this might be.

7. *What Is the Spouse, or the Partner, Like?* *(a question of truth)*

We are known by the company we keep, especially the people we keep closest to us. If you are thinking about hiring an important employee, consider inviting the candidate out to dinner with his or her spouse or partner. A related exercise is to ask how the people closest to you would describe your best and worst qualities. Does their list match up with your own? In all cases, spend the time to gather references not just from people listed by the candidate, but also from others with whom you might have common connections.

A variation of this question shows up in the Predictive Index self-assessment survey. The survey asks respondents to select attributes that they think a hypothetical friend might reasonably assign to them. How would people describe this person's best or worst characteristics? The survey takers of a Predictive Index test are able to see how they feel about themselves relative to how others perceive them. All people have a personal ledger of character traits. Are the people you're evaluating consistent in terms of how they see themselves versus how their closest friends see them?

8. Is There an Element of Struggle in the Person's History? How Does He Respond to Setbacks? (a question of compassion)

History matters, and so do personal histories. In my last book, my coauthors and I found that roughly two thirds of entrepreneurs who initiated and persevered in their ventures experienced some financial or social hardship or challenge early on in their lives. Early setbacks tend to shape character more than early successes, and developing resilience in response to adversity is a key predictor of success later in life.

I'm not saying anyone should willfully struggle or court failure. But if struggle is a necessary part of life, it's important to consider how someone transforms his or her low points into opportunities for learning. Why do people of great character excel at this in particular? There is no one simple answer, but there are common patterns—including codifying lessons, reflecting on what was inside and outside of their control, and asking themselves, "What would I do differently next time?"

9. What Has This Person Been Reading? (a question of wholeness)

Reading frames ideas, ignites new thoughts, and adds complexity and nuance to familiar perspectives. As we gain knowledge, we better comprehend the vastness of what we neither know nor fully understand. The

realization that so much of the universe is yet unknown should spark our intellectual curiosity. As E. O. Wilson once said, "Our sense of wonder grows exponentially. The deeper the knowledge, the deeper the mystery."[3] The most interesting, soulful people I know read often and widely. Reading also helps us connect to others via stories, metaphors, and parables. The better read someone is, the better she is able to use the powers of analogy and storytelling to clarify complex ideas and contextualize her place in the wider world.

The habit of reading one to two (or more) books a month, especially ones not directly related to your profession, enriches experience, expands curiosity, and allows for the combination of thoughts and lessons from a wide variety of sources. The world's most transformative ideas, from company creation to cultural evolution, emerge from multidisciplinary and well-read minds.

10. Would You Ever Want to Go on a Long Car Ride with This Person? (a question of truth and compassion)

This is a variant of the "Airport Test," which asks how you would feel to be stuck in an airport with a person. Can you imagine driving cross-country with this person? Why or why not? If you set aside professional skills, references, and other workplace commonalities, could the two of you get along, agree, laugh, or sit in silence? This question tests how you might feel about a person as a long-term colleague or partner. It reminds us to think hard about the "who" rather than the "what" of a person. Yes, competencies matter on the job for day-to-day tasks, but both the airport test and the car ride test ask us to reflect on the value of relationships in the long run.

Uncovering the "who" of another person requires allowing that person to get to know you as well. Are you willing to open up to a work colleague? Do you have something to hide? Do you fear others might think less of you if you break out of your workplace role? In this book I have attempted to show that humility and vulnerability are strengths. Remember this, too: common areas of interest are less important than shared values, shared standards, and shared authenticity.

11. Is the Person Comfortable with Idiosyncrasies?
(a question of wholeness)

Only rarely are people solely interesting because of what they do for a living. To use a baseball analogy, a person's identity has much more to do with his curveball than his fastball—more to do with his quirks, oddities, and eccentricities than his conventional qualities. Is this person at ease with idiosyncrasies, or is he embarrassed, self-conscious, even furtive? Does he hide or showcase these characteristics? We all function best when we feel free to be ourselves.

Now, in your head, ask this question of the person you're evaluating. How important does he think it is to conform with "the establishment"? How comfortable is he with your own and others' weirdness? Our most unusual traits make us who we are. In some cases, simply being true to ourselves—to our own idiosyncrasies—can make us good. One of the highest forms of truth is simply living as our real, true selves.

12. Is the Person Multidimensional or Multidisciplinary?
(a question of wholeness)

People who can't navigate between, around, and across diverse fields of learning and experience have drastically limited horizons of possibility. I was lucky to take several undergraduate courses at Harvard taught by the late evolutionary biologist Stephen Jay Gould. I vividly remember the week Professor Gould introduced the class to the concept of "spandrels," an architectural term used to describe the space between two arches. Gould later redefined the word in terms of evolution, describing it as an outcome that is an "accidental," positive by-product of some other evolutionary change, rather than an element of the "original" design. In birds, for example, feathers intended for thermal warmth were later adapted for flight. The takeaway: embrace in-between and unexpected creative spaces. Embrace the spandrels.

Like well-read people, multidisciplinary people have an unconventional approach to the world that opens up new possibilities and allows them to solve problems more creatively. So ask, do you sense that this person is multidimensional and multidisciplinary?

SPANDREL

· · · ·

I'm committed to developing tools that help us become better at judging people, both ourselves and others. If you can become a proficient judge of other people, chances are high you'll become a better judge of yourself; the reverse is also true.

Combining the values in the Goodness Pyramid with these dozen questions provides us with a language and practice that gives us a better sense of what goodness is really like. That said, the goal of this language and set of questions is not to provide a verbatim script with which to interrogate the goodness and character of a person. Instead, these resources give us a structured way to decide how we *feel* about someone when we reflect on how they live and embody the values in the Goodness Pyramid. If we ask these questions of the people who surround us—and more important, if we honestly ask these questions of ourselves—we will inevitably see that there is much work to be done on our journey and quest for goodness. With this understanding, how can we embrace the arduous road ahead and ask what we can do to increase the goodness of the world?

SUMMARY OF KEY POINTS FROM CHAPTER 12

• • • • • • •

• **It's difficult to judge other people's character and goodness, in large part because these values tend to express themselves over time.** We need to adopt a longitudinal view to get the truest sense of another person.

• **Our bias for familiarity and competency can interfere with our ability to see others' intrinsic goodness.** Naming these biases and identifying them in ourselves can help us look beyond them to appreciate the qualities in others that really matter.

• **Thinking about the values in the Goodness Pyramid and asking the right questions is the best way to get a gut sense of people.** Notice if the answers you hear *feel* right. The values within the Goodness Pyramid and the dozen questions are meant to guide your own intuition about goodness and good people.

13

WRAPPING IT UP: IT'S ALL UP TO YOU

When a dancer comes onstage, he is not just a blank slate
that the choreographer has written on. Behind him he has
all the decisions he has made in his life. Each time, he has
chosen, and in what he is onstage you see the result of those
choices. You are looking at the person he is, and the who,
at this point, he cannot help but be. Exceptional dancers,
in my experience, are also exceptional people, people with
an attitude toward life, a kind of quest, and an internal
quality. They know who they are, and they show this to
you, willingly.

MIKHAIL BARYSHNIKOV[1]

Practicing goodness isn't just a pleasantry, or a good idea; it's our duty. And accepting our duty as human beings is especially salient today, as we're at a point in history where institutional trust has declined, our country is divided, and extreme polarization is a daily theme in global news. Not to mention that our relationships, our waking hours, and most of our interactions have been compromised by the double-edged sword of an always-on digital environment.

All this is taking place in an era of widespread unease—even contempt—toward the business world. Old and new business scandals—Enron, Bernie Madoff, Volkswagen, Wells Fargo, and others—have made demonstrations like Occupy Wall Street into poignant and symbolic reminders of problems like increasing income inequality. But we also need to draw boundaries between inspired activism and unproductive cynicism. As Oscar Wilde's Lord Darlington said, a cynic is "someone who knows the price of everything and the value of nothing."[2]

On an institutional level, there may be no better place for goodness to breathe and spread its potential than in our workplaces. Is any place right now more in need of our Goodness Mantra and Goodness Pyramid and its accompanying values than business?

While we're on this subject, there's also a huge gulf in our understanding of how the broader world of business (from start-up to Fortune 500 boardrooms and social impact organizations) can collaborate with other types of organizations and institutions. On one side is the widespread belief that business and capitalism are possibly immoral, and on the other an assumption that business can do good only when it operates as an altruistic or nonprofit organization. Humanitarian and entrepreneur Dan Pallotta has written brilliantly about the stereotypes often perpetuated by these two sets of beliefs—neither of which is productive, and both of which hinder collaboration to find an efficient, innovative, and values-driven balance point.[3] Similar to the titles people wear, we need to break away from the labels we give to organizations—e.g., "businesses," "nonprofits," "institutions," "advocacy groups"—and focus instead on the core of what makes any place special: the people. It's time to recognize that we can find goodness anywhere, in anyone, and in any field, too.

Of course, no person—including the "good people" described in this book—is flawless. Humans are complex, and there will always be times when we're not proud of our actions. On any given day, any one of the five tensions we described in this book can override our innate goodness. In these moments, it's important to remember that goodness is a long-term commitment, and as such, impossible to get right all at once. We should judge our success and wholeness by the intention of our actions—by whether we're doing everything we can to be the best possible versions of ourselves, while helping others do the same.

I do know this much: by emphasizing good leadership and establishing values-driven cultures, we can move the needle on goodness—and show that goodness and the creation of economic value *can* coexist. One of our greatest assets in this country is our culture of entrepreneurship and innovation; we should use it for good. All leaders and workers have the power to create more goodness by changing their own organizations. But sometimes we forget we can all be leaders in our pursuit of goodness. We simply need to start with one another. Encouraging the values of truth, compassion, and wholeness in just one other person is the start of making change happen.

Real leadership begins with our willingness to ignite change in ourselves, then inspire change in others, before we collectively create the transformational changes we seek. We need leaders of competency *and* character who see their job as producing not only followers but future leaders. This kind of leader chooses goodness—and its values of truth, compassion, and wholeness—as a real lifelong commitment to do good not just when tested, but whenever possible.

Being good in this more holistic, values-centric manner is a way of *elevating* competency-based leadership, not swapping it out. If done right, leadership becomes a platform that creates more good—a *lot* more good. Why? Because *this* model of leadership is infused with truth and character. *This* model of leadership brings with it greater compassion and humanity. *This* model of leadership conveys more gratitude and wholeness. *This* model of leadership understands that in the end, above all else, it is about people, and about doing good with the people who surround us whenever the opportunity presents itself. It is, and always will be, about people, which is why by now we should all understand that our collective goal should be to foster the values of truth, compassion, and wholeness in ourselves and others to help create a virtuous cycle of good. It's a goal we should all participate in.

Our mandate, then, is to lead people in a manner that allows them to become leaders themselves. Along the way, help them feel that there is significance and meaning in who they are and in what they do. Do this, and you will create real change and enduring value in others. In turn, these same people will act in ways that benefit their companies while enhancing an overall culture of future goodness, as these lessons and behaviors transcend the boundaries of organizations and positively affect the rest of the world.

• • • •

We lack a common language that helps us define or describe good people; the only thing we know is that we want them around us! The language I put forth in our Good People Mantra and Goodness Pyramid is, I hope, the foundation of a clearer dialogue. Within the harder context of business, the topic of goodness may sound like soft stuff—how, you might ask, can goodness be linked to more concrete areas like product, growth, and profit?—but goodness is, I believe, the only real long-term advantage. The uniqueness, aura, and authenticity of what makes a culture special becomes more and more palpable over time. In fact, it becomes the basis for what makes any organization its own special organism. People and culture are what can sustain a business with superior growth and value over the long run. This is the new imperative for leadership: to recognize that businesses have an incredible opportunity to create transformative changes beyond their P&Ls, balance sheets, and stock prices by focusing on the people behind those things, and on an overall purpose that is bigger and more profound than any firm could ever be. Leaders need to go beyond being individual heroes to becoming champions of cultural systems and values.

Here's the thing: if you're willing to be patient over the long term, focusing on people first is, in fact, the *answer* to better P&Ls, stronger balance sheets, and more valuable stock prices. Consider any of the many companies that we profiled—from Nebraska Furniture Mart to Starbucks to Zappos to WD-40 and private companies like Trader Joe's and (we hope) Mini-Luxe. Over the long run, these businesses show us that enduring performance is the by-product of a deeper commitment to the organization's values, people, and the culture.

The choice is simple: either we choose to develop goodness for ourselves and surround ourselves with other people who are committed to developing and optimizing others, or we don't. The leaders who win are those who can consistently attract and evolve a pipeline of future talent. These leaders are in the business of bringing in the next generation of leadership. If you have any doubts, revisit some of the good people profiled in this book, then consider the ones in your circle. It takes a few short moments to recognize that the people in our lives, the ones we respect the most, have something more—*goodness*.

In these pages, I've argued that striving toward goodness, and surrounding ourselves with good people, is the only leadership decision that matters in business and in life. I've argued, too, that goodness begins with self-awareness, and is an ongoing, never-ending, frequently flawed work in progress. As the musician Amanda Palmer once said, "Goodness never comes in a perfect package. It's our ability to see that we are so flawed, and in the face of those flaws, still love ourselves and attempt to love each other."[4] Very few people lack the potential and capacity to produce profound positive impact on the world. Look around you. When you catch sight of the people you love and care about most, no doubt you believe they can do just about anything. Whether it's your children, your friends, your work colleagues, or the members of your community, I hope you believe, as I do, in the unbounded potential of the human spirit. Stop to consider the people who were and continue to be critical in shaping your own character, beginning, perhaps, with your own family, and branching out to your teachers, friends, church leaders, and business associates. These are the good people who chose *you*. To whom will you pass on the best of your own talents, abilities, and wisdom?

This brings me to the final and perhaps the most important reason for writing *Good People*. Ultimately, I believe that our existence is accompanied by the higher purpose of trying to do as much good as possible for as many people as possible. What role can each one of us play in becoming better not just at identifying and cultivating an affinity with good people, but in committing ourselves to helping those good people achieve what they might not see in themselves? What if we actively tried to influence the people closest to us in the most positive way possible? What if we made a conscious commitment to influence others in as beneficial a way as possible, while giving them tools to practice goodness whenever possible? What if we took a collective vow to attempt to change for the better the lives of ten people—to imprint whatever positivity we could onto them?

Ten people—that's all. Our efforts might range from helping them get into their chosen school to helping them improve at their jobs. It might involve helping them navigate an important relationship or counseling them on a suitable career path. Most important is that we select a set of people, and then commit to helping them learn everything we know, in the hopes they might someday make better decisions and in critical moments do the right thing. It would probably take one generation, at most two, to bring people together around a more common lens and language about the only decision that really matters—good people. Choose your ten, but also speak to as many people as possible about goodness, live and work by the values in the Goodness Pyramid and the Good People Mantra, try to hire for attitude, culture, and goodness as well as for competence, and take a lesson from Ben Franklin and ask that question: *What goodness have I done today?*

My hope is that by taking on this mission, goodness will become contagious. Together, we can create an exponential effect that alters our businesses, our communities, and ultimately, even our world in ways we can't yet even imagine. Have another look at the simple principles within the

GOOD PEOPLE MANTRA

BE
PEOPLE FIRST

HELP
OTHERS BECOME THE FULLEST VERSION OF THEMSELVES

COMMIT
BEYOND COMPETENCY TO THE VALUES OF GOODNESS

BALANCE
THE REALITIES AND TENSIONS OF GOODNESS

PRACTICE
GOODNESS WHENEVER POSSIBLE, NOT JUST WHEN TESTED

Good People Mantra. Can you commit to inspiring goodness in just ten people over the course of your lifetime?

This mantra is simple. There are five promises and ten people. Remember that transformative change begins with self-awareness. Next, it comes from defining, and practicing, goodness consistently across all facets of our lives as we attempt to reconcile the tensions that occasionally threaten to override it. Remember, too, that in whatever roles we play, we serve as mentors to one another. Every interaction we have influences another person, and the accumulation of these seemingly small encounters adds up to something greater than the sum of its parts. Goodness reveals itself in the context of others, and in the recognition that our organizations, cultures, and civilizations are interdependent in ways we cannot fully see or imagine. What we do on an individual level is usually much bigger than we can understand. As the photographer Paul Outerbridge once remarked, "No object of itself alone has color . . . If an object is dependent upon light for color, color must be a property of light. And so it is."[5] Just like color, we cannot be good by ourselves; we are in need of the light that comes from others.

It's fitting to conclude by quoting one of my mentors, Henry McCance, who has told me: "It sounds audacious, but if you can positively change these ten lives, and they in turn change ten, who in turn do the same, you really *can* change the world."[6]

Think about it: we all have inside us the potential to make great change happen, first in ourselves and then by encouraging the right values in as many others as possible. No matter how you choose to do this, in all cases the big questions remain: Will you choose goodness? Will you authentically seek goodness not just for yourself, but for the fulfillment of others?

Ten people, that's all. Who will your ten be?

AFTERWORD

· · · · · · ·

P utting our arms around the elusive topic of goodness and good people was a monumental task, so I wanted to provide background on the methodology that led to the Good People Mantra, the Goodness Pyramid, and the overall language we used throughout the book.

Self-reflection on life experiences. Any success I've had is the result of the guidance and inspiration I've received from many good people. Some of them are well known, others less so. I owe them all a debt of gratitude for the perspectives they've shared with me, which have shaped me and many of the ideas in this book. These personal relationships were, in fact, the starting point for what later became the driving purpose of *Good People*— to reflect on and acknowledge the family members, mentors, colleagues, and friends who have so positively impacted my life. In writing this book, I thought back on times I helped people, and on other times when I made poor judgment calls, especially about entrepreneurs and colleagues I've come to know while building businesses and venture investing. I wanted to identify what clicked when my firm and I made the right judgment about a person's character, and I wanted to explain why, in a small number of cases, we had missed out on someone's inner goodness. What could we have done differently in hindsight? A large part of this book is an effort to codify these assorted reflections and pass along as many lessons from them as possible.

Secondary research is obviously a key component of any nonfiction work, and this book is no exception. Through the centuries, much has been written about goodness in religion, psychology, and philosophy—from Christianity to Buddhism, from Jean Piaget to Abraham Maslow, and from Lao Tzu to Aristotle. So, why with all that's been written do we still so poorly understand the topic of good people, especially when it comes to business? Business leaders tend to discuss goodness and good people in terms of hard skills and competencies, with little reference to the "softer side" of values and culture. Yet there is a hard truth in soft things. Contemporary secondary sources—David Brooks's *Character*, Oliver Sacks's *Gratitude*, and many other business classics, including works by Steve Covey, Tom Peters, Daniel Goleman, and Ken Blanchard—have delved into the topic of goodness in business. These sources, alongside biographies of high-character leaders and other contemporary academic research articles, were valuable inputs to my thinking because they helped me to identify patterns and common threads in the principles underpinning goodness.

New primary research. The most gratifying work I did for *Good People* was the primary research my team and I conducted via interviews and survey work. We asked approximately one hundred men and women from diverse backgrounds and geographical locations to define what goodness means to them and give examples of people who helped shape them, both personally and professionally. We also collaborated with the nonprofit Shared Studios to capture internationally diverse perspectives on goodness. Shared Studios cofounders Amar Bakshi and Michelle Moghtader conceived of the idea of placing gold-painted shipping containers hooked up with audio and video technology in different parts of the world to serve as "pop-up studios" and connectivity portals. With the help of Shared Studios, we encouraged strangers from across the globe to engage in real-time conversations on the topic of goodness, answering questions like "What does goodness mean to you?" and "Do you have someone who has been particularly good to you?" The conversations shared by people living in Mexico City, Nashville, San Francisco, Afghanistan, and many other places brought to life the common themes that have shaped the language of goodness and good people in this book. Here is an excerpt from one conversation gathered through the portals:

MEXICO CITY: Who is a person important to your life?
NASHVILLE: I guess a person who has had a great impact on my life is my teacher from last year. She really helped me figure out who I am, what I like, and what I want to do with my life. How about you?

MEXICO CITY: Me? I think that there are two people. The first is my
grandma. She is full of love. She taught me many things, like that
you can really be a good person no matter what happens. The other
person is a teacher in high school. The same as your teacher, he
asked me things about who I am, what I want in my life.

Still, no technology replaces spending extended periods of time with
interview subjects. By far the deepest, most fascinating parts of our research were the self-stories and oral histories we uncovered over the
course of much longer, occasionally even multiday, interviews with a select group of highly regarded people. These in-depth interviews turned
into extended, open-ended, shared conversations that brought out some of
our most surprising, poignant, and valuable learnings on what it means
to be a good person.

For example, one of the most memorable oral histories came from a
person I've known for nearly two decades, a good friend whom I thought I
knew well (I'll call her Jane, though that's not her real name). I asked Jane
if she would be willing to share her perspectives on good people over the
course of a weekend. I'd always been impressed by the nontraditional path
Jane had followed, rising from a teenage office assistant to a member of the
senior management team of a well-known and highly respected corporation. While I already knew something about Jane's background going into
the interview, we ended up touching on topics and details she'd never discussed with anyone before. Many times we laughed, during other long
stretches we engaged in quiet but deep conversation, and there were moments when both of us just cried. It turned out to be one of the most beautifully authentic, revealing interviews I've ever conducted.

Jane didn't have an easy childhood. The child of two alcoholic parents,
she grew up in a family with little money and had worked since the age of
seventeen to survive. College wasn't an option. Her father went from beer
to vodka and ultimately died from an alcoholic seizure when he was forty-
eight. Jane had siblings, but she didn't want to talk about them much;
given her family's circumstances, she said simply, they never had a chance
to develop a normal relationship.

Jane remembered those early years through the prism of what she called "cloudy vagueness." Her memory was selective, but there were some memories, she told me, she wished would just slip away. Jane recounted watching her mother chase her drunk father around the house as he threatened to set fire to his clothes. She also remembered an unforgettably embarrassing day just weeks after she had landed her first real job. Her mother called her at work and summoned her home "to help." Jane had no choice but to tell her new boss that she had family issues she needed to attend to. When Jane got home, she saw her family's furniture scattered on the front lawn. "I saw it all laid out there in some humiliating, almost naked way. We had been evicted. We had no place to live." Shortly after, Jane realized the time had come for her to leave her childhood home.

Jane and I traced her various job stints, each of which accelerated her career development by allowing her to work with prestigious colleagues, bosses, and firms. Along the way, Jane learned to appreciate details, professionalism, and the gift of generosity—she recalled her first boss, who wrote Jane a check the day after she received the call to come home and help with the eviction. This same boss told Jane to take some time and return to work when she could. Her job would be waiting—she needed to resolve her family issues first.

Jane and I talked late into the night exchanging examples of people who exhibited varying degrees of goodness. We agreed without question that the good people we knew exhibited profound truth and self-awareness. Jane herself was no exception; when telling her oral history, she spoke about the centering role of faith in her life and the importance of a small set of good people who served as anchors when she needed them the most. "There were just times when I was most vulnerable—times when I felt low and insufficient, feeling there was no fork in the road to even take. I'm amazed I even survived those periods. But I know I was fortunate to have some of the right people around me."

Jane ended the conversation by expressing gratitude toward life and satisfaction with the strong, independent, and successful woman she has become. "The pieces of life have a funny way of coming back and fitting all together," she concluded. "That may be the best time. We just need to be good to ourselves and to others."

· · · ·

For a long time, I've believed that many people find goodness through struggle, hard-earned achievement, and resilience. Prior to interviewing Jane for this book, I could have never imagined the extent to which this was also true for her. I couldn't have picked a better person to color in the dimensions of this subject. Later, when I told a friend of mine—who happens to be a journalist—that my conversation with Jane felt like an NPR StoryCorps experience, he remarked that the interview reminded him of the approach taken by the late radio broadcaster Studs Terkel.

Studs Terkel had an inimitable ability to capture the oral histories of both influential and everyday Americans. Over the course of forty-five years as an author and host at Chicago's WFMT radio, he conducted over nine thousand hours of interviews. Terkel is one of my inspirations, so we did what we could to tease out our interview subjects' most concentrated essence and character in the spirit of a classic Terkel interview.

I encourage you to listen to the radio archives of Studs Terkel and conduct your own oral history interviews with the one to three people who have most fundamentally shaped you. Try to reserve a half day to a whole day with someone close to you. Find a garden, a table in an empty café, or even a quiet space in your home, and invite that person to play the role of the interviewee. Open by asking about her formative years and then move on to her greatest challenges, both personally and professionally. Try to uncover the people who influenced her, her lows of disappointment and pain, her highs of triumph and joy, and ask what she's trying to achieve now in her life—her true purpose and the path she envisages to get there. Bring out her oral history and narratives, then allow yourself to reverse roles and do the same.

In the process, you may find yourself asking the other person the question she's always wanted someone to ask her. Maybe she'll do the same for you. One question I learned from *New York Times* journalist Adam Bryant, and enjoyed asking in my own interviews, was "Which singular trait do you hope you have inherited from your mother, and which one from your father?" Another good question is one we asked in the Shared Studios shipping containers: "What is your earliest memory of goodness?" Allow yourself to be vulnerable in the conversation, and you'll receive vulnerability in return. The by-product of reciprocal vulnerability is that special, elusive something we all want from our conversations: real, authentic dialogue. Do this enough, and a set of patterns illustrating what makes for good people will emerge. You might also find, as we did, that men and women have more goodness in common than most of us realize. In the end, we're all people, and we can all be *good* people, too.

ACKNOWLEDGMENTS

． ． ． ． ． ． ．

I thought writing my second book would be a lot easier than writing my first, *Heart, Smarts, Guts, and Luck*. At least I knew this time around how much hard work it would take. That said, the writing process for *Good People* was meaningfully longer and deeper than anything I'd ever done before, and it required immense time and effort to settle into, research, and process the subject matter. Interviewing nearly one hundred people compelled me to dig deeper and learn as much about the subject as I could. To me, the experience proved beyond a doubt that goodness truly begets goodness. Good things tend to happen to good people, and good people have an ability to help goodness bloom in others.

This is why I first and foremost want to thank all the interviewees who spoke so generously and honestly about their work and lives, as well as all the other subjects who were portrayed as case studies or examples in this book. Whether it was an in-depth oral history that took place over several hours or numerous shorter interviews conducted in offices, cafés, hotels, and, yes, even shipping containers, I learned something different and new from each and every subject. This book could not have been written without your willingness to share your stories of goodness with openness, passion, and vulnerability. A million thanks to all of you for creating the foundational canvas, primary colors, and nuanced hues for this work.

Several of the interviews we conducted were with critical mentors, advisors, and colleagues of mine, including Tsun-yan Hsieh, Henry McCance, and Dick Harrington. I've mentioned or profiled almost all of my other mentors in this book, so I won't repeat all their names here. But I will say this to all the mentors who have graced my life: you know who you are, and I can't thank you enough for changing the trajectory of my professional and personal journey in ways I could never have imagined or done alone. If being good is about helping someone become a fuller, truer version of who they are, know that each one of you has done this for me. You are the good people who inspired me to explore this subject and write this book in the first place—and you motivate me to be better each day.

I'm not an author by trade, so the writing of *Good People* largely occurred between the hours of 9 p.m. and 7 a.m., plus weekends. My family members made meaningful sacrifices to help me succeed, so I want to give a super shout-out to them for their support as I embarked on yet another book project. Not only did you allow me that time, you also contributed to the book in a multitude of ways. To my seven-year-old twin daughters, Lexi and Stella: your mere presence inspires me to be as good as I possibly can. I hope to make up the time the three of us lost while I was writing this book with a strengthened perspective on what it really means to be good. To my nearly teenage son, Tyler: thank you for brainstorming with me on everything from subtitles to cover designs, especially on Saturday mornings at the museum, and for continually pushing me to answer the question "What is this book really about?" And, of course, to my wife, Laura: thank you for always pushing me to make my ideas and sentences clearer, and for your writing and editing skills, especially during the race to hand in the final manuscript.

My colleagues at my firm, Cue Ball, were amazingly supportive through every stage of this book's development. To all of you, I want to express my gratitude for your willingness to explore new ideas, deepen our collective self-awareness, and engage in conversations on the people-first philosophy and purpose that guides our firm. Not only did you provide a forum where I could further explore the topic of good people, many of you also concretely contributed to the development of those ideas. In the end, you are coauthors with me.

I'm extremely fortunate to have a core team that has worked with me since the inception of *Good People*, especially Christine Mastrangelo and Hilario Bango (and his firm, Martian Arts), who have served as content development partners and lent me creative inspiration on everything from interviews, to frameworks, to the artwork throughout the book. Thank you both for being there each step along the way! Together with our other colleagues, you gave me frequent and constructive feedback and sound editorial advice whenever I needed it.

Other members of the Cue Ball family also deserve special shout-outs. Tony Pino contributed early on to *Good People* and also undertook a Harvard Business School field study course for the book. Kercofa Francois, Cue Ball's people and community director, read early drafts and helped with chapter summaries. I also need to acknowledge one of our newer investment associates, Audrey Carson, who truly stepped up during the last few months of the manuscript submission period. Thank you, Audrey, for becoming a traffic cop of all the versions floating around, and for providing invaluable support through the editing and proofing process in the run-up to the book's launch. Finally, within the Cue Ball family, a huge thanks to my other partners John Hamel, Ali Rahimtula, Mats Lederhausen, and Brian Chu (who deserves a special thanks for reading and recommending edits to critical sections of the manuscript). And last but not least, thank you to all the interns who worked alongside me. I'd like to single out Teddy Lee for bringing clarity to the frameworks, especially the Goodness Pyramid; Julisa Salas and Michael Prince for their contributions to part two of the book on balancing tensions; Sebastian Christakis for his research and survey work; and Lauren Ge for her editing and fact-checking help.

I am also fortunate to have roped even more friends and good souls in on this project. To Amy Benzinger, who early on agreed to join our *Good People* team: you have no shortage of talents as an interdisciplinary entrepreneur and social media expert, but your sound advice on and contributions to *Good People*—including project management, interviewing, and your work on the website portal—always brought signal to whatever noise I was experiencing. Your enthusiasm for this endeavor has been infectious to all of us.

Then there was my friend Peter Smith, who I previously had the pleasure of working with alongside my coauthors on *Heart, Smarts, Guts, and Luck*. Perhaps more than anyone, Peter helped shape and sharpen many of my ideas. He also served as a psychotherapist and cheerleader along every step of the journey. Peter, you are one of the "good ones" and very much the real deal. I wonder how many people know that you are the secret weapon behind so many successful books, helping with everything from conceptualizing to writing to editing? I hope the secret does not get out *too* much, for the sake of my own future writing! You were the best developmental editor I could have ever wished for, and you helped me think hard about how to "take people on a 'ride' in a book." Peter, thanks for finding ways to push and focus me, and for doing it with velvet gloves, all while giving me the confidence to open up and find my voice.

Then, of course, there is my publishing team. I strongly believe that authors and their books benefit tremendously from finding the right publishing partner, and I count myself extremely lucky to have found that match with the Portfolio team at Penguin Random House. The editorial and production support showed consistent, authentic passion and care for this project, even as we passed through the classic phases of Bruce Tuckman's "forming, storming, norming, before performing" framework for teamwork.[1] I am very grateful to Adrian Zackheim, Portfolio's publisher and president, who sponsored this project, and to Stephanie Frerich, my day-to-day editor and project leader. Thank you, Stephanie, for believing in me and championing this book's cause from its first proposal. You and your colleague Merry Sun worked tirelessly on each draft and pushed me to aspire for a better, more cohesive product. Merry, you were one of those great supporters behind the scenes, setting up every meeting, reviewing every draft, and working side by side with Stephanie on the overall project plan. Thank you both! I also want to tuck in a quick thanks to our copy editor, Tricia Callahan, whose attention to detail made the book just plain better. I wish I could mention the many other members of the Portfolio team who pushed on various editorial and creative elements, but suffice it to say, you all were essential in clarifying my message and expressing it more beautifully. I'm truly grateful for your support. Lastly, let me just add that there is a reason Portfolio publishes so many of today's leading business books. I am humbled that you selected me, and appreciative of all the work you put in for *Good People*.

I also want to acknowledge my literary agent, Jim Levine, who believed in this project from the beginning and helped me frame a winning proposal. Jim, beyond placing *Good People* in the right publisher's hands, you were also critical to pushing the book's premise and making sure we stayed on point—up to and including your role-playing in mock interviews to ensure I would nail the core ideas behind the book! There wasn't a draft you didn't want to read and help improve, and I'm very grateful for your support and participation during the many content development and launch planning calls. No wonder you have so many great clients!

Finally, I want to applaud you, readers, for being engaged and interested in the topic of how to both better yourself and inspire and ignite goodness in others. The key message of this book is that we have a duty to help others become the fullest, truest versions of themselves. We need to move beyond settling for "hero-oriented leaders" of competency to demand "servant-oriented leaders" of character, who are committed to building cultural systems based on values. Consider taking up the challenge of helping at least one person, but hopefully ten or more people, realize their fullest potential and become the truest version of who they are—not just in competency, but also in character and values. To those of you who actually do take up this challenge, I can only offer the biggest thanks of all.

NOTES

· · · · · · ·

PART ONE: INTRODUCING GOODNESS AND GOOD PEOPLE

1   Marc Wright and Karuna Kumar, "How CEO Garry Ridge has made WD-40 a well-oiled machine," *SimplyCommunicate*, accessed October 2, 2016, https://www.simply-communicate.com/case-studies/communication/how-ceo-garry-ridge-has-made-wd-40-well-oiled-machine.

2   Employee engagement and satisfaction analysis by Peter Barron Stark Companies, cited by Garry Ridge, interview by Anthony K. Tjan, September 26, 2016.

3   Garry Ridge, interview by Anthony K. Tjan, September 26, 2016.

4   *Merriam-Webster Online*, s.v. "good," accessed October 3, 2016, http://www.merriam-webster.com/dictionary/good.

5   Tom Peters, quoted in Jacob Thomas, *Sustainable Leadership: Sourcing and Multiplying Happiness* (New Delhi: Partridge Publishing, 2016), accessed October 11, 2016, https://books.google.com/books?id=o6fJCwAAQBAJ.

CHAPTER 1: A FIRST ENCOUNTER WITH GOODNESS

1   "Living a Whole Life," LinHart Group, accessed October 11, 2016, http://linhartgrp.com/living-a-whole-life/.

2   "The Voting and Weight Machines," Morningstar, Inc., accessed October 2, 2016, http://news.morningstar.com/classroom2/course.asp?docId=142901&page=7.

3   Frank Litsky and John Branch, "John Wooden, Who Built Incomparable Dynasty at U.C.L.A., Dies at 99," *New York Times*, June 4, 2010, accessed October 2, 2016, http://www.nytimes.com/2010/06/05/sports/ncaabasketball/05wooden.html?_r=1#ucla-years.

4   John Wooden, "The difference between winning and succeeding," filmed February 2001, *TED* video, 17:36, accessed October 2, 2016, https://www .ted.com/talks/john_wooden_on_the_difference_between_winning_and _success?language=en.

5   "Wooden's Pyramid of Success," The John R. Wooden Course, accessed October 2, 2016, http://www.woodencourse.com/woodens_wisdom.html.

6   John Mackey, *Conscious Capitalism* (Boston: Harvard Business Review Press, 2013), 20, accessed November 16, 2016, https://books.google.com/books?id =KZvBAgAAQBAJ.

7   Robert Waldinger, "What Makes a Good Life? Lessons from the Longest Study on Happiness," TEDxBeaconStreet, November 2015, accessed October 3, 2016, https://www.ted.com/talks/robert_waldinger_what_makes_a _good_life_les- sons_from_the_longest_study_on_happiness?language=en#t-29391.

8   Robert Waldinger, interview by Anthony K. Tjan, September 8, 2016.

9   Kevin Kruse, "Norman Schwartzkopf: 10 Quotes on Leadership and War," *Forbes,* December 27, 2012, accessed October 11, 2016, http://www.forbes.com/ sites/kevinkruse/2012/12/27/norman-schwarzkopf-quotes/#43f8101027b3/.

10 Sydney Finkelstein, "Secrets of the Superbosses," *Harvard Business Review,* January/February 2016, accessed October 2, 2016, https://hbr.org/2016/01/ secrets-of-the-superbosses.

11 Sydney Finkelstein, *Superbosses: How Exceptional Leaders Master the Flow of Talent,* chapter 2 (New York: Portfolio Penguin, 2016), accessed November 17, 2016, https://books.google.com/books?id=OV5YCgAAQBAJ.

CHAPTER 2: A NEW FRAMEWORK AND LANGUAGE FOR GOODNESS

1   Eric Asimov, "Drinking Wine, From a Chore to a Choice," *New York Times,* January 31, 2013, accessed October 3, 2016, http://www.nytimes.com/2013 /02/06/dining/the-history-of-wine-drinking-from-a-chore-to-a-choice .html.

2   Erin Scala, "The History of the Sommelier," *Thinking-Drinking Blog,* January 1, 2014, accessed October 3, 2016, http://www.thinking-drinking.com/blog /the-history-of-the-sommelier.

3   Joann S. Lublin, "The Case for Humble Executives," *Wall Street Journal,* Oc- tober 20, 2015, accessed October 3, 2016, http://www.wsj.com/articles /the-case-for-humble-executives-1445385076.

4   Deepak Chopra, interview by Anthony K. Tjan, July 31, 2014.

5   "Legendary basketball coach Wooden dies," *CNN*, June 4, 2010, accessed October 11, 2016, http://www.cnn.com/2010/SPORT/06/03/basketball.wooden.obit/.

CHAPTER 3: THE FOUNDATION: TRUTH

1   Lao Tzu, quoted in R. A. Howard, C. D. Korver, and B. Birchard, *Ethics for the real world: Creating a personal code to guide decisions in work and life* (Cambridge, MA: Harvard Business Review Press, 2008), 51, accessed November 17, 2016, https://books.google.com/books?id=OqnrtQFfXb0C.

2   "Total number of Websites," Internet Live Stats, accessed October 11, 2016, http://www.internetlivestats.com/total-number-of-websites/.

3   Elizabeth Drake, "Ernest Hemingway: 10 quotes on his birthday," *Christian Science Monitor*, July 20, 2012, accessed October 11, 2016, http://www.csmonitor .com/Books/2012/0720/Ernest-Hemingway-10-quotes-on-his-birthday /True-nobility.

4   Simon Sinek, *Start with Why: How Great Leaders Inspire Everyone to Take Action* (New York: Portfolio/Penguin, 2009), accessed November 17, 2016, https://books.google.com/books?id=iyw6ul1x_n8C.

5   Jim Collins, "Level 5 Leadership: The Triumph of Humility and Fierce Resolve," *Harvard Business Review*, July/August 2005, accessed October 2, 2016, https:// hbr.org/2005/07/level-5-leadership-the-triumph-of-humility-and-fierce -resolve.

6   Mike Myers, "Myers: Creativity more important than fame," MSNBC, June 6, 2014, accessed October 2, 2016, http://www.msnbc.com/morning-joe /watch/myers-creativity-more-important-than-fame-274913347865.

7   Benjamin Franklin, *The Autobiography of Benjamin Franklin* (London: MacMillan & Co., 1921), 80, accessed October 11, 2016, https://books.google.com /books/about/Autobiography_of_Benjamin_Franklin.html?id= sooVAAAAYAAJ.

8   Peter Georgescu, *The Source of Success: Five Enduring Principles at the Heart of Real Leadership* (San Francisco: Jossey-Bass, 2005), 97, accessed October 19, 2016, https://books.google.com/books?id=F2rJlkLq-twC&dq.

9   Franklin, *The Autobiography of Benjamin Franklin*, 90.

10   Robert C. Roberts, "What Does It Mean to Be Intellectually Humble?," *Slate*, accessed October 12, 2016, http://www.slate.com/bigideas/what -do-we-know/essays-and-opinions/robert-roberts-opinion.

11 Billie Jean King, quoted in Isabelle Hamptonstone, *Hockey Confidence: Train Your Brain to Win in Hockey and in Life* (Vancouver: Greystone Books, 2016), 37, accessed November 16, 2016, https://books.google.com/books?id=6Uj4DAAAQBAJ.

12 Ellen Langer, "Conscious Choice and Mindful Living," panel with Peter Georgescu moderated by Anthony K. Tjan, Boston Book Festival, October 24, 2014.

13 Philip Zimbardo et al., "The Stanford Prison Experiment: A Simulation Study of the Psychology of Imprisonment," Stanford University, August 1971, accessed October 11, 2016, http://web.stanford.edu/dept/spec_coll/uarch/exhibits/spe/Narration.pdf.

14 Leslie Brunner, interview by Anthony K. Tjan, September 11, 2016.

15 Franklin, *The Autobiography of Benjamin Franklin*, 79.

16 Franklin, *The Autobiography of Benjamin Franklin*, 80.

17 Franklin, *The Autobiography of Benjamin Franklin*, 82, 85.

18 Annie Dillard, *The Writing Life* (New York: Harper & Row, 1989), 32.

19 Franklin, *The Autobiography of Benjamin Franklin*, 85.

CHAPTER 4: THE HUMAN FACTOR: COMPASSION

1 Thich Nhat Hanh, quoted in Irv Jacob, *Higher Truth* (Bloomington, IN: AuthorHouse, 2013), 379, accessed November 17, 2016, https://books.google.com/books?id=FNNnAgAAQBAJ.

2 Cancer Facts & Figures 2016, *American Cancer Association*, accessed October 3, 2016, http://www.cancer.org/acs/groups/content/@research/documents/document/acspc-047079.pdf.

3 Paul Kalanithi, *When Breath Becomes Air* (New York: Random House, 2016), 98, accessed November 17, 2016, https://books.google.com/books?id=Dg1sCQAAQBAJ.

4 Jack Erban, interview by Anthony K. Tjan, February 12, 2016.

5 Sherwin Nuland, *The Soul of Medicine* (New York: Kaplan, 2009).

6 General Stanley McChrystal and Chris Fussell, interview by Anthony K. Tjan, May 27, 2014.

7 Amy Toner, "How Employees Steal & How to Minimize It," *The NATSO Show 2017*, October 1, 2012, accessed October 2, 2016, http://www.natsoshow.org/2012/10/how-employees-steal-and-how-to-minimize-it/.

8 Barry Moltz, "7 Sneaky Ways Employees Steal and How to Prevent It," American Express Open Forum, November 12, 2013, accessed October 3, 2016, https://www.americanexpress.com/us/small-business/openforum/articles/7-sneaky-ways-employees-steal-and-how-to-prevent-it/.

9 *Literary Terms*, s.v. "empathy," accessed October 2, 2016, http://theliterarylink.com/definitions.html.

10 Carl Rogers, "01-Carl Rogers on Empathy," YouTube video, December 10, 2012, accessed October 2, 2016, https://www.youtube.com/watch?v=iMi7uY83z-U.

11 Robert Greenleaf, *Servant Leadership: A Journey into the Nature of Legitimate Power and Greatness* (New York: Paulist Press, 2002).

12 Mark Tatum, interview by Anthony K. Tjan, July 31, 2014.

13 Jørgen Vig Knudstorp, quoted in "5 Rules for CEOs to Simplify Their Job," *Chief Executive*, March 17, 2014, accessed October 11, 2016, http://chiefexecutive.net/5-rules-for-ceos-to-simplify-their-job/.

14 Edward O. Wilson, "One Giant Leap: How Insects Achieved Altruism and Colonial Life," *BioScience* 58, no. 1 (2008), accessed November 20, 2017, http://bioscience.oxfordjournals.org/content/58/1/17.

15 Elizabeth W. Dunn, Lara B. Aknin, and Michael I. Norton, "Spending Money on Others Promotes Happiness," Berkeley Greater Good Science Center, http://greatergood.berkeley.edu/images/application_uploads/norton-spendingmoney.pdf.

16 Adam Grant, *Give and Take: Why Helping Others Drives Our Success* (New York: Penguin, 2013).

17 His Holiness the Dalai Lama, preface to *The Power of Kindness: The Unexpected Benefits of Leading a Compassionate Life*, by Piero Ferrucci (New York: Penguin, 2006), ix, accessed October 11, 2016, https://books.google.com/books/about/The_Power_of_Kindness.html?id=SMcsDQAAQBA.

CHAPTER 5: THE ULTIMATE QUEST: WHOLENESS

1 Oliver Sacks, "My Own Life: Oliver Sacks on Learning He Has Terminal Cancer," *New York Times*, February 19, 2015, accessed October 2, 2016, http://www.nytimes.com/2015/02/19/opinion/oliver-sacks-on-learning-he-has-terminal-cancer.html.

2 George Tames, *The Loneliest Job: John F. Kennedy, New York Times*, 1961.

3   Graham T. Allison, *Essence of Decision: Explaining the Cuban Missile Crisis* (Boston: Little, Brown and Company, 1971), accessed November 17, 2016, https://books.google.com/books?id=aSk3ek0t54EC.

4   William Shakespeare, *Henry IV Part 2* (Boston: Cengage Learning, 1967), 91, accessed November 17, 2016, https://books.google.com/books?id=AG4h-0aUbmwC.

5   M. Scott Peck, *The Road Less Traveled, 25ᵗʰ Anniversary Edition: A New Psychology of Love, Traditional Values, and Spiritual Growth* (New York: Simon & Schuster, 2002, 2003), 83, 119, accessed November 17, 2016, https://books.google.com/books?id=KNyvQxE466kC.

6   Kevin Roberts, *Lovemarks: The Future Beyond Brands* (New York: powerHouse Books, 2004), book jacket.

7   "Our Story," Trader Joe's, accessed October 14, 2016, http://www.traderjoes.com/our-story.

8   "Doug Rauch: Former President of Trader Joe's," Leading Authorities, accessed October 11, 2016, http://www.leadingauthorities.com/speakers/doug-rauch.html.

9   Margaret M. Perlis, "4 Steps to Building an Enduring Brand: Lessons from Hermes," *Forbes*, October 11, 2012, accessed October 11, 2016, http://www.forbes.com/sites/margaretperlis/2012/10/11/4-steps-to-building-an-enduring-brand-lessons-from-hermes/#2313eb4a7160.

10 Bob Chavez, conversation with Anthony K. Tjan, September 17, 2015.

11 "Discover Lovemarks," Saatchi & Saatchi, accessed October 2, 2016, http://www.lovemarks.com/discover/lovemarks/.

12 Garry Ridge, interview by Anthony K. Tjan, September 26, 2016.

13 C. S. Lewis, *The Four Loves* (Boston: Houghton Mifflin Harcourt, 1971), accessed November 17, 2016, https://books.google.com/books?id=0qoftMnQ1rAC.

14 Casey Gerald, interview by Anthony K. Tjan, June 16, 2015.

15 "Remembering Jackie," National Baseball Hall of Fame, accessed October 11, 2016, http://baseballhall.org/discover/remembering-jackie.

16 Rick Reilly, "A Paragon Rising Above the Madness," *Sports Illustrated*, March 20, 2000, accessed October 2, 2016, http://www.si.com/vault/2000/03/20/8115557/a-paragon-rising-above-the-madness.

17 JetBlueCorpComm, "Our promise to you," YouTube video, 2:51, posted February 19, 2007, accessed November 29, 2016, https://www.youtube.com/watch?v=-r_PIg7EAUw.

18 Dr. Wayne W. Dyer, "Where Peace Lives," accessed October 11, 2016, http://www.drwaynedyer.com/blog/where-peace-lives/.

19 "A Word About Values," Trader Joe's, accessed October 4, 2016, http://www.traderjoes.com/fearless-flyer/article/2910.

20 Glen Stansberry, "10 Examples of Shockingly Excellent Customer Service," *American Express Open Forum*, May 4, 2010, https://www.americanexpress.com/us/small-business/openforum/articles/10-examples-of-shockingly-excellent-customer-service-1/.

21 Brené Brown, *Daring Greatly: How the Courage to Be Vulnerable Transforms the Way We Live, Love, Parent, and Lead* (New York: Gotham Books, 2012), 30, accessed November 17, 2016, https://books.google.com/books?id=K4naCwAAQBAJ.

22 Meghan Casserly, "Majority of Americans Would Rather Fire Their Boss Than Get a Raise," *Forbes*, October 17, 2012, accessed October 4, 2016, http://www.forbes.com/sites/meghancasserly/2012/10/17/majority-of-americans-would-rather-fire-their-boss-than-get-a-raise/#1f4a1f963d18.

23 Jane Austen, *Persuasion* (Boston: Little, Brown, and Company, 1899), 230, accessed November 17, 2016, https://books.google.com/books?id=Rk-4VAAAAYAAJ.

24 Ursula K. Le Guin, *The Dispossessed* (New York: HarperCollins Publishers Inc., 1974), 190.

25 Reinhold Niebuhr, "The Serenity Prayer," accessed August 11, 2016, http://skdesigns.com/internet/articles/prose/niebuhr/serenity_prayer/.

26 Jason G. Goldman, "Why Bronze Medalists Are Happier Than Silver Winners," *Scientific American*, August 9, 2012, accessed October 2, 2016, https://blogs.scientificamerican.com/thoughtful-animal/why-bronze-medalists-are-happier-than-silver-winners/.

27 "Herbert Simon," *Economist*, May 20, 2009, accessed August 11, 2016, http://www.economist.com/node/13350892.

28 Barry Schwartz and Andrew Ward, "Doing Better but Feeling Worse: The Paradox of Choice," *Positive Psychology in Practice* (2004), 86–104, accessed August 11, 2016.

29 Deepak Chopra, interview by Anthony K. Tjan, July 31, 2014.

30 David Brooks, *The Road to Character* (New York: Random House, 2015), accessed October 11, 2016, https://books.google.com/books/?id=PBedBAAAQBAJ&.

31 Abraham Maslow, *Toward a Psychology of Being* (Malden, MA: Blackwell, 1999), accessed November 17, 2016, https://books.google.com/books/?id =N1dqAAAAMAAJ.

PART TWO: BALANCING TENSIONS TO ACHIEVE GOODNESS

1 E. O. Wilson, *The Meaning of Human Existence* (New York: Liveright, 2014), accessed October 12, 2016, https://books.google.com/books?id=2yR0Aw AAQBAJ.

2 *Oxford Dictionaries*, s.v. "balance," accessed October 3, 2016, https://en .oxforddictionaries.com/definition/balance.

3 *Concise Oxford English Dictionary: Luxury Edition*, ed. Angus Stevenson and Maurice Waite, s.v. "balance" (New York: Oxford University Press, 2011), 100.

CHAPTER 6: PRAGMATISM VERSUS IDEALISM

1 Bono and Chris Anderson, "Congratulations, Bono," *TED Blog*, December 19, 2005, accessed October 3, 2016, http://blog.ted.com/congratulations//.

2 Carlton Tan, "Lee Kuan Yew Leaves a Legacy of Authoritarian Pragmatism," *The Guardian*, March 23, 2015, accessed October 3, 2016, https://www .theguardian.com/world/2015/mar/23/lee-kuan-yews-legacy-of-authoritarian -pragmatism-will-serve-singapore-well.

3 Rosalynn Carter, quoted in Nicole Fallon Taylor, "35 Inspiring Leadership Quotes," *Business News Daily*, September 9, 2015, accessed October 12, 2016, http://www.businessnewsdaily.com/7481-leadership-quotes.html.

4 Benjamin Hooks, quoted in Nicole Fallon Taylor, "35 Inspiring Leadership Quotes," *Business News Daily*, September 9, 2015, accessed October 12, 2016, http://www.businessnewsdaily.com/7481-leadership-quotes.html.

5 Eleanor Roosevelt, quoted in "Eleanor Roosevelt Biography," Biography On-line, accessed October 12, 2016, http://www.biographyonline.net/politicians /american/eleanor-roosevelt.html.

6 Nick Craig and Scott Snook, "From Purpose to Impact," *Harvard Business Review*, May 2014, accessed October 3, 2016, https://hbr.org/2014/05/from -purpose-to-impact.

7 "The Fantastic Five," Jumpcut, May 6, 2016, accessed October 17, 2016, https:// blog.jumpcutstudios.com/the-fantastic-five-404fa643cdff#.7ew060vzw.

8   Noam Wasserman, "Rich Versus King: The Entrepreneur's Dilemma," *Academy of Management Annual Meeting Proceedings*, August 2006, accessed August 11, 2016, http://www.hbs.edu/faculty/Pages/item.aspx?num=22821.

9   "Why Singapore Became an Economic Success," *Economist*, May 26, 2015, accessed October 3, 2016, http://www.economist.com/blogs/economist -explains/2015/03/economist-explains-23.

10 Zarina Hussain, "How Lee Kuan Yew Engineered Singapore's Economic Miracle," *BBC News*, March 24, 2015, accessed October 3, 2016, http:// www.bbc.com/news/business-32028693.

11 "UNDP and the Making of Singapore's Public Service: Lessons from Albert Winsemius," UNDP Global Centre for Public Service Excellence, 2015, accessed October 4, 2016, http://www.undp.org/content/dam/undp/library /capacity-development/English/Singapore%20Centre/Booklet_UNDP -SG50-Winsemius.pdf.

12 Zarina Hussain, "How Lee Kuan Yew Engineered Singapore's Economic Miracle."

13 Emily Jane Fox, "Sheryl Sandberg Responds to Rumors She Could Leave Facebook for Disney C.E.O. Job," *Vanity Fair*, June 2, 2016, accessed October 13, 2016, http://www.vanityfair.com/news/2016/06/sheryl-sandberg-disney-facebook.

14 Brad Stone, "Why Facebook Needs Sheryl Sandberg," *Bloomberg Businessweek*, May 12, 2011, accessed October 13, 2016, http://www.bloomberg.com/ news/articles/2011-05-12/why-facebook-needs-sheryl-sandberg.

CHAPTER 7: SHORT-TERMISM VERSUS LONG-TERMISM

1   Andrew Goodman, "Top 40 Buffett-isms: Inspiration to Become a Better Investor," *Forbes*, September 25, 2013, accessed October 4, 2016, http://www .forbes.com/sites/agoodman/2013/09/25/the-top-40-buffettisms -inspiration-to-become-a-better-investor/#64629744250d.

2   *PC Mag* Encyclopedia, s.v. "Amara's law," accessed October 4, 2016, http:// www.pcmag.com/encyclopedia/term/37701/amara-s-law.

3   Jeremey R. Gray, "A Bias Toward Short-Term Thinking in Threat-Related Negative Emotional States," *Perspectives on Social Psychology* 25, no. 1 (1999).

4   Andrew Bary, "What's Wrong, Warren?," *Barron's*, December 27, 1999, accessed October 4, 2016, http://www.barrons.com/articles/SB945992010127068546.

5   Andrew Bary, "What's Wrong, Warren?"

6   Michael Johnston, "19 Things That Actually Happened in 1999," Dividend Reference, accessed October 4, 2016, http://beforeitsnews.com/financial-markets/2015/05/19-things-that-actually-happened-in-1999-2829634.html.

7   Jordan Wathen, "Warren Buffett's 15-Minute Retirement Plan," The Motley Fool, January 6, 2016, accessed October 4, 2016, http://www.fool.com/investing/general/2016/01/06/warren-buffetts-15-minute-retirement-plan.aspx.

8   Barnaby J. Feder, "Rose Blumkin, Retail Queen, Dies at 104," *New York Times*, August 13, 1998, accessed October 4, 2016, http://www.nytimes.com/1998/08/13/business/rose-blumkin-retail-queen-dies-at-104.html?_r=1.

9   Richard Feloni, "Why Warren Buffett Considers the Deal He Made with an 89-Year-Old Woman One of the Best of His Career," *Business Insider*, May 1, 2015, accessed October 4, 2016, http://www.businessinsider.com/warren-buffett-and-mrs-b-rose-blumkin-2015-4.

10 Barnaby J. Feder, "Rose Blumkin, Retail Queen, Dies at 104."

11 Richard Feloni, "Why Warren Buffett Considers the Deal He Made with an 89-Year-Old Woman One of the Best of His Career."

12 J. R. R. Tolkien, *The Fellowship of the Ring: Being the First Part of The Lord of the Rings* (Boston: Houghton Mifflin Harcourt, 2012), accessed October 14, 2016, https://books.google.com/books/about/The_Fellowship_of_the_Ring.html?id=aWZzLPhY4ooC.

13 Tom Brady, interview by Anthony K. Tjan, August 9, 2014.

14 Tom Brady, interview by Anthony K. Tjan, August 9, 2014.

CHAPTER 8: VULNERABILITY VERSUS CONVICTION

1   Gabrielle Korn, "The Surprising History of Nail Salons & Vietnamese-American Women," *Refinery29*, July 16, 2014, accessed October 5, 2016, http://www.refinery29.com/2014/07/71245/vietnamese-american-nail-industry-documentary.

2   "Revenue from Nail Salon Services in the United States from 1998 to 2015," Statista, accessed October 5, 2016, https://www.statista.com/statistics/276605/revenue-nail-salon-services-united-states/.

"Number of Nail Salons in the United States from 2006 to 2015," Statista, accessed October 5, 2016, https://www.statista.com/statistics/276859/nail-salons-in-the-united-states/.

3 Brené Brown, "The Power of Vulnerability," filmed June 2010, *TED* video, 20:19, June 2010, accessed October 5, 2016, https://www.ted.com/talks/brene_brown_on_vulnerability?language=en.

4 Sarah Lewis, *The Rise: Creativity, the Gift of Failure, and the Search for Mastery* (New York: Simon & Schuster, 2015), 8, accessed November 17, 2016, https://books.google.com/books?id=hQHZAAAAQBAJ.

5 Anthony K. Tjan, "Vulnerability: The Defining Trait of Great Entrepreneurs," *Harvard Business Review*, October 6, 2009, accessed October 5, 2016, hbr.org/2009/10/vulnerability-the-defining-tra.

6 Chuck Salter, "Failure Doesn't Suck," *Fast Company*, May 1, 2007, accessed October 5, 2016, https://www.fastcompany.com/59549/failure-doesnt-suck.

7 Anthony K. Tjan, Richard J. Harrington, and Tsun-yan Hsieh, *Heart, Smarts, Guts, and Luck: What It Takes to Be an Entrepreneur and Build a Great Business* (Boston: Harvard Business Review Press, 2012), 87.

8 Dominic Barton, interview by Anthony K. Tjan, April 4, 2016.

9 Sara Maslin Nir, "The Price of Nice Nails," *New York Times*, May 7, 2015, accessed October 5, 2016, http://www.nytimes.com/2015/05/10/nyregion/at-nail-salons-in-nyc-manicurists-are-underpaid-and-unprotected.html.

CHAPTER 9: IDIOSYNCRASY VERSUS CONNECTEDNESS

1 "Remembering the King of Pop through this Quincy Jones' interview," Philemonowona, June 27, 2010, accessed October 13, 2016, https://philemonowona.com/2010/06/27/remembering-the-king-of-pop-through-this-quincy-jones-interview/.

2 Margo Feiden, interview by Anthony K. Tjan, April 3, 2014.

3 Glenn O'Brien, "History Rewrite," *Interview*, March 24, 2009, accessed August 22, 2016, http://www.interviewmagazine.com/culture/history-rewrite/.

4 "Oscar Levant," *Los Angeles Times*, accessed October 5, 2016, http://projects.latimes.com/hollywood/star-walk/oscar-levant/.

5 Joi Ito, "Rewarding Disobedience," MIT Media Lab on Medium, July 21, 2016, accessed October 5, 2016, https://medium.com/mit-media-lab/rewarding-disobedience-ae194d9f0785#.b5p8d4mj4.

6   "Why Did Steve Jobs Always Wear Black Turtlenecks & Jeans?," Gu-
    ruprasad's Portal, accessed October 5, 2016, http://guruprasad.net/posts/
    why-did-steve-jobs-always-wear-black-turtlenecks-jeans/.

7   "On a Scale of 1 to 10, How Weird Are You?," *New York Times*, January 9, 2010,
    accessed October 5, 2016, http://www.nytimes.com/2010/01/10/business
    /10corner.html?_r=0.

8   Peter Carbonara, "Hire for Attitude, Train for Skill," *Fast Company*, August
    31, 1996, accessed October 13, 2016, https://www.fastcompany.com/26996/
    hire-attitude-train-skill.

9   "Southwest Corporate Fact Sheet," Southwest, accessed October 17, 2016,
    http://swamedia.com/channels/Corporate-Fact-Sheet/pages/corporate-fact
    -sheet.

10 Jalāl ad-Dīn Muhammad Rūmī, quoted in Brian Groves, *Coaching, Performing
    and Thinking at Work* (Milan, Italy: EDUCatt, 2014), 70, accessed November
    17, 2016, https://books.google.com/books?id=0-U-AwAAQBAJ.

11 Mark Twain, "How to Tell a Story and Others," Project Gutenberg, accessed
    October 5, 2016, http://www.gutenberg.org/files/3250/3250-h/3250-h.htm.

12 Somi, interview by Anthony K. Tjan, May 18, 2016, Nomad Hotel, New York.

13 E. O. Wilson, *Biophilia* (Cambridge, MA: Harvard University Press, 1984),
    10, accessed November 17, 2016, https://books.google.com/books?id=CrD
    qGK wMFAkC.

14 John Maeda, interview by Anthony K. Tjan, March 4, 2016.

15 Charlie Munger, interview by Anthony K. Tjan, April 9, 2016.

16 Katherine Collins, *The Nature of Investing: Resilient Investment Strategies
    Through Biomimicry* (New York: Routledge, 2014), accessed November 17,
    2016, https://books.google.com/books?id=uNRXBAAAQBAJ.

17 Kurt Vonnegut, *Player Piano* (New York: Library of America, 2012), ac-
    cessed October 13, 2016, https://libcom.org/library/player-piano-kurt-
    vonnegut.

CHAPTER 10: GRIT VERSUS ACCEPTANCE

1   *Fire Rescue Magazine*, "Remembering the Worcester 6," Firefighter Nation/
    Fire Rescue Magazine, December 3, 2010, accessed October 5, 2016, http://
    my.firefighternation.com/profiles/blogs/remembering-the
    -worcester-6?q=profiles/blogs/remembering-the-worcester-6.

Firehouse, "Interview with Worcester District Chief Mike McNamee," You-Tube video, 16:46, posted May 21, 2015, accessed October 5, 2016, https://www.youtube.com/watch?v=KvEGV8NveHo.

2 Stephan H. Haeckel, *Adaptive Enterprise: Creating and Leading Sense-and-Respond Organizations* (Boston: Harvard Business School Press, 1999), accessed November 17, 2016, https://books.google.com/books?id=pkrFugJBAn4C.

3 Mike Berardino, "Mike Tyson Explains One of His Most Famous Quotes," *Sun Sentinel*, November 9, 2016, accessed October 14, 2016, http://articles.sun-sentinel.com/2012-11-09/sports/sfl-mike-tyson-explains-one-of-his-most-famous-quotes-20121109_1_mike-tyson-undisputed-truth-famous-quotes.

4 Steven Callahan, *Adrift: 76 Days Lost at Sea* (Boston, MA: Houghton Mifflin Harcourt, 2002), accessed November 17, 2016, https://books.google.com/books?id=3nmIoSY6AZ4C.

PART THREE: THE IMPERATIVE TO PUT GOODNESS INTO PRACTICE

1 William Shakespeare, *Julius Caesar* (Plain Label Books, 2010), 39, accessed November 17, 2016, https://books.google.com/books?id=xkhkfRJh8ewC.

2 Tony Hsieh, interview by Anthony K. Tjan, February 16, 2016.

3 Kurt Vonnegut, *Mother Night* (New York: Delta Trade, 1999).

CHAPTER 11: BEYOND ORDINARY MENTORSHIP

1 Alan Hicks and Davis Coombe, *Keep On Keepin' On*, directed by Alan Hicks (New York: RADiUS-TWC, 2015), DVD.

2 Kathryn Shattuck, "Something in Common With His Mentor: Talking to Justin Kauflin," *New York Times*, September 26, 2014, accessed October 4, 2016, http://www.nytimes.com/2014/09/28/movies/talking-to-justin-kauflin.html.

3 Amy Adkins, "Majority of U.S. Employees Not Engaged Despite Gains in 2014," Gallup, January 28, 2015, accessed October 5, 2016, http://www.gallup.com/poll/181289/majority-employees-not-engaged-despite-gains-2014.aspx.

4 James Levine, e-mail message to Anthony K. Tjan, September 25, 2016.

5 Belle Rose Ragins, John L. Cotton, and Janice S. Miller, "Marginal Mentoring: The Effects of Type of Mentor, Quality of Relationship, and Program Design on Work and Career Attitudes," *Academy of Management* 43, no. 6 (2000), 1177–94.

6   Belle Rose Ragins, John L. Cotton, and Janice S. Miller, "Marginal Mentoring: The Effects of Type of Mentor, Quality of Relationship, and Program Design on Work and Career Attitudes."

7   Keith Ferrazzi, interview by Anthony K. Tjan, February 27, 2016.

8   "Millennials at Work: Reshaping the Workplace," PwC, accessed October 5, 2016, https://www.pwc.com/gx/en/managing-tomorrows-people/future-of-work/assets/reshaping-the-workplace.pdf.

9   Mats Lederhausen, conversation with Anthony K. Tjan, June 15, 2013.

10 Dr. Wayne W. Dyer, "Letting Go," accessed October 5, 2016, http://www.drwaynedyer.com/blog/letting-go/.

11 Mike Myers, *Supermensch: The Legend of Shep Gordon* (New York: A&E IndieFilms, 2013), DVD.

12 Shep Gordon, interview by Anthony K. Tjan, May 1, 2016.

13 Tsun-yan Hsieh, interview by Anthony K. Tjan, December 4, 2015.

CHAPTER 12: BECOMING A BETTER JUDGE OF PEOPLE

1   Rita Mae Brown, *Alma Mater* (New York: Ballantine Books, 2002), 108, accessed November 17, 2016, https://books.google.com/books?id=y7oRR-poeatoC.

2   Anthony K. Tjan, "Becoming a Better Judge of People," *Harvard Business Review*, June 17, 2013, accessed October 5, 2016, https://hbr.org/2013/06/becoming-a-better-judge-of-peo.html.

3   Edward O. Wilson, *Biophilia* (Cambridge, MA: Harvard University Press, 1986), 10.

CHAPTER 13: WRAPPING IT UP: IT'S ALL UP TO YOU

1   Mikhail Baryshnikov, quoted in Bob Deutsch, "The Secret Lives of Start-Ups," *Huffington Post*, November 18, 2014, accessed October 14, 2016, http://www.huffingtonpost.com/bob-deutsch/the-secret-lives-of-start_b_5845988.html.

2   Oscar Wilde, *Lady Windemere's Fan*, act 3, scene 1 (Minneapolis: Filquarian, 2007), 78, accessed November 17, 2016, https://books.google.com/books?id=oVHinWsVQrQC.

3   Dan Pallotta, *Uncharitable—How Restraints on Nonprofits Undermine Their Potential* (Boston: UPNE, 2010), accessed November 17, 2016, https://books.google.com/books?id=RkQIIKzMjowC.

4   Amanda Palmer, interview by Anthony K. Tjan, February 17, 2016.

5   Paul Outerbridge, quoted in "Color Temperature & Color Rendering Index DeMystified," Lowel EDU, accessed October 17, 2016, http://lowel.tiffen.com/edu/color_temperature_and_rendering_demystified.html.

6   Henry McCance, interview by Anthony K. Tjan, On Cue, June 17, 2014.

ACKNOWLEDGMENTS

1   Bruce W. Tuckman, "Developmental Sequence in Small Groups," *Psychological Bulletin* 63: 6 (1965), 384–99, accessed December 7, 2016, http://openvce.net/sites/default/files/Tuckman1965DevelopmentalSequence.pdf.

INDEX

....

Aboriginal culture of Australia, 133
acceptance. *See* grit versus acceptance
accountability, 55–56, 171–72
agape, 101
Aknin, Lara, 82
Allison, Graham, 92
altruism, self-rewarding aspects of, 82
apologies, 105
Apple, 74
Aristotle, 2, 259
arrogance, 171
artists, 179
Austen, Jane, 108
authenticity, 242
authoritarianism, 52–53

balance, importance of, 18, 23–24,
    26, 117
Barton, Dominic, 6, 174, 221, 243
Baryshnikov, Mikhail, 251
biases, awareness of, 50–51, 52–53, 74,
    202, 242
biomimicry, principles of,
    190–91
Blake, Frank, 35
Blakely, Sara, 192
Blanchard, Ken, 1–2, 78
Blumkin, Rose, 147
Bono, 127
bosses, 22, 108, 230. *See also* mentors and
    mentoring
Brady, Tom, 150–53
brands and branding, 96–99
Branson, Richard, 192
Brooks, David, 114
Brown, Brené, 107, 168, 169
Brown, Rita Mae, 237
Brunner, Leslie, 58, 78, 80–81
Bryant, Adam, 230, 263
Buddhism, 171
Buffett, Warren, 54, 83, 144–47, 192
Bush, Jonathan, 58–59
Butterfield, Stewart, 192

Callahan, Steve, 199–200, 202, 203
cancer diagnoses, 67–71
Carter, Rosalynn, 132
Chanel, 63
Chaplin, Charlie, 83
Chappellet, Molly, 17
character
    and leadership, 21, 71, 253
    placing a premium on, 22–23, 26
    and setbacks, 245
Chavez, Robert, 97, 98
Chen, Perry, 192
Chiat, Jay, 16, 22, 23, 74
children, 86–87, 156–57
Chipotle, 168
Chopra, Deepak, 37, 114
Clow, Lee, 74
collaboration, 84, 180–81, 252
Collins, Jim, 47, 48
Collins, Katherine, 190–91
communication and storytelling, 186–88
compassion, 36–37, 67–89
    and business goals, 21
    and connectedness, 193
    as cornerstone quality, 31, 34, 39
    and empathy, 36, 72–73, 73, 77–81, 89
    in framework of Goodness Pyramid, 31,
        33, 34, 73
    and generosity, 36, 72–73, 73, 81–87, 89
    and good judgement of others, 242–44,
        245, 246
    and grit versus acceptance, 201
    and leadership, 71, 88, 89, 253
    and mentoring, 228
    and openness, 36, 72–73, 73, 89
    of physicians, 67–71
    and realistic expectations, 110
    and respect, 103–4
    tensions against, 121, 178
competency
    bias toward, 238, 249
    goodness compared to, 3
    and leadership, 24, 26, 71
    and mentoring, 215–16, 235

competency *(cont.)*
  prioritizing clan and culture over, 15
  values prioritized over, 18, 21–23, 26,
    28, 213
confidence, 171–72, 242–43
Confucius, 101
connectedness versus idiosyncrasy, 121,
    177–93
  balance between, 121, 191–92, 193
  in business practices, 183–85
  and collaboration, 180–81
  and communication, 186–88
  and Feiden, 177–78
  love/hate relationship between, 182
Conscious Capitalism (Mackey), 12
convenience, bias for, 149–50
conviction, 171–72. *See also* vulnerability
    versus conviction
Cook, Tim, 83
counterfactual thinking, 110
Craig, Nick, 133, 135
creativity, 179, 192
criticism of others, 104
Cuban missile crisis, 92
Cue Ball
  attitude toward failure at, 58
  feedback at, 56
  long-term vision of, 143–44
  and mentoring, 220–21, 223
  and MiniLuxe, 162–66, 167, 174–75, 180
  people-first policy of, 14
  priority setting at, 55
  and ShapeUp, 154
culture, corporate, 97–98, 135–36, 183–84
Cummings, E. E., 180
curiosity, 189, 190
cynicism, 252

Dalai Lama, 87
Daring Greatly (Brown), 169
Darwin, Charles, 81
decision-making
  active versus passive, 202–3
  difficult, 172–73
  distributed model of, 75, 77
  R.I.S.E. approach to, 122–25, 139–40,
    153–55, 167–68, 201, 204
  of satisficers versus maximizers, 111–12
  and wisdom, 109
decorum, exercising, 103–4, 117
Dickinson, Emily, 179–80
Dillard, Annie, 62
discipline for long term, 150–53
disobedience, ethical, 181–82
dissention, 182
diversity, 181
Doriot, George, 19

dot-com boom, 41, 144–45, 146
dreams, 138, 142, 156
Dunn, Elizabeth, 82
Dyer, Wayne, 105, 230
Dyson, James, 170, 171

ego-integrity, 113
empathy, 77–81
  in framework of Goodness Pyramid, *33*,
    72–73, *73*
  and mentoring, 228
  and non-phatic language, 79–80, 89
  practice of, 36
  and storge, 101
  tensions against, 178
energy balance, 243
Erban, Jack, 17, 69–71, 72, 74
Erikson, Erik, 3, 113, 233
eros, 100–101
expectations, realistic, 110–11
extrinsic rewards, 84, 100, 114

failures, 58–59, 170–71, 245
families, 211–13
feedback, 56–57, 65, 242
Feiden, Margo, 177–78, 227
Ferrazzi, Keith, 218
Ferrucci, Piero, 87
financial crisis of 2008, 144–45
The Four Loves (Lewis), 100–101
Frank, Anne, 157
Franklin, Benjamin, 48, 49, 59–63, 256

Gandhi, Mahatma, 173
Gates, Bill and Melinda, 83
generosity, *33*, 36, 72–73, 81–87, 89, 228
Georgescu, Peter, 48–49
Gerald, Casey, 102
Gilovich, Thomas, 110
Give and Take (Grant), 83
Giving Pledge, 83
golden rule, 106–7
Goldworm, Dawn, 17
Goldworm, Samantha, 17
"good" and "goodness" (terms), 2–3,
    39, 206–7
good judgement of others, 237–49
  biases that compromise, 238–39, 249
  and Goodness Pyramid, 239, *240*, 248
  questions to develop, 241–47, 249
Goodness Pyramid
  cornerstone qualities of, 31, 39 (*see also*
    compassion; truth; wholeness)
  framework of, 29–32, *33*, 39, *240*
  and good judgement of others, 239, 248

as ideal, 38
and intentions, 38
language of, 31–32, 39, 254
and mentoring, 225, 227, 231
values of, 29, 34–38, 39
See also tensions
Goodnight, Jim, 84–85, 188
"good people" (term), 30, 206–7
Good People Mantra, 15–25
language of, 254
and mentoring, 213, 227
principles of, 17–25, *18*, 213, *256, 257*
and tensions, 120–21
Good to Great (Collins), 47
Goodwin, Doris Kearns, 140–41
Gordon, Shep, 231–32
Gould, Glenn, 182
Gould, Stephen Jay, 247
Graham, Benjamin, 10
Grant, Adam, 83
gratitude, *33*, 91, 253
Greeks, ancient, 100–101, 216
Greenleaf, Robert, 78
grit versus acceptance, 121, 195–204
balance between, 121, 197, 201–3, 204
and Callahan, 199–200
and R.I.S.E. approach to decision-making,
201, 204
and "sense and respond" strategy, 198–99,
201–2
and Worcester, Mass. fire, 195–96,
199, 203

Haeckel, Stephan, 198–99
Hamel, John, 103, 163
Hancock, Herbie, 17, 87–88, 116–17
Hanh, Thich Nhat, 67
happiness, 13, 82, 99–100
Harrington, Dick, 14, 16, 106, 148–49, 230
Hassenfeld, Alan, 178–79
health, 13
Heart, Smarts, Guts, and Luck (Tjan), 50,
100, 101
Hedren, Tippi, 161–62, 175
Helping People Win at Work (Ridge and
Blanchard), 2
Hemingway, Ernest, 46
Hermès, 63, 97–98
Hirschfeld, Al, 83
Holstee, 99
honesty, *33*
Hooks, Benjamin, 132
Hsieh, Tony, 74–75, 183, 184, 206
Hsieh, Tsun-yan
and mentoring, 6–9, 16, 220, 221, 223, 233
value generated by, 10
humanity, 21, 184. *See also* compassion

human resource departments, 72
humility, *33, 35,* 41, 46–51, 64, 65, 229

idealism, 23, 129, 141, 142. *See also*
pragmatism versus idealism
idiosyncrasy, 178, 179–80, 181–85, 193,
247. *See also* connectedness versus
idiosyncrasy
IKEA, 63
influences, negative, 52–53
innovation, 184
inside-out love, 98–99
integrity, *33, 35,* 36, 57–63, 64, 65, 103
intentions, 38, 242
Internet, 41–43, 146, 187
intrinsic versus extrinsic rewards, 84,
100, 114
Ito, Joi, 181, 191

Jay, Stef, 15
JetBlue Airways, 104–5
Jobs, Steve, 182
Johnson, Cathy Viscardi, 16
Jones, Bill T., 178–79
Jones, Quincy, 177
journaling, 54–55, 65, 115
Jumpcut, 135–36

Kalanithi, Paul, 68–69
Kalliarekos, Kosmo, 223
Kauflin, Justin, 209–11
Keep On Keepin' On (2014), 209–11
Kennedy, John F., *91,* 91–92, 94, 112, 129
Kennedy, Robert, 92, 112
kindness, 105, 115, 229–30
King, Billie Jean, 50
King Henry IV (Shakespeare), 93
Knell, Gary, 187
Knudstorp, Jørgen Vig, 81
Kumar, Rajiv, 153–55

Lady Gaga, 182
Laliberté, Guy, 189, 192
Langer, Ellen, 51–52, 75–76
language for goodness, 27–39
and Goodness Pyramid, 31–32, 39, 254
and perception, 32
Lao Tzu, 41, 259
Larsen, Norman, 1
leaders and leadership
apologies from, 105
and balance, 117
and branding, 98
and character, 21, 24, 26, 71, 253

leaders and leadership *(cont.)*
  and compassion, 71, 88, 89, 253
  of competency, 24, 26, 71
  and connectedness versus idiosyncrasy,
      185, 187, 193
  and core values, 26
  decision-making of, 64
  difficulties of, 91–92
  as forces of change, 28
  humanity as shown by, 21
  humility in, 47–48
  and integrity, 57
  loneliness of, 91–92, 93, 117
  with long-term vision, 158
  optimism of, 114–15
  and people-first policy, 64
  as platform for goodness creation, 253
  and producing future leaders, 253
  and purpose statements, 133–35
  and qualities of goodness, 34
  and respect, 105–6, 108
  sacrifices required by, 93
  Schwarzkopf on, 21
  and self-actualization, 117–18
  and self-awareness, 35
  servant model of, 78–79, 101, 117
  and soft skills, 47
  truth as foundation of, 53, 64, 65, 253
  and values, 23
  and wholeness, 93, 95, 253
learning, culture of, 58–59
Lederhausen, Mats, 16, 95–96, 144, 166, 168,
      220–21
Lee, Kuan Yew, 127–29, 130, 138–40
legacy, mentoring as, 233–34
Le Guin, Ursula K., 108
Levant, Oscar, 179, 192
Levine, James, 213
Lewis, C. S., 100, 101
Lewis, Sarah, 169–70
Lincoln, Abraham, 140–41
listening
  with empathy, 78, 79–81
  talk-to-listen ratio, 242–43
Lobo, Vernon, 16, 221–22
The Loneliest Job (Tames), 91
long-termism. *See* short-termism versus
      long-termism
love, *33*, 37, 93, 95–102, 115, 117
lovemarks versus trade/brandmarks, 96–99
Lu, Li, 59, 145

Mackey, John, 12–13, 95
Madey, Scott, 110
Maeda, John, 156, 188–89, 238
mantra. *See* Good People Mantra
Maslow, Abraham, 3, 31, 115, 117–18, 259

maximizers, 111–12
McCance, Henry, 16, 24–25, 77, 220, 257
McDonald's, 168
McFerrin, Bobby, 114
McKinsey & Company, 6–9, 41, 174, 182, 221
McNamee, Mike, 196, 199, 203
meditation, 54, 65
Medvec, Victoria, 110
mentors and mentoring, 209–36
  and accountability, 55–56
  as advocates, 218, 226, 230
  of author, 16–17
  defined, 216
  demands of, 234
  developing others through, 20–21, 26, 213
  and empathy, 78
  five critical questions of, 224–26, 231, 235
  for goodness, 215–16, 235
  and Goodness Pyramid, 225, 227, 231
  and Good People Mantra, 17–18, 213
  and Gordon, 231–32
  guiding principles of, 227–30, 231
  and Hsieh, 6–9, 220, 221, 223, 233
  as legacy, 233–34
  as a mensch, 231–32, 235–36
  parents and family members as, 211–13
  reciprocity in, 20–21
  relationships as basis of, 7, 210, 211–15,
      227, 230, 231, 235
  reverse, 219–20
  roles of, 216–20, 235
  and success of mentees, 14–15
  and ten-people commitment, 255–57
  Terry–Kauflin relationship, 209–11
  and values, 215, 220
  wise counsel from, 113
millennials, 156, 211, 219–20, 223
Mindfulness (Langer), 51
MiniLuxe, 162–66, 167, 174–75, 180
Minsky, Marvin, 2, 32, 149
Mintzberg, Henry, 199
MIT Media Lab, 181, 191
multidimensional/multidisciplinary
      thinking, 184, 188–91, 193, 201, 247
Munger, Charlie, 146–47, 163, 189–90
Musk, Elon, 83
Myers, Mike, 47, 231

nail salons, 161–66, 167, 174–75
Nebraska Furniture Mart, 147, 254
Neeleman, David, 104–5
Net Promoter Scores (NPS), 106
New York Times, 28–29, 74, 174–75
Ng, Kaming, 41–42, 180, 203, 206
Niebuhr, Reinhold, 109, 112
Nir, Sarah Maslin, 174
Nohria, Dean, 24

Nohria, Nitin, 16, 71
Norton, Michael, 82
Nuland, Sherwin, 71

Olympic medal winners, 110
On the Origin of Species (Darwin), 81
openness, 74–77
  in framework of Goodness Pyramid, *33*,
    72–73, *73*
  and grit versus acceptance, 201–2
  and mentoring, 228
  mind-set of, 36, 89
  pride as enemy of, 229
  tensions against, 178
optimism, 114, 228, 243
Outerbridge, Paul, 257
Oxman, Neri, 17, 178–79

Pallotta, Dan, 252
Palmer, Amanda, 255
The Paradox of Choice (Schwartz and
    Ward), 112
parents, 211–13
passive/active vulnerability, 170
Patagonia, 63
pattern recognition, 190
Peck, M. Scott, 96
peer pressure, positive, 52
people-first policy
  and decision-making of executives, 64
  and Good People Mantra, 19
  and grit versus acceptance, 201
  of mentors, 213
  proactive application of, 17, 19, 26
  and servant leadership, 101
perception and language, 32
Perón, Eva Duarte de, 157
personal development, 17–18
Peters, Tom, 4
Pfortmüller, Fabian, 99, 224
phatic language, 79–80, 89, 177
philia, 101
physicians and compassion, 67–71
Piaget, Jean, 156–57, 259
Pike, Valerie, 17
Porter, Michael, 31
Porter, Stephen, 86
The Power of Kindness (Ferrucci), 87
practicing goodness opportunistically,
    24–25, 26, 213
pragmatism versus idealism, 121, 127–42
  balance between, 23, 121, 130–32,
    140–41, 142
  as complementary, 130
  and dance between strategy and execution,
    138–40, 142

and mentoring, 229
and purpose statements, 132–37, 142
Predictive Index self-assessment survey, 245
pride, 49, 50, 65, 171, 229
problem solving, 189–90, 193
profits, 3, 10, 12, 15
pro-social behavior, 82–84
psychometric tests, 55, 65, 242
punctuality, 103
purpose
  clarity of, 174, 176, 201, 204
  purpose-driven organizations, 156
  statements of, 132–37, 142
pyramid of goodness. *See* Goodness Pyramid

Ragins, Belle Rose, 214, 215–16
Rauch, Doug, 97
reading, 115, 202, 245–46
realists, 18, 23–24
reality and vision, 131–32
reflection, 63, 115, 134, 242
respect, *33*, 37, 93, 102–8, 117
rewards, extrinsic versus intrinsic, 84,
    100, 114
"rich versus king" dilemma, 137
Ridge, Garry, 1–2, 10, 64, 78, 171
The Rise (Lewis), 169–70
R.I.S.E. approach to decision-making
  and grit versus acceptance, 201, 204
  and pragmatism versus idealism, 139–40
  process of, 122–25
  and short-termism versus long-termism,
    153–55
  and vulnerability versus conviction,
    167–68
risk taking, 58–59, 169, 170, 172, 176. *See
    also* vulnerability versus conviction
The Road to Character (Brooks), 114
Roberts, Robert, 49, 96–97, 98
Robinson, Jackie, 102
Rockefeller, David, 83
Rocket Chemical Company, 1–2
Rogers, Carl, 78
Roosevelt, Eleanor, 132
routines, 62–63
rules and policies, 76
Rumi, 185

Saatchi & Saatchi, 98
Sacks, Oliver, 91
Safdie, Moshe, 17
Sandberg, Sheryl, 141
Sapir, Edward, 32
SAS, 84–85
satisficers, 111–12
schedules, 62–63

Schiller, Friedrich, 182
Schwartz, Barry, 112
Schwarzkopf, Norman, 21
self-actualization, 115, 117–18
self-awareness, 50–57
  and confidence, 171
  in framework of Goodness Pyramid, 33
  of Franklin, 61
  and good judgement of others, 241–42
  and grit versus acceptance, 202, 204
  and leadership, 35
  and openness, 75
  practices to strengthen, 54–57, 65
  and purpose statements, 135
  and truth, 64
  and values, 137
selflessness, 33, 36
serenity prayer, 109, 112
servant leadership, 78–79, 101, 117
setbacks, responses to, 245
Shakespeare, William, 93, 205
ShapeUp, 153–55
Shared Studios, 260, 264
shareholders, 12–13
short-termism versus long-termism, 121,
    143–59
  and Amara's law, 145, 155–56
  balance between, 121
  and bias for short term, 143–45,
    147–50, 159
  and Brady, 150–53
  and Buffett, 144–47
  and discipline for long term, 150–53
  and people as long-term investments,
    146–47
  and R.I.S.E. approach to decision-making,
    153–55
Simon, Herbert A., 111
Sinek, Simon, 46
Singapore, 127–29, 130, 138–40
"Smartest Person in the Room Syndrome"
    (SPRS), 106
Snook, Scott, 133, 135
soft concepts and skills, 3, 17, 21–22, 47, 75
Somi, 187
Sotomayor, Sonia, 17, 85
SoulCycle, 63
The Soul of Medicine (Nuland), 71
The Source of Success (Georgescu), 49
Southwest Airlines, 63, 183–84
spandrels, 247, 248
speed, bias for, 149–50
spouses and partners, 244–45
stakeholders, 12–13, 100
standards of behavior and accountability,
    55–56
Stanford Prisoner Experiment, 53
Starbucks, 254

Start with Why (Sinek), 46
storge, 101
storytelling, 186–88
success, redefining, 10–15
Superbosses (Finkelstein), 22
Supermensch (2013), 231

Tames, George, 91
Tatum, Mark, 80
Team of Rivals (Goodwin), 140–41
tensions (countervailing forces), 120–22,
    213. *See also* connectedness versus
    idiosyncrasy; grit versus acceptance;
    pragmatism versus idealism; short-
    termism versus long-termism;
    vulnerability versus conviction
Terkel, Studs, 263
Terry, Clark "CT," 209–11
Thomas of Aquinas, Saint, 101
Thomson Corporation, 14, 16, 106, 148–49
Tolkien, J. R. R., 147
Trader Joe's, 63, 97, 98, 106–7
truth, 35–36, 41–65
  as cornerstone quality, 31, 34, 39
  as foundation of goodness, 41
  in framework of Goodness Pyramid, 31,
    33, 34, 75
  and good judgement of others,
    242–43, 246
  and humility, 33, 35, 41, 46–51, 64, 65
  and integrity, 33, 35, 36, 57–63, 64, 65
  role of, in leadership, 53, 64, 65, 253
  and self-awareness, 33, 35–36, 50–57, 64,
    65, 75, 241–42
  tensions against, 121, 129–30, 142, 178
Twain, Mark, 186
24 x 3 Rule, 74, 114–15, 228, 243
Tyson, Mike, 199

values
  as anchor for dreams, 135–37, 138
  defining, 34–38
  and ego-integrity, 113
  of employees, 4
  of families, 212–13
  in framework of Goodness Pyramid, 29,
    31, 33
  and good judgement of others, 249
  and grit versus acceptance, 201
  and leadership, 23
  and mentoring, 215, 220, 228
  and open mind-sets, 76–77
  placing a premium on, 26
  practicing, 24
  prioritized over competencies, 18,
    21–23, 28

and self-awareness, 137
and vulnerability, 169
vision, 131–37
Vonnegut, Kurt, 191–92, 206
vulnerability versus conviction, 121, 161–76
   balance between, 121
   and clarity of purpose, 174, 176
   and confidence and conviction, 171–72, 176
   and decision-making, 172–73
   defining *vulnerability*, 168–69
   and failures, 170–71
   and nail salon venture, 161–66, 167, 174–75
   and passive/active vulnerability, 170, 176
   power in vulnerability, 168–71, 176
   reconciling, 166–68
   and R.I.S.E. approach to decision-making, 167–68
   and risk taking, 169, 170, 172, 176
   and values of goodness, 173

Waldinger, Robert, 13
Walton, Bill, 104
Ward, Andrew, 112
Wasserman, Noam, 137
Waters, Alice, 22
WD-40
   attitude toward mistakes at, 47–48
   culture of, 3, 254
   employee satisfaction at, 1, 3, 99
   failed prototypes of, 171
   mentoring at, 2
   people-first policy at, 1–2
   performance of, 10
   values of, 136
   See also Ridge, Garry

wealth/control trade-offs, 137
Weinberg, Brad, 153–54
When Breath Becomes Air (Kalanithi), 68–69
Whole Foods, 12–13, 95
wholeness, 37–38, 91–118
   as cornerstone quality, 31, 34, 39
   and ego-integrity, 113–14
   in framework of Goodness Pyramid, 31, 33, 34, 93, 94, 117
   and good judgement of others, 243, 245–46, 247
   and grit versus acceptance, 197
   and leadership, 93, 95, 253
   and love, 33, 37, 93, 95–102, 115, 117
   ongoing quest for, 116, 117
   and respect, 33, 37, 93, 102–8, 117
   tensions against, 121, 178
   and wisdom, 33, 37–38, 93, 108–13, 117
Whorf, Benjamin, 32
Wilson, E. O., 81, 119, 188, 189, 246
wine, terminology of, 28–29
Winsemius, Albert, 139–40
wisdom, 33, 37–38, 93, 108–13, 117
Wolfe, Tom, 182
Wooden, John, 11–12, 103–4, 198
Worcester, Mass. fire, 195–96, 199
writing down plans and priorities, 54–55, 65, 115
The Writing Life (Dillard), 62

Zappos, 74–75, 136, 183, 184, 254
ZEFER, 42–46, 221–22
Zimbardo, Philip, 53, 206
Zuckerberg, Mark, 141